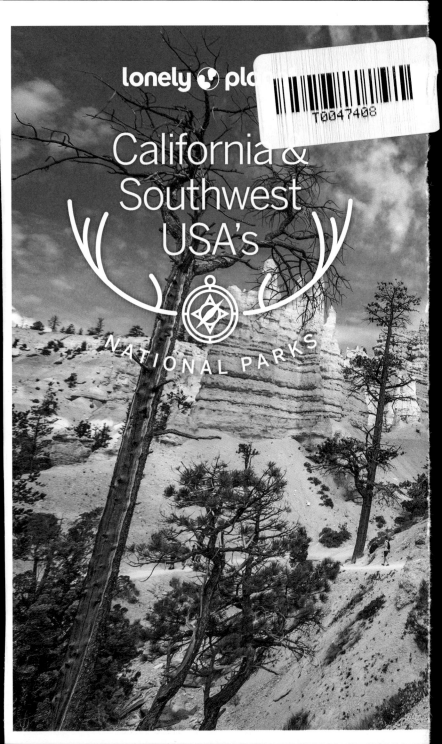

lonely ⊕ pla

T0047408

California &
Southwest
USA's

NATIONAL PARKS

Contents

Plan Your Trip

California & Southwest
USA's National Parks
Top 12.........................4
Need to Know...........16
Month by Month.......18
Get Inspired..............21
Health & Safety.......22
Clothing &
Equipment...............24
California & Southwest
USA's National Parks
Overview..................26
Road Trips................28
Best Hiking..............32
Best Wildlife &
Nature Watching.....34
Best Family
Experiences.............36
Best Adventures......38

California   41
Channel Islands........ 44
Death Valley.............. 50
Joshua Tree.................56
Classic Road Trip: Palm
Springs & Joshua Tree
Oases...........................62
Kings Canyon.............. 68
Hike: Mist Falls.............74
Classic Hike: Rae Lakes
Loop.............................78

Lassen Volcanic..........82
Pinnacles.................... 88
Redwood..................... 90
Classic Road Trip:
Northern Redwood
Coast............................ 96
Sequoia......................102
Hike: Monarch Lakes 106
Hike: General Sherman
Tree to Moro Rock......108
Yosemite.....................112
Hike: Vernal & Nevada
Falls.............................118
Hike: Cathedral
Lakes...........................120
Classic Road Trip:
Yosemite, Sequoia &
Kings Canyon.............124

The Southwest   131
Arches.........................134
Big Bend.....................140
Classic Road Trip: Big
Bend Scenic Loop..... 146
Bryce Canyon..........152
Drive: Scenic Bryce
Canyon........................ 156
Classic Hike: Under the
Rim Trail...................... 162
Canyonlands............164
Capitol Reef.............170
Drive: Highway 24...... 174

In Focus
The Parks Today...226
History..................228
Outdoor
Activities...............234
Wildlife..................240
Conservation........245
Landscapes &
Geology.................248

Special Features
Diverse
Landscapes........... 86
Incredible
Rock Formations. 206

Carlsbad Caverns...178
Grand Canyon..........180
Hike: Widforss Trail....186
Hike: Hermit Trail.......187
Great Basin..............190
Guadalupe
Mountains................192
Mesa Verde..............198
Petrified Forest.......204
Saguaro....................208
Zion............................210
Drive: Scenic Zion
Canyon........................ 216
Classic Hike: The
Narrows: Top Down... 220
White Sands............. 222

COVID-19

We have re-checked every business in this book before publication to ensure that it is still open after the COVID-19 outbreak. However, the economic and social impacts of COVID-19 will continue to be felt long after the outbreak has been contained, and many businesses, services and events referenced in this guide may experience ongoing restrictions. Some may be temporarily closed, have changed their opening hours and services, or require bookings; some unfortunately could have closed permanently. We suggest you check with venues before visiting for the latest information.

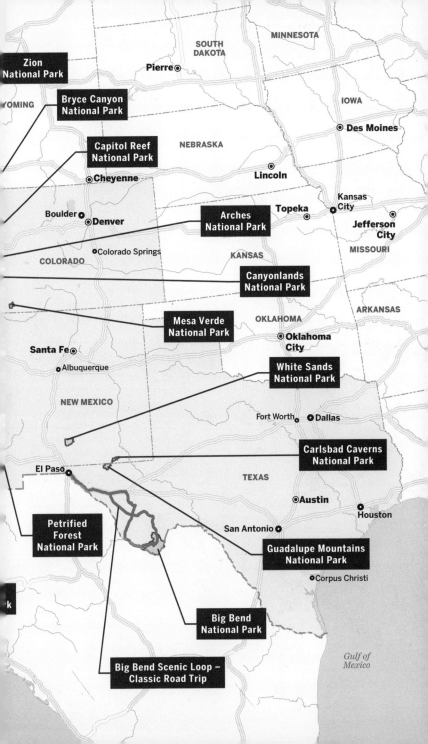

Welcome to California & Southwest USA's National Parks

The national parks are the very essence of the US. The 63 carefully protected natural enclaves reflect every facet of this vast, complex and magnificently diverse country.

National parks are America's big backyards. No visit to California and the Southwest would be complete without a visit to at least one of these remarkable natural treasures, rich in unspoiled wilderness, rare wildlife and history.

The parks represent American ideals at their best. The ability to enjoy these special places today may seem like a matter of course, but the establishment of the National Park System was no sure thing. Challenges have been present on every step of the way, and many threatened to derail the entire experiment. But, until now, the best instincts of a nation have prevailed.

California and the Southwest make a contribution to the national park story far out of proportion to their size. The creation of White Sands National Park in New Mexico in late 2019 brought to 22 the number of national parks in the region, which is more than one-third of the national total of 63. California has nine national parks, more than any other US state, while Utah comes in third (behind Alaska) with five.

And within these 22 parks are some of the USA's most storied natural wonders, from the tallest trees on earth standing sentinel on Pacific shores to the bizarre saguaro cacti, petrified forests and Joshua trees. Or from the astonishing rock formations and waterfalls of Yosemite to the hallucinatory shapes rising from the deserts of Utah. And yes, all the way to and around the Grand Canyon and back again. Whether you drive, hike, kayak or climb these fabulous places, it's impossible not to be inspired by the call of these national parks to explore nature.

The USA's national parks are the very essence of the country

Queen's Gardens Trail, Bryce Canyon National Park
UNAI HUIZI PHOTOGRAPHY/SHUTTERSTOCK ©

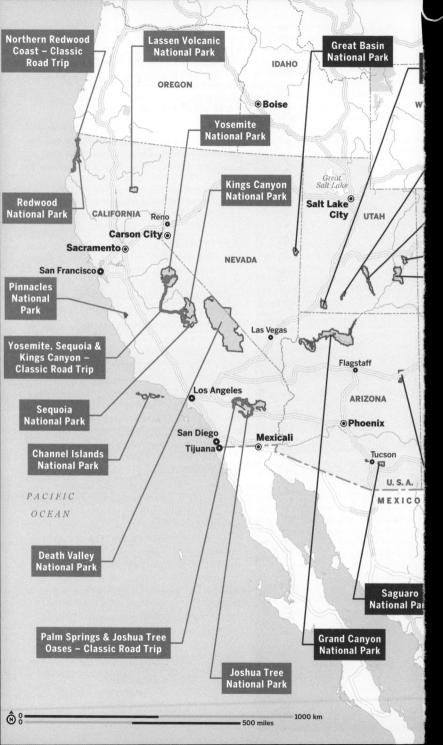

Northern Redwood Coast – Classic Road Trip

Lassen Volcanic National Park

Great Basin National Park

IDAHO

OREGON

⊙ **Boise**

Yosemite National Park

Kings Canyon National Park

Great Salt Lake

Redwood National Park

CALIFORNIA Reno

Salt Lake City ⊙ UTAH

Carson City ⊙

Sacramento ⊙

San Francisco ⊙

NEVADA

Pinnacles National Park

Las Vegas ⊙

Yosemite, Sequoia & Kings Canyon – Classic Road Trip

Flagstaff ⊙

Sequoia National Park

Los Angeles ⊙

ARIZONA

⊙ **Phoenix**

Channel Islands National Park

San Diego ⊙ **Mexicali** ⊙

Tijuana ⊙

Tucson ⊙

PACIFIC OCEAN

U.S.A.

MEXICO

Saguaro National Park

Death Valley National Park

Palm Springs & Joshua Tree Oases – Classic Road Trip

Grand Canyon National Park

Joshua Tree National Park

⊗N 0
0

1000 km

500 miles

Prickly Pear, California

Plan Your Trip
California & Southwest USA's National Parks Top 12

PIXELSHOP/SHUTTERSTOCK ©

Yosemite Valley, Yosemite

In Yosemite Valley, the National Park System's crown jewel, massive granite rock formations tower thousands of feet over the Merced River. Wild creeks plummet from the cliff tops, creating a spectacle of waterfalls unlike anywhere on earth. And presiding over it all stand iconic and mighty sentinels of rock, including El Capitan, Half Dome, the Royal Arches, the Three Brothers and Cathedral Rocks.

MICHAEL SEWELL/VISUAL PURSUIT/GETTY IMAGES ©

CB_TRAVEL/SHUTTERSTOCK ©

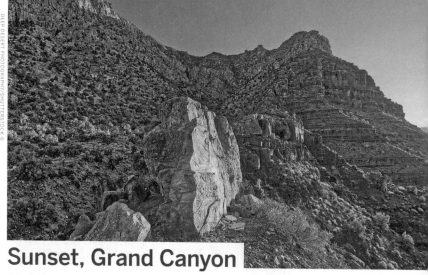

DEEP DESERT PHOTOGRAPHY/SHUTTERSTOCK ©

Sunset, Grand Canyon

Of all the places in the world to watch the sun set, few can measure up to the Grand Canyon. Lipan Point is one of the finest spots to do it. Or, if you're feeling leisurely, simply grab a drink and a porch swing on the patio of El Tovar lodge, where you can watch the sunset in style.

2

KYLE SPARKS/GETTY IMAGES ©

Rock Climbing, Joshua Tree

Whether you're a rock-climbing novice or a bouldering goddess, you'll find heaven above earth in Joshua Tree. With more than 8000 established routes, this is one of the world's key climbing destinations. There are classes for beginners, and the 400-plus climbing formations offer endless fun for seasoned enthusiasts. Amid the giant boulders and sweaty climbers, the bizarre Joshua trees themselves lend the scenery an otherworldly character.

3

4

The Narrows, Zion

Check your claustrophobia at the door and prepare to get wet on this hike up Virgin River into a 2000ft-deep slot canyon. As you make your way upriver, the cliffs press inward, towering higher and higher until, finally, you reach Wall Street, where the width of the canyon narrows to under 30ft and this astonishing place takes on a special kind of magic.

5

Bryce Amphitheater, Bryce Canyon

Proof that nature has a wild imagination, hoodoos are one of the strangest formations on the planet. From the rim of southern Utah's Bryce Amphitheater you can look down upon thousands of these bizarre, ancient rock spires as they tower out of the so-called Silent City, a conglomeration of hoodoos so vast that you'd be forgiven for thinking you'd landed on another planet. Sunrise over the amphitheater is one of life's treats.

GALYNA ANDRUSHKO/SHUTTERSTOCK ©

LORDRUNAR/GETTY IMAGES ©

BRYAN MULLENNIX/GETTY IMAGES ©

Cliff Palace, Mesa Verde

This grand engineering achievement, the largest cliff dwelling in North America, has 217 rooms and 23 kivas, and once provided shelter for 250 to 300 Ancestral Pueblo people. To access it, visitors must climb down a stone stairway and four 10ft ladders, as part of an hour-long ranger-led tour. It's a great place to puzzle out the clues left by its former inhabitants – who vacated the site in 1300 CE for reasons still not fully understood.

6

ALEXEY ULASHCHICK/SHUTTERSTOCK ©

Dante's View, Death Valley

The deserts of California and the Southwest have many extraordinary viewpoints, but few can match the drama of Dante's View. This perspective-altering lookout from high atop the Black Mountains gazes out across Death Valley, and from here you can see the highest (Mt Whitney) and lowest (Badwater) points in the lower 48. It's a view that changes with the seasons, painted in vivid hues in summer, moody and grey in the depths of a desert winter.

7

Tree hugging, Redwood Forests

Hugging a tree never came so naturally as it does in California's sun-dappled groves of ancient redwoods, the world's tallest trees. These gentle giants are quintessentially Californian: their roots may be shallow, but they hold each other up and reach dizzying heights. Even a short stroll on the soft forest floor beneath them puts the rest of the world into perspective.

PATRICK LEITZ/GETTY IMAGES ©

YAYA ERNST/SHUTTERSTOCK ©

STASS GRICKO/500PX/
GETTY IMAGES ©

9

Lassen Volcanic National Park

Anchoring the Cascades' chain of volcanoes to the south, this alien landscape bubbles over with roiling mud pots, noxious sulfur vents and steamy fumaroles. But Lassen also delights the senses with colorful cinder cones and azure crater lakes. Ditch the crowds and head to this off-the-beaten-path destination to discover fresh peaks to be conquered, pristine waters for dipping, forested campgrounds for comfort and boardwalks through Bumpass Hell that will leave you awestruck.

JFCREATIVES/GETTY IMAGES ©

DOUGLAS KLUG/GETTY IMAGES ©

DOUGLAS KLUG/GETTY IMAGES ©

Watching Wildlife, Channel Islands

Tossed like lost pearls off the coast, the Channel Islands have a history of habitation stretching back thousands of years. Marine life thrives on these islands, from coral reefs to giant elephant seals. Enjoy fantastic sea kayaking in Channel Islands National Park, or plan a posh getaway at the harborfront hotels of Catalina Island.

10

JEFF R CLOW/GETTY IMAGES ©

Arches & Canyonlands National Parks

More than 2000 sandstone arches cluster within just 119 sq miles at Arches, a cauldron of geologic wonders including a balanced rock, a swath of giant fins and one span that's so photogenic it's emblazoned on Utah license plates. Just south is stunning Canyonlands, a maze of plateaus, mesas and canyons as forbidding as it is beautiful.

11

DOUG MEEK/SHUTTERSTOCK ©

Carlsbad Caverns National Park

The elevator descends the length of the Empire State Building, and then the doors open to reveal a subterranean village: a snack bar, water fountains, restrooms and, most impressive, the 255ft-high Big Room where geologic wonders line a 1.25-mile path. It's also home to 400,000 Mexican free-tailed bats from April to October.

12

Plan Your Trip
Need to Know

When to Go

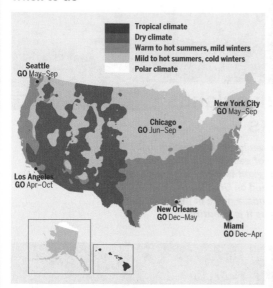

Tropical climate
Dry climate
Warm to hot summers, mild winters
Mild to hot summers, cold winters
Polar climate

Seattle
GO May–Sep

New York City
GO May–Sep

Chicago
GO Jun–Sep

Los Angeles
GO Apr–Oct

New Orleans
GO Dec–May

Miami
GO Dec–Apr

High Season (Jun–early Sep)

○ High-country sectors in the mountainous parks are guaranteed to be open.

○ July and August are crowded; reservations are a must.

Shoulder (May–mid-Jun & mid-Sep–Oct)

○ Waterfalls in Yosemite and elsewhere are at their peak in spring.

○ High-elevation roads are still closed in spring.

Low Season (mid-Sep–May)

○ Rain is possible in coastal regions, but rarely constant.

○ Expect cooler weather and fewer crowds at Bryce and Grand Canyon.

Entry Fees

Seven-day pass from free to per vehicle/pedestrian $35/20.

America the Beautiful Annual Pass

$80 per vehicle valid for all national parks for 12 months from purchase. Buy through National Park Service (#888-275-8747, ext 1; www.nps.gov).

ATMs

Most parks have at least one ATM; widely available in gateway towns.

Credit Cards

Major credit cards widely accepted; Forest Service, BLM and other campgrounds accept cash and/or checks only.

Cell Phones

Coverage inside parks is inconsistent at best.

Wi-Fi

Some park lodges have wireless. Outside the parks, most cafes and hotels offer free wireless. Chain hotels sometimes charge.

Tipping

Tip restaurant servers 15–20%; porters $2 per bag; hotel maids $2 to $5 per night.

Daily Costs

Budget: Less than $150

- Camping & RV site: $15–45
- Park entrance fee: free–$35
- Cheap self-catering food or cafe/diner meal: $6–15
- Park shuttle: free

Midrange: $150–250

- Double room in midrange hotel: $100–250
- Popular restaurant dinner for two: $30–60
- Car hire per day: from $30

Top End: More than $250

- Double room in a top-end hotel: from $200
- Dinner in a top restaurant: $60–100

Advance Planning

Twelve months before Reserve campsites and historic lodge accommodations.
Six months before Reserve hotel rooms in satellite towns if visiting in summer. Book flights.
Three months before Start training if planning to backpack. If you haven't reserved sleeping arrangements, do so.
One month before Secure rental car. Take your own car in for a safety inspection and tune-up if planning a long drive.

Useful Websites

Lonely Planet (www.lonelyplanet.com/usa) Destination information, hotel reviews, traveler forum and more.
National Park Service (NPS; www.nps.gov) Gateway to America's greatest natural treasures, its national parks.

Accommodations

Campsites Reservation and first-come, first-served sites both available in all parks. Flush toilets are common, hot showers are not. Full hookups for RVs usually found outside parks.
Park Lodges Wonderful experience. Many have wi-fi.
B&Bs Available in gateway towns outside parks; often excellent and usually include wi-fi.
Hotels Occasionally inside parks; most in gateway towns. Nearly all have wi-fi.

Arriving at a National Park

Information Pick up a park newspaper at the entry kiosk and hang onto it; they're packed with useful information.
Camping If you're going for a first-come, first-served site, head straight to the campground. For weekends, try to arrive no later than mid-morning Friday.
Parking People not spending the night inside a park may find parking difficult. Arrive early, park and take free shuttles whenever possible.
Visitor Centers Best places to start exploring the parks. Purchase books and maps, ask rangers questions, check weather reports and trail and road conditions.

Getting Around

Car Most convenient way to travel between the parks. A few park roads are gravel. Traffic inside some parks can be horrendous, especially in summer.

Park Shuttles Many parks have excellent shuttle systems with stops at major visitor sites and trailheads.

Bicycles Some parks have rentals. Good for getting around developed areas. Elsewhere, roads can be steep and shoulders narrow.

Plan Your Trip
Month by Month

January

Skiers and snowboarders descend on ski resorts across the region. The deserts of the southwest welcome travelers seeking warmer climes and saguaro-dotted landscapes.

🎬 Sundance Film Festival

If you're visiting Utah's national parks, head for Park City, UT, which unfurls the red carpet for a week of cutting-edge films (festival.sundance.org).

February & March

February is the height of ski season; meanwhile, low-desert wildflowers bloom, whales migrate off the California coast, and dude ranches saddle up in southern Arizona. In March beaches warm up, for spring break!

April

As wildflower season peaks in the high desert, the southern desert bursts into song. Shoulder season in the mountains and *along the coast brings lower hotel prices. Weather in the desert parks is beautiful.*

☉ Wildflower Season

Spring (March through May) is wildflower season in the desert, including Death Valley, Zion and sometimes Joshua Tree. Check www.desertusa.com for wildflower bloom reports or the National Park Service websites for wildflower walks, talks and celebrations.

☆ Coachella Valley Music & Arts Festival

Headliners, indie rockers, rappers and cult DJs converge outside Palm Springs for a three-day musical extravaganza (www.coachella.com) usually held over two weekends in mid-April. Book well ahead – this festival is huge.

Above: Egyptian Theater, Sundance Film Festival

PURERADIANCEPHOTO/SHUTTERSTOCK ©

KEVIN SUTTON/SHUTTERSTOCK ©

◉ Yosemite Waterfalls

Most people who visit Yosemite in July and August have no idea – until they get there – that the Valley's famous falls are but a trickle of their springtime selves. April, May and June are the best months to see the falls in full force.

🚶 National Park Week

For an entire week every April, admission to the national parks is free. Early in the year, the US president announces when National Park Week will fall that year. Many of the parks also host free activities.

May

Temperatures in Zion, Bryce, Grand Canyon, Yosemite Valley, Death Valley and Joshua Tree are delightful. Summer crowds have yet to materialize, waterfalls are at their peak, and rivers and streams are high.

☆ Joshua Tree Music Festival

Over a long weekend in May, numerous bands rock Joshua Tree Lake Campground

★ Top Events

Spring Wildflowers, April

Joshua Tree Music Festival, May

Yosemite Waterfalls, April

National Park Week, April

Meteor Showers, August

during a family-friendly indie music fest (www.joshuatreemusicfestival.com). It's followed by a soulful roots celebration in mid-October.

June

It's still possible to beat the crowds of summer in early June. By late June, the parks are jammed but the weather is stellar in many of them. Upper-elevation roads are still closed in the Sierras.

Above: Cyclists in dust storm, Burning Man (p20)

☆ Utah Shakespeare Festival

Near Zion National Park, Cedar City kicks off its three-month-long Shakespeare Festival (www.bard.org) in late June, bringing famed actors to the stage for dozens of top-notch performances.

July

High elevation sectors of the Sierras begin opening. It's prime hiking time in the high country, where wildflowers are at their peak. Desert parks, including Grand Canyon, are sweltering.

☉ Summer Wildflowers

There's nothing like hiking through high-country meadows blanketed in wildflowers. In parts of Yosemite, wildflowers bloom intensely during the short growing season between snows.

August

Hello crowds! It's the height of summer, it's blazing hot, and every hotel and campsite is reserved. First-come, first-served campgrounds are your best bet. Head to the high-country, where the weather is superb.

☉ Meteor Showers

Mid-August is the best time to catch the Perseid meteor showers in action, with a digital camera or just your own two eyes. Head away to remote desert locales like Joshua Tree and Death Valley national parks for the best visibility.

September

The crowds begin to thin and if you don't mind brisk evenings, daytime temperatures are bearable again. It's a particularly nice time for an overnight hike to the bottom of the Grand Canyon.

✵ Burning Man

In 2019 some 79,000 people attended this outdoor celebration of self-expression known for its elaborate art displays, barter system, blowing sand and final burning of the man. This temporary city (www.burningman.org) rises in the Nevada desert before Labor Day.

✵ Navajo Nation Fair

The country's largest Native American fair (navajopeople.org/blog), with a rodeo, a parade, dances, songs, arts, crafts and food, is held in mid-October in Window Rock, AZ.

October

In Yosemite in particular, fall color is nothing short of fabulous. Grand Canyon, Zion, Joshua Tree and Death Valley are especially beautiful. Crowds are nonexistent and the temperatures are dropping quickly. High-elevation sectors are closed.

✵ Pioneer Days

On the third weekend in October, Twenty-nine Palms, near Joshua Tree National Park, celebrates Pioneer Days (www.visit29.org) with an Old West–themed carnival featuring a parade, arm-wrestling and a giant chili dinner.

November

Winter is creeping in quickly. The best parks to visit are those in southern Utah, Arizona and the California deserts, where the weather is cool but still beautiful.

✵ Death Valley '49ers

In early or mid-November, Furnace Creek hosts this historical encampment (www.deathvalley49ers.org), featuring cowboy poetry, campfire sing-alongs, a gold-panning contest and a Western art show.

December

Winter is well under way in most of the parks. High-elevation roads and park sectors are closed, and visitor-center and business hours are reduced. Think snowshoeing and cross-country skiing.

✵ National Audubon Society Christmas Bird Count

Every year around Christmastime, thousands of people take to the wilds to look for and record birds for the Audubon Society's annual survey (www.audubon.org/conservation/science/christmas-bird-count). Many of the parks organize a count and rely on volunteers to help. Check the National Park Service websites for information.

Plan Your Trip
Get Inspired

MAXIMUM FILM/ALAMY STOCK PHOTO ©

Read

o **In the National Parks**
(2010) Reading Ansel Adams is the next best thing to being there.

o **Our National Parks**
(1901) The words of John Muir inspired a nation to embrace national parks.

o **Ranger Confidential: Living, Working & Dying in the National Parks**
(2010) Former park ranger Andrea Lankford takes you behind the scenes of park life.

o **Wildlife in America**
(1959) Peter Matthiessen's classic on America's wildlife story.

o **Desert Solitaire** (1968) Edward Abbey's nature writing arose from his work as a ranger in Utah's Arches National Park.

Above: Reese Witherspoon, *Wild*, 2014

Watch

o **The National Parks, America's Best Idea**
(2009) Ken Burns' 12-hour PBS miniseries is a must.

o **American Experience: Ansel Adams** (2004) Inspire your snapshots with this PBS documentary.

o **Vacation** (1983) Perfect comedy kick-starter for any family vacation.

o **Wild** (2014) A recently divorced woman throws caution to the wind to undertake a hike of self-discovery on the Pacific Crest Trail.

o **Free Solo** (2018) Epic documentary that follows Alex Honnold's free-climbing ascent of Yosemite's El Capitan.

Listen

o **Anthology of American Folk Music**
(1952) Dig into the blues, folk and country roots of America with Harry Smith.

o **Joshua Tree** (1987) Crank up this U2 classic, whether you're heading to Joshua Tree or not.

o **Beautiful Maladies**
(1998) Nothing spells 'road trip' like a good Tom Waits tune.

o **This Land is Your Land: The Asch Recordings, Vol 1** (1997) Woodie Guthrie sings everything from 'This Land is Your Land' to 'The Car Song'.

Plan Your Trip
Health & Safety

FRANTIC00/SHUTTERSTOCK ©

Before You Go

If you require medications bring them in their original, labeled containers. A signed and dated letter from your physician describing your medical conditions and medications, including generic names, is a good idea. If carrying syringes or needles, be sure to have a physician's letter documenting their necessity.

Some of the walks in this book are physically demanding and most require a reasonable level of fitness. Even if you're tackling the easy or easy–moderate walks, it pays to be relatively fit, rather than launch straight into them after months of fairly sedentary living. For the demanding walks, fitness is essential. If you have any medical problems, or are concerned about your health in any way, it's a good idea to have a full checkup before you start walking.

In the Parks

Visiting city dwellers will need to keep their wits about them in order to minimize the chances of suffering an avoidable accident or tragedy. Dress appropriately to the conditions, tell people where you are going, don't try for a big expedition without prior experience, and, above all, respect the wilderness and the inherent dangers it conceals.

Crime is far more common in big cities than in sparsely populated national parks. Nevertheless, use common sense: lock valuables in the trunk of your vehicle, especially if you're parking it at a trailhead overnight, and never leave valuables in your tent.

Walk Safety – Basic Rules

o Allow plenty of time to accomplish a walk before dark, particularly in winter.

o Study the route carefully before setting out, noting the possible escape routes and the point of no return (where it's quicker to continue than to turn back). Monitor your progress during the day against your estimated walk time, and watch the weather.

o It's wise not to walk alone. Always leave details of your intended route, number of people in your group and expected return time with someone responsible before you set off, and let that person know when you return.

○ Before setting off, make sure you have a relevant map, compass and whistle, and that you know the weather forecast for the next 24 hours. In remote, high-altitude areas, always carry extra warm, dry layers of clothing and plenty of high-energy food.

Avalanches

Avalanches are a threat during and following storms, in high winds and during temperature changes, particularly in spring. Educate yourself about the danger before setting out into the backcountry of the Sierra Nevada in particular. Signs of avalanche activity include felled trees and slides.

If you are caught in an avalanche, your chance of survival depends on your ability to keep yourself above the flowing snow and your companions' ability to rescue you. The probability of survival decreases rapidly after half an hour, so each member of the party should carry an avalanche beacon, a sectional probe and a collapsible shovel.

Altitude

To prevent acute mountain sickness:

○ Ascend slowly – have frequent rest days, spending two to three nights at each rise of 3300ft (1000m). If you reach a high altitude by trekking, acclimatization takes place gradually and you are less likely to be affected than if you fly directly to high altitude.

○ It is always wise to sleep at a lower altitude than the greatest height reached during the day, if possible. Once above 9800ft (3000m), take care not to increase the sleeping altitude by more than 985ft (300m) per day.

○ Drink extra fluids. The mountain air is dry and cold and moisture is lost as you breathe; evaporation of sweat may occur unnoticed and result in dehydration.

★ Water Purification

To ensure you are getting safe, clean drinking water in the backcountry you have three basic options:

Boiling Water is considered safe to drink if it has been boiled for at least a minute. This is best done when you set up your camp and stove in the evening.

Chemical Purification There are two types of chemicals that will purify water: chlorine or iodine. You can choose from various products on the market. Read the instructions carefully first, be aware of expiration dates and ensure you are not allergic to either chemical.

Filtration Mobile devices can pump water through microscopic filters and take out potentially harmful organisms. If carrying a filter, take care it doesn't get damaged in transit, read the instructions carefully and always filter the cleanest water you can find.

○ Eat light, high-carbohydrate meals.

○ Avoid alcohol and sedatives.

Rescue & Evacuation

If someone in your group is injured or falls ill and can't move, leave somebody with them while someone (or more) goes for help. They should take clear written details of the location and condition of the victim, and of helicopter landing conditions. If there are only two of you, leave the injured person with as much warm clothing, food and water as it's sensible to spare, plus the whistle and torch. Mark the position with something conspicuous – an orange bivvy bag, or perhaps a large stone cross on the ground.

Left: Yosemite National Park

Plan Your Trip
Clothing & Equipment

Deciding what gear is essential for a trip and what will only weigh you down is an art. Smartphone apps, new filtration systems and battery chargers are changing the game. Don't forget essentials, but be ruthless when packing, since every ounce counts when you're lugging your gear up a steep mountain.

Layering

The secret to comfortable walking is to wear several layers of light clothing, which you can easily take off or put on as you warm up or cool down. Most walkers use three main layers: a base layer next to the skin, an insulating layer, and an outer-shell layer for protection from wind, rain and snow.

For the upper body, the base layer is typically a shirt of synthetic material that wicks moisture away from the body and reduces chilling. The insulating layer retains heat next to your body, and is usually a (windproof) fleece jacket or sweater. The outer shell consists of a waterproof jacket that also protects against cold wind.

For the lower body, the layers generally consist of either shorts or loose-fitting trousers, thermal underwear ('long johns') and waterproof overtrousers.

When purchasing outdoor clothing, one of the most practical fabrics is merino wool. Though pricier than other materials, natural wool absorbs sweat, retains heat even when wet, and is soft and comfortable to wear. Even better, it doesn't store odors like other sports garments, so you can wear it for several days in a row!

Waterproof Shells

Jackets should be made of a breathable, waterproof fabric, with a hood that is roomy enough to cover headwear, but that still allows peripheral vision. Other handy features include underarm zippers for easy ventilation and a large map pocket with a heavy-gauge zipper protected by a storm flap.

Waterproof pants are best with slits for pocket access and long leg zips so that you can pull them on and off over your boots.

Footwear

Running shoes are OK for walks that are graded easy or moderate. However, you'll probably appreciate, if not need, the support and protection provided by hiking boots for more demanding walks. Nonslip soles (such as Vibram) provide the best grip.

Buy boots in warm conditions or go for a walk before trying them on, so that your feet can expand slightly, as they would on a hike. Carry a pair of sandals to wear at night for getting in and out of tents easily, at rest stops or when fording waterways.

Gaiters help to keep your feet dry in wet weather and on boggy ground; they can also deflect small stones or sand and maintain leg warmth. The best are made of strong fabric, with a robust zip protected by a flap, and secure easily around the foot.

Walking socks should be free of ridged seams in the toes and heels.

Backpack & Daypacks

For day walks, a day pack (30L to 40L) will usually suffice, but for multiday walks you will need a backpack of between 45L and 90L capacity. Even if your pack is billed as waterproof, use heavy-duty liners.

Tent

A three-season tent will fulfill most walkers' requirements. The floor and the outer shell, or fly, should have taped or sealed seams and covered zips to stop leaks. The weight can be as low as 2.2lb (1kg) for a stripped-down, low-profile tent, and up to 6.6lb (3kg) for a roomy, luxury, four-season model.

Dome- and tunnel-shaped tents handle windy conditions better than flat-sided tents.

Map & Compass

You should always carry a good map of the area in which you are walking, and know how to read it. Before setting off on your

★ Bear Spray

Some of the hikes/activities in the parks take you through bear country. As a last resort, bear spray (pepper spray) has been used effectively to deter aggressive bears, and park authorities often recommend that you equip yourself with a canister when venturing into backcountry. Be sure to familiarize yourself with the manufacturer's instructions before use, and only use as a last resort (ie, on a charging bear approximately 30–50ft/9–15m away from you). Most shops in or around the parks stock bear spray. Prices typically range from US$35 to US$45; some places also rent it by the day. It is best kept close at hand on a belt around your waist.

walk, ensure that you are aware of the contour interval, the map symbols, the magnetic declination (difference between true and grid north), plus the main ridge and river systems in the area and the general direction in which you are heading.

On the trail, try to identify major landforms such as mountain ranges and valleys, and locate them on your map to familiarize yourself with the geography.

Buy a compass and learn how to use it. The attraction of magnetic north varies in different parts of the world, so compasses need to be balanced accordingly. Compass manufacturers have divided the world into five zones. Make sure your compass is balanced for your destination zone.

There are also 'universal' compasses on the market that can be used anywhere in the world.

Left: Sequoia National Park

California & Southwest USA's National Parks Overview

NAME	STATE	ENTRANCE FEE
Arches National Park (p134)	Utah	7-day pass per vehicle $30
Big Bend National Park (p140)	Texas	7-day pass per vehicle $25
Bryce Canyon National Park (p152)	Utah	7-day pass per vehicle $35
Canyonlands National Park (p164)	Utah	7-day pass per vehicle $30
Capitol Reef National Park (p170)	Utah	7-day pass per vehicle $15
Carlsbad Caverns National Park (p178)	New Mexico	3-day pass per adult/child $12/free
Channel Islands National Park (p44)	California	Free
Death Valley National Park (p50)	California	7-day pass per vehicle $35
Grand Canyon National Park (p180)	Arizona	7-day pass per vehicle $35
Great Basin National Park (p190)	Nevada	Free
Guadalupe Mountains National Park (p192)	Texas	7-day pass per adult/child $5/free

National Parks............ p26
Road Trips................... p28

DESCRIPTION	GREAT FOR...
Giant sweeping arcs of sandstone frame snowy peaks and desert landscapes; explore the park's namesake formations in a red-rock wonderland.	
Traversing Big Bend's 1252 sq miles, you come to appreciate what 'big' really means. This is a land of incredible diversity, and vast enough to allow a lifetime of discovery.	
Bryce Canyon's sights are nothing short of otherworldly: repeated freezes and thaws have eroded soft sandstone and limestone into a landscape that's utterly unique.	
A forbidding and beautiful maze of red-rock fins, bridges, needles, spires, craters, mesas and buttes, Canyonlands is a crumbling, decaying beauty – a vision of ancient earth.	
Giant slabs of chocolate-red rock and sweeping yellow sandstone domes dominate the landscape of Capitol Reef, which Freemont Indians called the 'Land of the Sleeping Rainbow.'	
Scores of wondrous caves hide under the hills at this unique national park. The cavern formations are an ethereal wonderland of stalactites and fantastical geological features.	
Tossed like lost pearls off the coast, the Channel Islands are California's last outpost of civilization; the islands have earned themselves the nickname 'California's Galápagos.'	
The name itself evokes all that is harsh and hellish, yet closer inspection reveals water-sculpted canyons, windswept sand dunes, palm-shaded oases, jagged mountains and wildlife aplenty.	
The Grand Canyon embodies the scale and splendor of the American West, captured in its dramatic vistas and inner canyons.	
Rising abruptly from the desert, and dominating Great Basin National Park, 13,063ft Wheeler Peak creates an awesome range of life zones and landscapes within a very compact area.	
Guadalupe Mountains National Park is a Texas high spot, both literally and figuratively. At 8749ft, Guadalupe Peak is the highest point in the Lone Star State.	

NAME	STATE	ENTRANCE FEE
Joshua Tree National Park (p56)	California	7-day pass per vehicle $30
Kings Canyon National Park (p68)	California	7-day pass per vehicle $35
Lassen Volcanic National Park (p82)	California	7-day pass per vehicle $25 ($10 in winter)
Mesa Verde National Park (p198)	Colorado	7-day pass per vehicle $15-20
Petrified Forest National Park (p204)	Arizona	7-day pass per vehicle $20
Pinnacles National Park (p88)	California	7-day pass per vehicle $30
Redwood National Park (p90)	California	Free
Saguaro National Park (p208)	Arizona	7-day pass per vehicle $15
Sequoia National Park (p102)	California	7-day pass per vehicle $35
White Sands National Park (p222)	New Mexico	7-day pass per vehicle $25
Yosemite National Park (p112)	California	7-day pass per vehicle $35
Zion National Park (p210)	Utah	7-day pass per vehicle $35

Road Trips

NAME	STATE	DISTANCE/DURATION
Big Bend Scenic Loop (p146)	Texas	690 miles / 5–7 days

DESCRIPTION	GREAT FOR...
Like figments from a Dr Seuss book, Joshua trees welcome visitors to this park where the Sonora and Mojave Deserts converge.	
Kings Canyon is one of North America's deepest canyons, plunging over 8000ft.	
Anchoring the southernmost link in the Cascades' chain of volcanoes, this alien landscape bubbles over with roiling mud pots, noxious sulfur vents, steamy fumaroles, colorful cinder cones and crater lakes.	
Shrouded in mystery, Mesa Verde is a fascinating, if slightly eerie place, with a complex of cliff dwellings, some accessed by sheer climbs.	
Home to an extraordinary array of fossilized ancient logs and the multicolored sandscape of the Painted Desert.	
Pinnacles National Park is a study in geologic drama, with craggy monoliths, sheer-walled canyons and ancient volcanic remnants.	
The world's tallest living trees have been standing here from time immemorial; prepare to be impressed.	
An entire army of the majestic saguaro plant is protected in this two-part desert playground.	
With trees as high as 20-story buildings, this is an extraordinary park with soul-sustaining forests and vibrant wildflower meadows.	
With dazzling white sands, these ethereal dunes are a highlight of any trip to New Mexico.	
It's hard to believe so much natural beauty can exist in the one place. The jaw-dropping head-turner of USA national parks, Yosemite garners the devotion of all who enter.	
From secret oases of trickling water to the hot-pink blooms of a prickly pear cactus, Zion's treasures turn up in the most unexpected places.	

DESCRIPTION	ESSENTIAL PHOTO
Big Bend National Park and the endless vistas straight out of an old Western are reason enough to make this trip. But you'll also have plenty of fun along the way, exploring quirky small towns, minimalist art and astronomy parties.	Prada Marfa, a quirky roadside art installation.

NAME	STATE	DISTANCE/DURATION
Northern Redwood Coast (p96)	California	150 miles / 3–4 days
Palm Springs & Joshua Tree Oases (p62)	California	170 miles / 2–3 days
Yosemite, Sequoia & Kings Canyon (p124)	California	450 miles / 5–7 days

DESCRIPTION	ESSENTIAL PHOTO
Hug a 700-year-old tree, stroll moody coastal bluffs and drop in on roadside attractions of yesteryear on this trip through verdant redwood parks and personality-packed villages.	Misty redwoods clinging to rocky Pacific cliffs at Del Norte Coast Redwoods State Park.
Southern California's deserts can be brutally hot, barren places – escape to Palm Springs and Joshua Tree National Park, where shady fan-palm oases and date gardens await.	Sunset from Keys View
Drive up into the lofty Sierra Nevada, where glacial valleys and ancient forests overfill the windshield scenery. Go climb a rock, pitch a tent or photograph wildflowers and wildlife.	Yosemite Valley from panoramic Tunnel View.

Plan Your Trip
Best Hiking

BLAZG/SHUTTERSTOCK ©

TOP RIGHT: BENNY MARTY/SHUTTERSTOCK © BOTTOM: ALEKS2.2/SHUTTERSTOCK ©

Above: The Golden Canyon, Death Valley National Park; top left: Angels Landing, Zion National Park

Nothing captures the spirit of national parks quite like hiking. Trails crisscross the parks, offering access to scenic mountain passes, waterfalls and quiet corners. Then there's the 2663-mile, Canada-to-Mexico Pacific Crest Trail that passes through seven national parks...

Grandview Trail, Grand Canyon

A rugged and steep trail with switchbacks of cobblestone and epic canyon views.

Vernal & Nevada Falls, Yosemite

Take in unmatched views of Yosemite's most stunning waterfalls.

Angels Landing, Zion

Exposed scrambling and unrivaled panoramas on a chain-assisted climb to heaven.

Golden Canyon, Death Valley

Hike through narrow canyons past magical golden rocks up to glorious Zabriskie Point.

Monarch Lakes, Sequoia

Head out into the gorgeous backcountry of Sequoia National Park on this 8.4-mile trek.

Boy Scout Trail, Joshua Tree

Disappear into the Wonderland of Rocks labyrinth with plenty of Joshua trees to enjoy.

Top right: Nevada Falls bridge, Yosemite National Park

Plan Your Trip
Best Wildlife & Nature Watching

LEFT: HAVESEEN/SHUTTERSTOCK ©, TOP RIGHT: THOMAS TORGET/SHUTTERSTOCK © BOTTOM RIGHT: ADRIANA MARGARITA LARIOS ARELLANO/SHUTTERSTOCK ©

Above: General Sherman Tree, Sequoia National Park

North America is home to creatures both great and small and the USA's national parks are by far the best places to see them.

Sequoia
Hike the 6-mile General Sherman Tree to Moro Rock Trail and watch for black bears.

Channel Islands
Watch for whales, sea lions and abundant shorebirds just off the California coast.

Redwoods
Get to know Redwood's population of Roosevelt elk, with whales also possible from December to March.

Big Bend
Head down the Rio Grande Valley with binoculars looking for the Big Bend's 450 bird species.

Sequoia
Pay homage to the largest living tree on earth, the vast General Sherman.

Top: Green jay; Bottom: Black bears

Plan Your Trip
Best Family Experiences

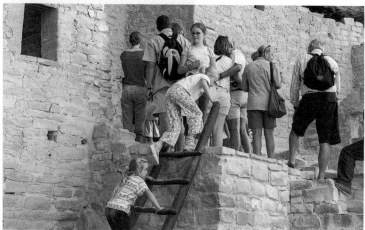

ROB CRANDALL/SHUTTERSTOCK ©

TOP RIGHT: NATURAL HISTORY COLLECTION/ALAMY STOCK PHOTO ©. BOTTOM: MARGARET WIKTOR/SHUTTERSTOCK ©

Above: Petrified Forest National Park; top left: Cliff Palace, Mesa Verde National Park

There's something inherently gratifying about bringing kids to a national park, most of which offer educational programs and activities designed to engage children in the environment around them.

Rock Climbing, Yosemite Mountaineering School

The world's holy grail of rock climbing, made accessible to all. The school is a gold mine of opportunity, and a constructive way to turn the kids loose for a day.

Cave Tour, Lehman Cave

Explore the magical underground caverns of Big Basin National Park on a guided tour.

Stargazing, Carlsbad Caverns

Take advantage of clear desert skies and let the experts introduce you to outer space in all its glory.

Petrified Forest

Introduce your children to deep time they can understand with entire forests turned to stone.

Cliff Palace, Mesa Verde

Like a movie set from *Lord of the Rings*, these cliff-face dwellings never fail to inspire wonder.

Top right: Yosemite Mountaineering School, Yosemite National Park

Plan Your Trip
Best Adventures

DHUGHES9/GETTY IMAGES ©

TOP RIGHT: ERSHOV_MAKS/GETTY IMAGES ©; BOTTOM: NICK OCEAN PHOTOGRAPHY/GETTY IMAGES ©

Above: Canyoneering, Zion National Park; top left: Santa Elena Canyon, Big Bend National Park

The USA's national parks have no shortage of spectacular settings for a bit of adventure, and you don't have to be Bear Grylls to enjoy what the American wild has to offer.

Rafting the Colorado River, Grand Canyon

Rafting this stretch of the Colorado River is a virtual all-access pass to the Grand Canyon, in all its wildness, peace and ancient glory.

River Trips, Big Bend

Whether it's white-water rafting or canoeing, the canyons of the Rio Grande in Big Bend National Park have an adventure to suit all levels of expertise and courage.

Canyoning, Zion

Rappelling 100ft over the lip of a sandstone bowl, tracing a slot canyon's sculpted curves, staring up at a ragged gash of blue sky – canyoning is beautiful, dangerous and sublime all at once.

The Maze, Canyonlands

Few areas of backcountry are at once so accessible and so challenging in a 4WD as the 30-sq-mile tangle of canyons in aptly named Canyonlands.

Hermit Trail, Grand Canyon

Leave behind the Grand Canyon crowds and hike this challenging two-day, 18.4-mile one-way trek into the canyon backcountry.

Top right: Canyonlands National Park

CALIFORNIA

In This Chapter

Channel Islands 44
Death Valley 50
Joshua Tree 56
Kings Canyon 68
Lassen Volcanic 82
Pinnacles 88
Redwood 90
Sequoia 102
Yosemite 112

California

From misty forests to sun-kissed beaches, the Golden State is an all-seasons outdoor playground with more national parks than anywhere else in the United States. California has it all: the arid expanses of the Mojave Desert reach almost to the Pacific's underwater kelp forests, while mighty redwoods line the northern coast. Hike among desert wildflowers in spring, dive into the Pacific in summer, mountain bike through fall foliage and ski down wintry mountains.

Don't Miss

o Roaming from waterfalls to granite monoliths in Yosemite Valley (p112)

o Gazing up at gigantic trees in Redwood (p90)

o Being awed by Death Valley's dunes and mountains (p50)

o Exploring otherworldly Lassen Volcanic National Park (p82)

o Toiling up stairs to reach Sequoia's spectacular Moro Rock (p104)

o Hiking or climbing at subalpine Tuolumne Meadows (p115)

When to Go

Summer's high season (June to August) sees prices rise by 50% or more in many parks. But it's low season in the hot desert regions.

Crowds and prices drop during the shoulder seasons (April to May and September to October). It's wetter in spring and drier in autumn, but generally mild at these times.

Winter (November to March) is peak season in SoCal's deserts. But elsewhere it's low season, with room rates lowest along the coast. In the mountains, expect chilly temperatures, rainstorms and heavy snow.

Previous page: Yosemite National Park (p112)
SUNDRY PHOTOGRAPHY/SHUTTERSTOCK ©

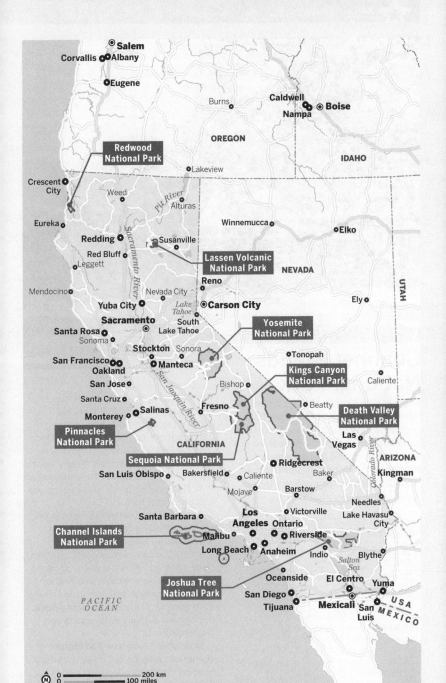

TRAVEL STOCK/SHUTTERSTOCK ©

Sea lions

Channel Islands National Park

This chain of islands off the Southern California coast is rich in unique flora and fauna, tide pools and kelp forests, and home to 23 endemic terrestrial animal species and 578 varieties of native plant. This raw, end-of-the-world landscape is an inspiring place to hike, kayak and whale-watch.

The archipelago's four northern islands, San Miguel, Santa Rosa, Santa Cruz and Anacapa, along with tiny southern Santa Barbara, comprise Channel Islands National Park.

Anacapa Island, actually three separate islands, is the best option if you're short on time. Go kayaking, diving, tide-pooling and watch sea lions here.

Santa Cruz is the largest island at 96 sq miles, claiming two mountain ranges and the park's tallest peak, Mt Diablo (2450ft). You can swim, snorkel, dive and kayak here, and there are plenty of hiking options starting from Scorpion Anchorage. Beach, canyon and grasslands hiking trails abound on 84-sq-mile **Santa Rosa**, but high winds make water sports very challenging.

Meanwhile, 14-sq-mile **San Miguel** guarantees solitude, but its westernmost location means it's often shrouded in fog. Some sections are off-limits to visitors.

Great For...

State
California

Entrance Fee
Free

Area
390 sq miles

Bat star and orange cup corals, Santa Cruz Island; Overleaf: Anacapa Island

STEVENHULLPHOTOGRAPHY/SHUTTERSTOCK ©

CARLOS GANDIAGA/SHUTTERSTOCK ®

 Channel Islands History

Originally, the Channel Islands were inhabited by Chumash tribespeople, who were forced to move to mainland Catholic missions by Spanish military forces in the early 1800s. The islands were subsequently taken over by Mexican and American ranchers during the 19th century and the US military in the 20th century, until conservation efforts began in the 1970s and '80s.

Scenic & Whale-Watching Cruises

The main provider of boats for Channel Islands visits is Island Packers (p48), with day trips and overnight camping excursions available. Boats mostly set out from Ventura but a few go from nearby Oxnard. It also offers wildlife cruises year-round, including seasonal whale-watching from late December to mid-April (gray whales) and mid-May through mid-September (blue and humpback whales).

Water Sports

Aquasports (805-968-7231; www.islandkayaking.com) offers day and overnight kayaking trips to Santa Cruz, Anacapa and along the coast near Santa Barbara, led by professional naturalists. Book ahead to rent kayaks and SUPs from **Channel Islands Kayak Center** (805-984-5595; www.cikayak.com; 1691 Spinnaker Dr, Ventura; by appointment only). It can also arrange a private guided kayaking tour of Santa Cruz or Anacapa.

Wildlife & Nature

Human beings have left a heavy footprint. Erosion was caused by overgrazing livestock, rabbits fed on native plants, and the US military even used San Miguel as a practice bombing range. In 1969 an offshore oil spill engulfed the northern islands.

But the future isn't all bleak. Brown pelicans have rebounded on West Anacapa and Santa Barbara, while on San Miguel, native vegetation has returned a half-century after overgrazing sheep were removed.

Essential Information

When to Go
In summer, island conditions are hot, dusty and bone-dry. Better times to visit are during the spring wildflower bloom or in early fall, when the fog clears. Winter can be stormy, but it's also great for wildlife-watching, especially whales.

Sleeping & Eating
Each island has a primitive year-round **campground** (reservations 877-444-6777; www.recreation.gov; tent sites $15) with pit toilets and picnic tables. Water is only available on Santa Cruz Island. Advance reservations are required for all island campsites.

There's nowhere to buy food on the islands so bring a picnic (and take out all your trash).

Visitor Center
Channel Islands National Park Visitor Center (Robert J Lagomarsino Visitor Center; 805-658-5730; www.nps.gov/chis; 1901 Spinnaker Dr, Ventura; 8:30am-5pm) is on the mainland at the far end of Ventura Harbor. A free video gives some background.

Getting There & Around
You can access the national park by taking a boat from Ventura or Oxnard or a plane from Camarillo. Trips may be canceled anytime due to high surf or weather conditions. Reservations are essential for weekends, holidays and summer trips. **Island Packers** (805-642-1393; http://islandpackers.com; 1691 Spinnaker Dr, Ventura; Channel Island day trips from $59, wildlife cruises from $68) offers regularly scheduled boat services.

The open seas on the boat ride out to the Channel Islands may feel choppy to landlubbers. To avoid seasickness, sit outside on the lower deck, keep away from the diesel fumes in the back, and focus on the horizon.

Alternatively, you can take a scenic flight to Santa Rosa or San Miguel with **Channel Islands Aviation** (805-987-1301; www.flycia.com; 305 Durley Ave, Camarillo). ∎

Humpback whale off Channel Islands

ATSUOBABA/GETTY IMAGES ©

THIERRY HENNET/GETTY IMAGES ©

Zabriskie Point

Death Valley National Park

The name evokes all that is harsh, hot and hellish – a punishing, barren and lifeless place. Yet closer inspection reveals that nature is putting on a truly spectacular show: singing sand dunes, boulders moving across the desert floor, extinct volcanic craters, stark mountains rising to 11,000ft and plenty of wildlife.

Great For...

State
California

Entrance Fee
7-day pass per car/motorcycle/person on foot or bicycle $35/25/15

Area
5270 sq miles

Dramatic Viewpoints

Southeast of Furnace Creek is **Zabriskie Point**, for spectacular views across golden badlands eroded into pleats and gullies. It was named for a manager of the Pacific Coast Borax Company and also inspired the title of Michelangelo Antonio's 1970s movie. Early morning is the best time to visit.

Twenty miles south is 5475ft-high **Dante's View**, gazing out on the entire southern Death Valley basin from the top of the Black Mountains. On very clear days, you can simultaneously see the highest (Mt Whitney) and lowest (Badwater) points in the contiguous USA. Allow about 1½ hours for the round-trip from the turnoff at Hwy 190.

Scenic Drives

About 9 miles south of Furnace Creek, the 9-mile, one-way **Artists Drive** scenic loop offers 'wow' moments around every turn; it's best done in the late afternoon when exposed minerals and volcanic ash make the hills erupt in fireworks of color.

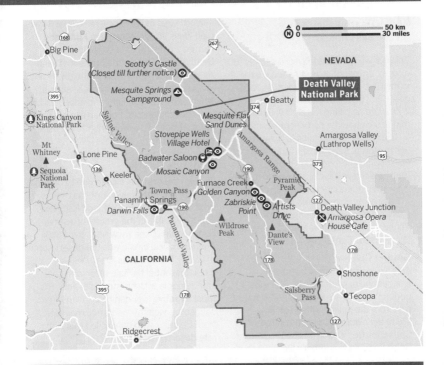

Dante's View

Death Valley's Best Hikes

This is a land of superlatives: it's the hottest, driest and lowest national park in the USA. There are also palm-shaded oases and plenty of endemic wildlife, so it's rewarding hiking terrain if you don't mind some bouldering or scrambling.

The best time for hiking is November to March. Steer clear in summer, except on higher-elevation mountain trails, which are usually snowed in during winter. Adequate water is essential.

Easy hikes do exist, and families can pick up a free fun-for-all-ages *Junior Ranger Activity Booklet* at the Furnace Creek Visitor Center (p54).

Golden Canyon

This trail network winds through a wonderland of golden rocks. The most popular route is a 3-mile out-and-back trek from the main trailhead off Hwy 178 to the oxidized iron cliffs of Red Cathedral. Combining it with the Gower Gulch Loop adds another mile.

Wildrose Peak

This moderate-to-strenuous trail begins near the charcoal kilns off Wildrose Canyon Rd and ascends to Wildrose Peak (9064ft), which has a stunning vista. The 8.4-mile round-trip hike is best in spring or fall.

Mosaic Canyon Trail

West of Stovepipe Wells Village, a 2.3-mile gravel road leads to Mosaic Canyon, where you can hike and scramble past smooth multihued rock walls. Colors are sharpest at midday.

Darwin Falls

This natural-spring-fed year-round cascade plunges into a gorge, embraced by willows that attract migratory birds. Look for the (unmarked) turnoff about 0.75 miles west of Panamint Springs, then follow the dirt road for 2.5 miles to the parking area. The 1-mile hike to the first waterfall requires some climbing over rocks and crossing small streams.

Northwest of Furnace Creek, near Stovepipe Wells Village, **Mesquite Flat Sand Dunes** are the most accessible dunes in Death Valley. This undulating sea of sand rises to 100ft high next to the highway and is most photogenic at sunrise or sunset when bathed in soft light and accented by long, deep shadows. Keep an eye out for animal tracks. Full-moon nights are especially magical.

Scotty's Castle

Though the castle is closed due to flood damage and not likely to until further notice, there are special 'Flood Recovery Tours' available in the grounds (reservations required, see www.nps.gov/deva). This whimsical castle was the desert home of Walter E Scott, alias 'Death Valley Scotty,' a quintessential tall-tale teller who captivated people with his stories of gold. His most lucrative friendship was with Albert Johnson, a wealthy insurance magnate from Chicago, who bankrolled this elaborate desert oasis in the 1920s.

CHECUBUS/SHUTTERSTOCK ©

NADIA YONG/SHUTTERSTOCK ©

Top: Mesquite Flat Sand Dunes; Bottom: Scotty's Castle

Essential Information

Sleeping

Camping is plentiful but if you're looking for a place with a roof, in-park options are limited, pricey and often booked solid in springtime. Alternative bases are the gateway towns of Beatty (40 miles from Furnace Creek), Lone Pine (40 miles), Death Valley Junction (30 miles) and Tecopa (70 miles). Options a bit further afield include Ridgecrest (120 miles) and Las Vegas (140 miles).

Death Valley National Park Campgrounds (www.nps.gov/deva; campsites free-$36) The National Park Service (NPS) operates nine campgrounds on a first-come, first-served basis (exception: Furnace Creek between mid-October and mid-April). Campsites fill by midmorning on some weekends, especially during the spring wildflower bloom.

Mesquite Springs Campground (📞760-786-3200; www.nps.gov/deva; Hwy 190; per site $14) In the northern reaches of the park, this first-come, first-served campground has 30 spaces. At an elevation of 1800ft, it's also a lot cooler than the desert floor. Sites come with fire pits and tables, and there's water and flush toilets.

Stovepipe Wells Village Hotel (📞760-786-2387; www.deathvalleyhotels.com; 51880 Hwy 190, Stovepipe Wells; RV sites $33.30, r $140-210; ✳@🛜🏊) The 83 rooms at this private resort have beds draped in quality linens and accented with cheerful Native American–patterned blankets. There's a small pool and the on-site cowboy-style restaurant serves breakfast and dinner daily, with lunch available in the next-door saloon.

Eating & Drinking

There are restaurants and stores for stocking up on basic groceries and camping supplies in Furnace Creek, Stovepipe Wells Village and Panamint Springs. Hours vary seasonally; some close in summer.

Amargosa Opera House Cafe (📞760-852-4432; www.amargosacafe.org; Death Valley Junction; mains $9-19, pie per slice $5; ⏰8am-3pm Mon,

Fri, Sat & Sun, 6:30-9pm Sat) 🍴 This charmer in the middle of nowhere gets you ready for a day in Death Valley with hearty breakfasts or healthy sandwiches, but truly shows off its farm-to-table stripes at dinnertime on Saturdays. Combine with a tour of (or show at) the late Marta Becket's kooky opera house. Excellent coffee to boot.

Badwater Saloon (📞760-786-2387; www.deathvalleyhotels.com; 51880 Hwy 190, Stovepipe Wells Village; ⏰11:30am-9pm or later) Light meals and bar snacks are served at this colorful bar with Old West knickknacks, cold draft beer and Lynyrd Skynyrd on the jukebox.

Information

Furnace Creek is Death Valley's commercial hub, with the park's main visitor center, a general store, gas station, post office, ATM, wi-fi, golf course, lodging and restaurants.

There is no public transportation to Death Valley. Coming from Las Vegas, it's about 120 miles via Hwy 160 or 140 miles via I-95 and Hwy 373. Coming from Hwy 395, you can reach Furnace Creek in about 100 miles from Lone Pine via Hwy 190 or in 120 miles from Ridgecrest via Hwys 178 and 190. From I-15, get off at Baker and head 115 miles north via Hwy 127.

Gas is available 24/7 at Furnace Creek and Stovepipe Wells Village and from 7am to 9:30pm in Panamint Springs. Prices are much higher than outside the park, especially at Panamint.

Cell towers provide service at Furnace Creek and Stovepipe Wells but there's little to no coverage elsewhere in the park.

Visitor Center

Furnace Creek Visitor Center (📞760-786-3200; www.nps.gov/deva; ⏰8am-5pm; 🛜) has engaging exhibits on the park's ecosystem and the indigenous tribes as well as a gift shop, clean toilets, (slow) wi-fi and friendly rangers to answer questions and help you plan your day. Check the schedule for ranger-led activities. ■

Top left: Stovepipe Wells Village Hotel store; Top right: Amargosa Opera House; Bottom: Furnace Creek Visitor Center

S BORISOV/SHUTTERSTOCK ©

Joshua Tree National Park

Taking a page from a Dr Seuss book, the whimsical Joshua trees (actually tree-sized yuccas) welcome visitors to this park at the transition zone between two deserts. Rock climbers know 'JT' as California's best place to climb, hikers seek out shady oases, and mountain bikers are hypnotized by desert vistas.

Great For...

State
California

Entrance Fee
7-day pass per car/motorcycle/person on foot or bike $30/25/15

Area
1235 sq miles

Hiking

Just about anyone can enjoy a clamber on the cluster of rocks at the **Hidden Valley Trail**. An easy 1-mile trail loops around and back to the parking lot and picnic area.

For immersion into the Wonderland of Rocks, a striking rock labyrinth, embark on the challenging, 8-mile one-way **Boy Scout Trail** linking Indian Cove and Park Blvd (near Quail Springs picnic area). Arrange for pick-up at the other end.

The moderate 3-mile **Fortynine Palms Oasis Trail** allows an escape from the crowds; the trailhead is at the end of Canyon Rd that veers off 29 Palms Hwy/Hwy 62.

Cycling

Bikes are not permitted on hiking trails, but only on public paved and dirt roads that are also open to vehicles, including 29 miles of backcountry. Popular routes include challenging **Pinkham Canyon Rd**, starting from the Cottonwood Visitor Center, and the long-distance **Black Eagle Mine Rd**,

Boy Scout Trail

LEFT: DENNIS SILVAS/SHUTTERSTOCK © RIGHT: JOEL CARILLET/GETTY IMAGES ©

Prophetic Trees

It was Mormon settlers who named the Joshua trees because the branches stretching up toward heaven reminded them of the biblical prophet Joshua pointing the way to the promised land. In springtime, the trees send up a huge single cream-colored flower.

6.5 miles further north. **Queen Valley** has a gentler set of trails with bike racks along the way, so people can lock up their bikes and go hiking, but it's busy with cars, as is the bumpy, sandy and steep **Geology Tour Rd**. There's also a wide-open network of dirt roads at **Covington Flats**.

Rock Climbing

JT's rocks are famous for their rough, high-friction surfaces; from boulders to cracks to multipitch faces, there are more than 8000 established routes. Some of the most popular climbs are in the Hidden Valley area.

Joshua Tree Rock Climbing School (☎760-366-4745; www.joshuatreerockclimbing. com; 63439 Doggie Trail, Joshua Tree; 1-day course from $195) and **Vertical Adventures** (☎949-854-6250, 800-514-8785; www.verticaladven tures.com; courses from $155; ☻Sep-May) offer guided climbs and climbing instruction.

Left: Joshua trees
Right: Fortynine Palms Oasis Trail

Essential Information

Sleeping

Unless you're day-tripping from Palm Springs, set up camp inside the park or base yourself in the desert communities linked by 29 Palms Hwy/Hwy 62 along the park's northern perimeter. Twenty-nine Palms and Yucca Valley have mostly national chain motels, while pads in Joshua Tree have plenty of charm and character.

Camping

Of the park's eight campgrounds, only **Cottonwood** (Pinto Basin Rd; per site $20) and **Black Rock Canyon** (Joshua Lane; per site $20) have potable water, flush toilets and dump stations. **Indian Cove** (Indian Cove Rd; per site $20) and Black Rock accept reservations from October through May. The others are first-come, first-served and have pit toilets, picnic tables and fire grates. None have showers, but there are some at **Coyote Corner** (6535 Park Blvd; ⊙9am-6pm) in Joshua Tree. Details are available at www.nps.gov/jotr or ☑760-367-5500.

Between October and May, campsites fill by Thursday noon, especially during the springtime bloom. If you arrive too late, there's overflow camping on Bureau of Land Management (BLM) land north and south of the park as well as in private campgrounds.

Backcountry camping is allowed 1 mile from any road or 500ft from any trailhead. There is no water in the park, so bring one to two gallons per person per day for drinking, cooking and personal hygiene. Campfires are prohibited to prevent wildfires and damage to the fragile desert floor. Free self-registration is required at a backcountry board inside the park, where you can also leave your car.

Lodgings

Sacred Sands (☑760-424-6407; www.sacred sands.com; 63155 Quail Springs Rd, Joshua Tree; studio/ste $339/369, 2-night minimum; ❋ 🛜) 🍃 In an isolated, pin-drop-quiet spot, these two desert-chic suites are the ultimate romantic retreat, each with a private outdoor shower, hot tub, sundeck and earthen straw-bale walls. There are astounding views across the desert hills and into the national park. Owners Scott and Steve are gracious hosts. It's 4 miles south of 29 Palms Hwy (via Park Bl), 1 mile west of the park entrance.

Eating

La Copine (www.lacopinekitchen.com; 848 Old Woman Rd, Flamingo Heights; mains $10-16; ⊙9am-3pm Thu-Sun) It's a long road from Phila-delphia to the high desert, but that's where Nikki and Claire decided to take their farm-to-table brunch cuisine from pop-up to brick and mortar. Their roadside bistro serves zeitgeist-capturing dishes such as the signature salad with smoked salmon and poached egg, homemade crumpets and gold milk turmeric tea. Expect a wait on weekends.

Drinking & Entertainment

Joshua Tree Coffee Company (☑760-974-4060; www.jtcoffeeco.com; 61738 29 Palms Hwy/Hwy 62, Joshua Tree; ⊙7am-6pm) Organic and locally roasted, this spotless outfit makes some of the best coffee in JT. It's sold in places around the valley but roasted right here in the little hipster cafe with outdoor seating.

Pappy & Harriet's Pioneertown Palace (☑760-365-5956; www.pappyandharriets.com; 53688 Pioneertown Rd, Pioneertown; mains $6-15; ⊙11am-2am Thu-Sun, from 5pm Mon) For local color, toothsome BBQ, cheap beer and kick-ass live music, drop in at this textbook honky-tonk in Pioneertown, a movie set turned living town. Monday's open-mike nights (admission free) are legendary and often bring out astounding talent. From Thursday to Saturday, local and national talent takes over the stage.

Getting There & Away

Joshua Tree has three park entrances. Access the west entrance from the town of Joshua Tree, the north entrance from Twentynine Palms and the south entrance from I-10. The park's northern half harbors most of the attractions.

Top left: Coyote Corner; Top right: Pappy & Harriet's Pioneertown Palace; Bottom: Indian Cove

Palm Springs & Joshua Tree Oases

Southern California's deserts can be brutally hot, barren places – escape to Palm Springs and Joshua Tree National Park, where shady fan-palm oases and date gardens await.

Duration 2–3 days

Distance 170 miles

Best Time to Go
February to April for spring wildflower blooms and cooler temperatures.

Essential Photo
Sunset from Keys View.

Best for Solitude
Hike to the Lost Palms Oasis.

❶ Palm Springs

Hollywood celebs have always counted on Palm Springs as a quick escape from LA. Today, this desert resort town shows off a trove of well-preserved mid-Century Modern buildings. Stop at the **Palm Springs Visitors Center** (☑760-778-8418, 800-347-7746; www.visitpalmsprings.com; 2901 N Palm Canyon Dr; ☉9am-5pm), inside a 1965 gas station by modernist Albert Frey, to pick up a self-guided architectural tour map. Then drive uphill to clamber aboard the **Palm Springs Aerial Tramway** (☑760-325-1391, 888-515-8726; www.pstramway.com; 1 Tram Way; adult/child $26/17, parking $5; ☉1st tram up 10am Mon-Fri, 8am Sat & Sun, last tram down 9:45pm daily, varies seasonally), which climbs nearly 6000 vertical feet from the hot Sonoran Desert floor to the cool, even snowy San Jacinto Mountains in less than 15 minutes. Back down on the ground, drive south on Palm Canyon Dr, where you can hop between art galleries, cafes, cocktail bars, trendy restaurants and chic boutiques. For a dose of culture, check out the latest exhibit at the excellent **Palm Springs Art Museum** (☑760-322-4800; www.psmuseum. org; 101 Museum Dr; adult/student $12/5, all free 4-8pm Thu; ☉10am-5pm Sun-Tue & Sat, noon-9pm Thu & Fri).

The Drive » Drive north out of downtown Palm Springs along Indian Canyon Dr for 7 miles, passing over the I-10. Turn right onto Dillon Rd, then after 2.5 miles turn left onto Palm Dr, which heads north into central Desert Hot Springs.

❷ Desert Hot Springs

In 1774 Spanish explorer Juan Bautista de Anza was the first European to encounter the desert Cahuilla tribe. Afterward, the Spanish name Agua Caliente came to refer to both the indigenous people and the natural hot springs, which still flow restoratively through the town of Desert Hot Springs (www.visitdeserthotsprings.com), where hip boutique hotels have appeared atop healing waters bubbling up from deep below. Imitate Tim Robbins in Robert Altman's film *The Player* and have a mud bath at **Two Bunch Palms Spa Resort** (☑760-676-5000; www.twobunchpalms.com/spa; 67425 Two Bunch Palms Trail; day-spa package from $195; ☉by reservation 9am-7pm Tue-Thu, 9am-8:30pm Fri, 8am-8:30pm Sat, 8am-7pm Sun & Mon) ✐, which sits atop an actual oasis. Bounce between a variety of pools and sunbathing areas, but maintain the code of silence (actually, whispers only).

The Drive » Head west on Pierson Blvd back to Indian Canyon Dr. Turn right and drive northwest through the dusty outskirts of Desert Hot Springs. Turn right onto Hwy 62 Eastbound toward Yucca Valley; after about 4 miles, turn right onto East Dr and

look for signs for Big Morongo Canyon
Preserve.

❸ Big Morongo Canyon Preserve

An oasis hidden in the high desert, Big
Morongo Canyon Preserve is a bird-
watching hot spot. Tucked into the Little
San Bernardino Mountains, this stream-fed
riparian habitat is flush with cottonwood
and willow trees. Nearly 250 bird species
have been identified here, including over
70 that use the area as breeding grounds.
Tramp along wooden boardwalks through
marshy woodlands as hummingbirds
flutter atop flowers and woodpeckers
hammer away.

The Drive » Rejoin Hwy 62 Eastbound
past Yucca Valley, with its roadside
antiques, vintage shops, art galleries and
cafes, to the town of Joshua Tree about
16 miles away, which makes a good place
to base yourself for the night. At the

intersection with Park Blvd, turn right and
drive 5 miles to Joshua Tree National Park's
west entrance. Make sure you've got a full
tank of gas first.

❹ Hidden Valley

It's time to jump into **Joshua Tree National
Park**, a wonderland of jumbo rocks
interspersed with sandy forests of Joshua
trees (related to agave plants). Revel in
the scenery as you drive along the winding
park road for about 8 miles to the Hidden
Valley picnic area. Turn left and drive past
the campground to the trailhead for **Barker
Dam**. Here a kid-friendly nature trail loops
for just over a mile past a pretty little
artificial lake and a rock incised with Native
American petroglyphs. If you enjoy history
and Western lore, check with the national
park office whether ranger-led walking
tours of nearby **Keys Ranch** (📞760-367-
5500; www.nps.gov/jotr; tour adult/child $10/5;
🕑tour schedules vary) are offered during

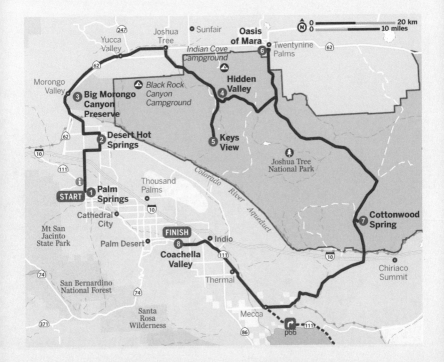

your stay. Pioneer homesteaders tried their hand at cattle ranching, mining and desert farming here in the 19th century.

The Drive » Backtrack to Park Blvd, turn left and head south again past jumbled rock formations and fields of spiky Joshua trees. Take the well-signed right turn toward Keys View. You'll pass several trailheads and roadside interpretive exhibits over the next 5.5 miles leading up to the viewpoint.

❺ Keys View

Make sure you embark at least an hour before sunset for the drive up to Keys View (5185ft), where panoramic views look into the **Coachella Valley** and reach as far south as the shimmering Salton Sea or, on an unusually clear day, Mexico's Signal Mountain. Looming in front of you are **Mt San Jacinto** (10,800ft) and **Mt San** **Gorgonio** (11,500ft), two of Southern California's highest peaks, often snow-dusted even in spring. Down below snakes the shaky **San Andreas Fault**.

The Drive » Head back downhill to Park Blvd. Turn right and wind through the park's Wonderland of Rocks (where boulders call out to scampering kids and serious rock jocks alike), passing more campgrounds. After 10 miles, veer left to stay on Park Blvd and drive north for 8 miles toward the town of Twentynine Palms onto Utah Trail.

❻ Oasis of Mara

Drop by Joshua Tree National Park's **Oasis Visitor Center** (www.nps.gov/jotr; 74485 National Park Dr, Twentynine Palms; ⏰8:30am-5pm) for its educational exhibits about Southern California's desert fan palms. These palms are often found growing along

MIKE VER SPRILL/SHUTTERSTOCK ©

Top: Oasis Visitor Center; Bottom left: Keys View; Bottom right: Ladder-backed woodpecker

SANDRA FOYT/ALAMY STOCK PHOTO ©

TAKAHASHI PHOTOGRAPHY/SHUTTERSTOCK ©

Detour:
Salton Sea

Start: **7** Cottonwood Spring

Driving along Hwy 111 southeast of Mecca, it's a most unexpected sight: California's largest lake in the middle of its largest desert. It was created by accident in 1905 when spring flooding breached irrigation canals built to bring water from the Colorado River to the farmland in the Imperial Valley. Marketed to mid-20th-century tourists as the 'California Riviera' with beachfront vacation homes, the Salton Sea has been mostly abandoned because agricultural runoff has increased the lake's salinity to the point where few fish species can survive. An even stranger sight is folk-art **Salvation Mountain** (📞760-624-8754; www.salvationmountain inc.org; 603 E Beal Rd, Niland; donations accepted; ⊙dawn-dusk), an artificial hill covered in acrylic paint and found objects and inscribed with Christian religious messages. It's outside Niland, about 3 miles east of Hwy 111 en route to Slab City.

onto Pinto Basin Rd for a winding 30-mile drive southeast to Cottonwood Spring.

7 Cottonwood Spring

On your drive to Cottonwood Spring, you'll pass from the high Mojave Desert into the lower Sonoran Desert. At the **Cholla Cactus Garden**, handily labeled specimens burst into bloom in spring, including unmistakable ocotillo plants, which look like green octopus tentacles adorned with flaming scarlet flowers. Turn left at the Cottonwood Visitor Center for a short drive east past the campground to Cottonwood Spring. Once used by the Cahuilla, who left behind archaeological evidence such as mortars and clay pots, the springs became a hotbed for gold mining in the late 19th century. The now-dry springs are the start of the moderately strenuous 7.5-mile round-trip trek out to **Lost Palms Oasis**, a fan-palm oasis blessed with solitude and scenery.

The Drive » Head south from Cottonwood Springs and drive across the I-10 to pick up scenic Box Canyon Rd, which burrows a hole through the desert, twisting its way toward the Salton Sea. Take 66th Ave west to Mecca, then turn right onto Hwy 111 and drive northwest ('up valley') toward Indio.

8 Coachella Valley

The hot but fertile Coachella Valley is the ideal place to find the date of your dreams – the kind that grows on trees, that is. Date farms let you sample exotic-sounding varieties like halawy, deglet noor and zahidi for free, but the signature taste of the valley is a rich date shake from certified-organic **Oasis Date Gardens** (www.oasisdate.com) or the 1920s pioneer **Shields Date Garden** (www.shieldsdate garden.com). ∎

fault lines, where cracks in the earth's crust allow subterranean water to surface. Outside the visitor center, a gentle half-mile nature trail leads around the **Oasis of Mara**, where Serrano peoples once camped. Ask for directions to the trailhead off Hwy 62 for the 3-mile, round-trip hike to **Fortynine Palms Oasis**, where a sun-exposed dirt trail marches you over a ridge, then drops you into a rocky gorge, doggedly heading down past barrel cacti toward a distant speck of green.

The Drive » Drive back south on Utah Trail and re-enter the park. Follow Park Blvd south, turning left at the first major junction

Cottonwood Spring

PAWO/SHUTTERSTOCK ©

General Grant Tree Trail

Kings Canyon National Park

Rugged Kings Canyon offers true adventure to those who crave verdant trails, rushing streams and gargantuan rock formations. The camping, back-country exploring and climbing are superb, and Kings Canyon Scenic Byway twists through some of California's most dramatic scenery.

Great For...

State
California

Entrance Fee
7-day pass per vehicle/person on foot or bicycle $35/20

Area
721 sq miles

❶ General Grant Grove

This sequoia grove off Generals Hwy is astounding. The paved half-mile **General Grant Tree Trail** is an interpretive walk that visits a number of mature sequoias, including the 27-story **General Grant Tree**. This giant holds triple honors as the world's second-largest living tree, a memorial to US soldiers killed in war and the nation's official Christmas tree since 1926. The nearby **Fallen Monarch**, a massive, fire-hollowed trunk you can walk through, has been a cabin, hotel, saloon and stables.

To escape the bustling crowds, follow the more secluded 1.5-mile **North Grove Loop**, which passes wildflower patches and bubbling creeks as it gently winds underneath a canopy of stately sequoias, evergreen pines and aromatic incense cedars.

The magnificence of this ancient sequoia grove was nationally recognized

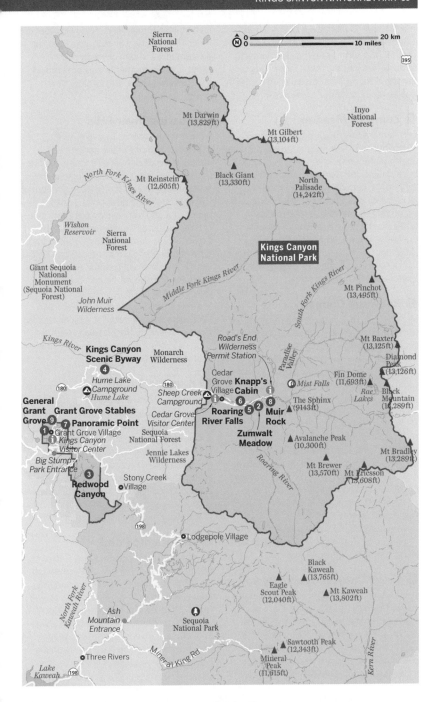

in 1890 when Congress first designated it General Grant National Park. It took another half-century for this tiny parcel to be absorbed into the much larger Kings Canyon National Park, established in 1940 to prevent damming of the Kings River.

❷ Zumwalt Meadow

This verdant meadow, bordered by the Kings River and soaring granite walls, offers phenomenal views. In the early morning, the air hums with birdsong, the sun's rays light up the canyon, and mule deer and black bears can often be spotted foraging among the meadow's long grasses, wildflowers and berry bushes. Following the partly shaded, easy loop nature trail (1.5 miles), with boardwalk sections and a few benches for resting, gives you a quick snapshot of the canyon's beauty.

❸ Redwood Canyon

More than 15,000 sequoias form one of the world's largest groves of these giant trees. In an almost-forgotten corner of the park, this secluded forest lets you revel in the grandeur of the trees away from the crowds while you hike mostly moderate trails. What you won't find here, however, are any of the California coast's redwood trees – that's what early pioneers mistook these giant sequoias for, hence the erroneous name.

For the best view, hike to the summit of Big Baldy. Alternatively, you can walk in the forest via trailheads at the end of a bumpy 2-mile dirt road (closed in winter) that starts across from the Hume Lake/Quail Flat signed intersection on the Generals Hwy, just over 5 miles southeast of Grant Grove Village. There's also a good spot for a picnic before heading out on a hike.

❹ Kings Canyon Scenic Byway

Connecting Grant Grove and Cedar Grove in Kings Canyon, this 31-mile roller-coaster road, also known as Hwy 180, surely ranks as one of the most spectacular in the US. This jaw-dropping scenic drive enters one of North America's deepest canyons, traversing the forested Giant Sequoia National Monument and shadowing the Kings River all the way to Road's End. The descent into the canyon involves some white-knuckle moments; turnouts provide superb views and a chance to let other drivers pass.

❺ Roaring River Falls

A five-minute walk on a paved trail (0.3 miles) leads to one of the park's most accessible waterfalls, a 40ft chute gushing into a granite bowl. In late spring and sometimes in early summer, the strength of this cascade won't disappoint. Look for the parking lot and trailhead on the south side of Hwy 180, about 3 miles east of Cedar Grove Village, slightly closer to Road's End. It's a great spot to stretch your legs after a long drive. You can clamber over the boulders and dip your toes in the pool at the bottom of the falls.

There's also access to the River Trail here, a pleasant almost-flat walk along the riverbed reaching the Zumwalt Meadow Loop (1.6 miles) and continuing a further mile onto Road's End.

❻ Knapp's Cabin

During the 1920s, wealthy Santa Barbara businessman George Knapp built this simple wood-shingled cabin to store gear in during his extravagant fishing and camping excursions in Kings Canyon. From a signed roadside pullout on Hwy 180, about 2 miles east of the village, a very short trail leads to this hidden building, the oldest in Cedar Grove. Come around dusk, when the views of the glacier-carved canyon are glorious.

❼ Panoramic Point

For a breathtaking view of Kings Canyon, head 2.3 miles up narrow, steep and winding Panoramic Point Rd (trailers and RVs aren't recommended), which branches off Hwy 180. Follow a short paved trail uphill from the parking lot to the viewpoint, where precipitous canyons and the snowcapped peaks of the Great Western Divide unfold below you. Snow closes the road to vehicles during winter, when it becomes a cross-country ski and snowshoe route.

Hikers may access the road when snow levels are low. From the visitor center in Grant Grove, follow the paved side road east, turning left after 0.1 miles, then right at the John Muir Lodge.

❽ Muir Rock

On excursions to Kings Canyon, John Muir would allegedly give talks on this large, flat river boulder, a short walk from the Road's End parking lot and less than a mile past Zumwalt Meadow. A sandy river beach here is taken over by gleeful swimmers in midsummer. Don't jump in when the raging waters, swollen with snowmelt, are dangerous. Ask at the Road's End ranger station (p76) if conditions are calm enough for a dip.

❾ Horseback Riding

Just north of General Grant Grove in Kings Canyon, pint-sized **Grant Grove Stables** (☏559-335-9292; Hwy 180; trail rides from $40; ☉mid-Jun–early Sep) is a summer-only operation offering one- and two-hour trail rides. Short and overnight rides (reservations required) are available from **Cedar Grove Pack Station** (☏559-565-3464; www.facebook.com/CedarGrovePackStation; Cedar Lane, Cedar Grove; 1/2hr ride $40/75, overnights (2-night minimum) from $350; ☉late May–mid-Oct).

Zumwalt Meadow; Overleaf: Panoramic Point

NATALIEJEAN/SHUTTERSTOCK ©

PURESTOCK/ALAMY STOCK PHOTO ©

Hike Mist Falls

TRY MEDIA/SHUTTERSTOCK. ©

A satisfying long walk along the riverside and up a natural granite staircase highlights the beauty of Kings Canyon. The waterfall is thunderous in late spring and possibly into early summer, depending on the previous winter's snowpack.

Bring plenty of water and sunscreen on this hike, which gains 600ft in elevation before reaching the falls. Get an early morning start because the return trip can be brutally hot on summer afternoons, and also to beat the crowds of big families.

The trail begins just past the Road's End wilderness permit station (p76), crossing a small footbridge over **Copper Creek**. Walk along a sandy trail through sparse cedar and pine forest, where boulders rolled by avalanches are scattered on the canyon floor. Keep an eye out for black bears. Eventually the trail enters cooler, shady and

Duration 3–5 hours

Distance 9.2 miles round-trip

Difficulty Moderate

Start & Finish Road's End

Nearest Town/Junction Cedar Grove Village

Transportation Car

low-lying areas of ferns and reeds before reaching a well-marked, three-way junction with the Woods Creek Trail, just shy of 2 miles from Road's End.

Turn left (north) toward Paradise Valley and begin a gradual climb that runs parallel to powerful cataracts in the boulder-saturated Kings River. Stone-framed stairs lead to a granite knob overlook, with wide southern views of **Avalanche Peak** and the

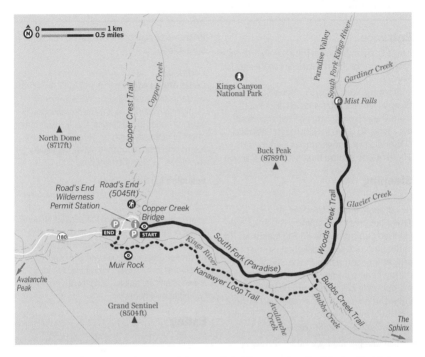

oddly pointed **Sphinx**, another mountain peak, behind you.

Follow cairns up the rock face and continue briefly through shady forest to reach **Mist Falls**, one of the park's largest waterfalls, with a fine spray to cool down warm hikers. Warning: don't wade above the waterfall or swim below it due to the danger of rockfall and swift water currents, especially during snowmelt runoff. In late summer, the river downstream from the falls may be tame enough for a dip – use your own best judgment, however.

Retrace your steps, around 2.5 miles downhill, to the three-way trail junction. Instead of returning directly to Road's End, you can bear left and cross the bridge over the **Kings River** (pictured), briefly joining the Bubbs Creek Trail. After less than a quarter-mile, turn right onto the untrammeled Kanawyer Loop Trail, which is mostly flat. After crossing **Avalanche Creek** (you may need to wade through or cross via a makeshift bridge), the tree canopy opens up to show off sprawling talus slopes along the Kings Canyon's southern walls.

Muir Rock and its late-summer swimming hole come into view across the river before you make a short climb to the River Trail junction. Turn right and walk across the red footbridge, below which is another favorite late-summer swimming hole. Follow the path back to the paved highway, turning right to walk back to the Road's End parking lot.

Essential Information

Entrance

Kings Canyon National Park's only entrance station, not far from Grant Grove Village, is Big Stump.

From the west, Kings Canyon Scenic Byway (Hwy 180) travels 53 miles east from Fresno to Big Stump. From the south, it's a long 46-mile drive through Sequoia National Park along sinuous Generals Hwy. There are no shuttle buses in Kings Canyon.

Sleeping

Camping

All campsites are first-come, first-served. There are great free, uncrowded and unde-veloped campgrounds off Big Meadows Rd in the Sequoia National Forest, some of the only empty campsites in the Sierra Nevada during peak summer season. Free roadside car camping is also allowed near Hume Lake, but no campfires are allowed without a permit (available from the Kings Canyon Visitor Center in Grant Grove).

Sunset Campground (www.nps.gov/seki; Hwy 180; tent & RV sites $22; ☺late May-early Sep) Grant Grove's biggest campground has 157 sites and is a five-minute walk from the village. Ranger campfire programs run in summer. Two large group sites are also available (with space for 15 to 30 people). Flush toilets, water, bear-proof lockers, fire rings and picnic benches are available.

Hume Lake Campground (www.recreation.gov; Hume Lake Rd; tent & RV sites $27; ☺mid-May–mid-Sep) Almost always full, this campground operated by California Land Management offers around 65 relatively uncrowded, shady campsites at 5250ft. It's on the lake's northern shore and has picnic tables, campfire rings, flush toilets and drinking water. Reservations are highly recommended.

Sheep Creek Campground (www.nps.gov/seki; Hwy 180; tent & RV sites $18; ☺late May–mid-Sep) Just a short walk west of the visitor center and village, Cedar Grove's second-biggest camp-ground, with 111 sites, has shady waterfront loops that are especially popular with RVers. Flush

toilets, water, bear-proof lockers and restrooms are available.

Lodgings

Cedar Grove Lodge (☏559-565-3096; www.visitsequoia.com; 86724 Hwy 180; r from $147; ☺mid-May–mid-Oct; ✴☎) The only indoor sleeping option in the canyon, this riverside lodge offers 21 motel-style rooms. Three ground-floor rooms with shady furnished patios have spiffy river views, TVs and kitchenettes.

Sequoia High Sierra Camp (☏866-654-2877; www.sequoiahighsierracamp.com; off Forest Rte 13S12; tent cabins for 2 $500; ☺early Jun–mid-Sep) A mile's hike deep into the Sequoia National Forest is this off-the-grid, all-inclusive resort. Canvas bungalows are spiffed up with pillow-top mattresses, feather pillows and cozy wool rugs. Restrooms and a shower house are shared. Reservations are required and there's usually a two-night minimum stay.

Eating

Markets in Grant Grove and Cedar Grove Villages have a limited selection of grocer-ies. Each village also has a restaurant, the best being **Grant Grove Restaurant** (Hwy 180; mains $8-30; ☺7-10am, 11:30am-3:30pm & 5-9pm late May-early Sep, until 8pm Apr-late May & early Sep-Oct; ☎) ✐.

Information

Cedar Grove Visitor Center (☏559-565-3793; Hwy 180; ☺9am-5pm late May-late Sep) Small, seasonal visitor center in Cedar Grove Village.

Kings Canyon Visitor Center (☏559-565-4307; Hwy 180; ☺9am-5pm) The park's main facility in Grant Grove Village.

Road's End Wilderness Permit Station (Hwy 180; ☺usually 7am-3:30pm late May-late Sep) Dispenses wilderness permits, rents bear-proof canisters and sells a few trail guides and maps between late May and late September. It's 6 miles east of Cedar Grove Village, at the end of Hwy 180.

General Grant Grove

DAVID H. CARRIERE/GETTY IMAGES ©

CLASSIC HIKES

Rae Lakes Loop

The best backpacking loop in Kings Canyon traverses some of the Sierra Nevada's finest landscapes. The route takes in sun-blessed forests and meadows, crosses one mind-bending pass and skirts a chain of jewel-like lakes beneath the Sierra crest, joining the famous John Muir Trail partway along.

Duration 5 days

Distance 42 miles

Difficulty Hard

Start & Finish Road's End

Nearest Town Cedar Grove Village

Transportation Car

For good reason, this five-day hike is one of the park's most popular trails. Note: one of the bridges on this trail has washed out, making the trail impossible to complete unless you trek at the height of summer when the South Fork of the Kings River is at its lowest.

DAY 1: Road's End to Middle Paradise Valley (7 miles)

The Rae Lakes Loop kicks off with a 4.5-mile hike along the Woods Creek Trail from **Road's End** (5045ft) to **Mist Falls**. Rocky switchbacks lead into the shadier forest. The trail levels out at **Paradise Valley**, less than 2 miles north. The Kings River's South Fork flows through forested meadows,

inviting you to linger at the backpacker campsites in **Lower Paradise Valley** (6600ft). Continue through mixed-conifer forest just over a mile further to **Middle Paradise Valley** (6700ft).

DAY 2: Middle Paradise Valley to Woods Creek (9 miles)

The trail gradually ascends alongside a grassy meadow before dropping back to the river in **Upper Paradise Valley** (6800ft). Forested campsites appear before the confluence of the Kings River's South Fork and Woods Creek, about 1.5 miles from Middle Paradise Valley.

The South Fork Kings River Bridge above Paradise Valley washed out during the winter of 2016–17. At the time of writing, construction of a replacement bridge had not yet begun. It may be possible to cross this section of river in late summer, after a hot spell, when water levels are at their lowest. However, proceed with caution – crossing the South Fork of the Kings River can be extremely hazardous. The trail steadily ascends through a valley above Woods Creek. Less than 4 miles from the river crossing, the trail rolls into **Castle Domes Meadow** (8200ft).

The trail re-enters pine forest. At the signposted **John Muir Trail (JMT) junction** (8500ft), turn right and cross Woods Creek on the suspension bridge. Backpacker campsites sprawl south of the bridge.

DAY 3: Woods Creek to Middle Rae Lake (8 miles)

Heading south, the JMT rolls easily across open slopes along the west side of Woods Creek's South Fork. Crossing a small stream, the trail rises over rocky terrain to a small meadow. At the next crossing, a bigger stream cascades over a cleft in the rock. Foxtail pines dot the dry slope above the trail as it continues up to **Dollar Lake** (10,220ft), about 3.5 miles from the Woods Creek crossing. There's a striking view of **Fin Dome** (11,693ft) above Dollar Lake (camping strictly prohibited).

Skirting Dollar Lake's west shore, the JMT continues up to arrive at larger **Arrowhead Lake** (10,300ft) and enchanting **Lower Rae Lake** (10,535ft). The gently rolling trail crosses several small side streams and passes a spur trail to a seasonal ranger station. Continue to the signed turnoff for campsites above the eastern shore of **Middle Rae Lake** (10,540ft).

DAY 4: Middle Rae Lake to Junction Meadow (8 miles)

Return to the JMT and turn right (south). Walk along the northern shore of **Upper Rae Lake** (10,545ft). Cross the connector stream between the lakes. At a signed trail junction, keep straight ahead on the JMT, which continues south up well-graded switchbacks above the west side of Upper Rae Lake. More switchbacks take you to a tarn-filled basin, from where Glen Pass is visible ahead on the dark, rocky ridgeline. The trail passes several small mountain lakes, then rises to narrow **Glen Pass**

(11,978ft), almost 3 miles from Middle Rae Lake.

Gravelly but well-graded switchbacks take you down from Glen Pass toward a pothole tarn. Filter water here – the next reliable water is not until the Bullfrog Lake outlet a few miles ahead. Head down the canyon until the trail swings south, then contours high above Charlotte Lake. A connector trail to Kearsarge Pass appears about 2.5 miles from Glen Pass, after which you'll soon reach a four-way junction with the main Charlotte Lake (northwest) and Kearsarge Pass (northeast) Trails. Continue straight (south).

At the head of Bubbs Creek, cross a low rise and then start descending, passing a junction. The scenic descent twice crosses the outlet from Bullfrog Lake to reach **Lower Vidette Meadow** (9480ft). Leaving the JMT, turn right (southwest) and follow the trail down Bubbs Creek past campsites and crossing several streams and a large rockslide. The trail drops to Bubbs

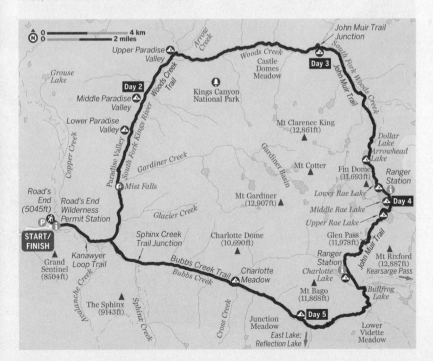

Creek, continuing to aspen-filled **Junction Meadow** (8500ft). Past the signed junction with the East and Reflection Lakes Trails, you'll find grassy campsites.

DAY 5: Junction Meadow to Road's End (10 miles)

The Bubbs Creek Trail meanders down the valley to Charlotte Creek, about 3.5 miles from Junction Meadow, continuing creek-side downhill for three more miles to the **Sphinx Creek Trail junction** (6240ft).

Continuing straight ahead, the Bubbs Creek Trail descends steeply, providing sweeping views. At the canyon floor, the trail crosses braided Bubbs Creek over wooden footbridges. Just beyond the steel **Bailey Bridge** is the Paradise Valley Trail junction. Turn left (west) and retrace your steps from day one for less than 2 miles to **Road's End**. ■

ED CALLAERT/ALAMY STOCK PHOTO ©

Top: Glen Pass; bottom left: Paradise Valley; bottom right: Mist Falls

RDOM THE AGENCY/ALMY STOCK PHOTO ©

STRAYSTONE/SHUTTERSTOCK ©

NADIA YONG/SHUTTERSTOCK ©

Bumpass Hell boardwalk

Lassen Volcanic National Park

Offering a glimpse into the earth's fiery core, this alien landscape bubbles over with roiling mud pots, noxious sulfur vents, steamy fumaroles, colorful cinder cones and crater lakes. The region was once a meeting point for Native American tribes; some indigenous people still work closely with the park.

Great For...

State
California

Entrance Fee
7-day entry per vehicle $25 ($10 in winter)

Area
166 sq miles

The dry, smoldering, treeless terrain within this national park stands in stunning contrast to the cool, green conifer forest that surrounds it. That's the summer; in winter tons of snow ensure you won't get too far inside its borders. Still, entering the park from the southwest entrance is to suddenly step into another world.

Hwy 89, the road through the park, wraps around **Lassen Peak** on three sides and provides access to dramatic geothermal formations, pure lakes, gorgeous picnic areas and remote hiking trails.

Hiking
In total, the park has 150 miles of hiking trails, including a 17-mile section of the Pacific Crest Trail. Experienced hikers can attack the **Lassen Peak Trail**; it takes at least 4½ hours to make the 5-mile round-trip but the first 1.3 miles up to the Grand-view viewpoint is suitable for families. The 360-degree view from the top is stunning,

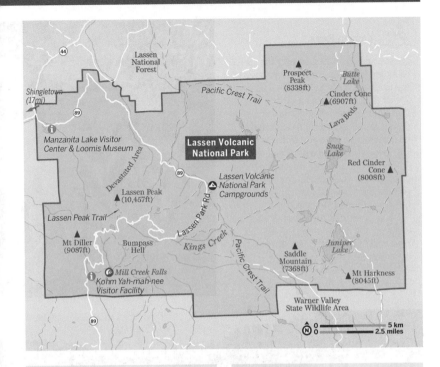

Lassen National Forest

44

Shingletown (17mi)

89

ⓘ Manzanita Lake Visitor Center & Loomis Museum

Devastated Area

89

Lassen Peak Trail

Lassen Peak ▲ (10,457ft)

Prospect Peak ▲ (8338ft)

Pacific Crest Trail

Butte Lake

Cinder Cone ▲(6907ft)

Lava Beds

Lassen Volcanic National Park

Snag Lake

Red Cinder Cone ▲ (8008ft)

Lassen Volcanic ⛺ National Park Campgrounds

Lassen Park Rd

Kings Creek

Pacific Crest Trail

▲ Mt Diller (9087ft)

Bumpass Hell

Mill Creek Falls ⓘ Kohm Yah-mah-nee Visitor Facility

Juniper Lake

▲ Saddle Mountain (7368ft)

▲ Mt Harkness (8045ft)

Warner Valley State Wildlife Area

89

Ⓝ 0 _____ 5 km
0 _____ 2.5 miles

SUNDRY PHOTOGRAPHY/SHUTTERSTOCK ©

Lassen Peak Trail

Essential Information

From the north on Hwy 89, you won't see many gas/food/lodgings signs after Mt Shasta City. Aside from the eight developed **campgrounds** (☑518-885-3639, reservations 877-444-6777; www.recreation.gov; tent & RV sites $12-24) in the park, there are many more in the surrounding Lassen National Forest. The nearest hotels and motels are in Chester, which accesses the south entrance of the park. There are some basic services near the split of Hwy 89 and Hwy 44, in the north.

There are a few basic places to eat in the small towns surrounding the park but, for the most part, you'll want to pack provisions.

Lassen Peak

Lassen Peak rises 2000ft over the surrounding landscape to 10,457ft above sea level. Lassen's dome has a volume of half a cubic mile, making it one of the world's largest plug-dome volcanoes. Classified as an active volcano, its most recent large eruption was in 1915, when it spewed a giant cloud of smoke, steam and ash 7 miles into the atmosphere. The national park was created the following year to protect the newly formed landscape.

Some areas destroyed by the blast, including the aptly named Devastated Area northeast of the peak, are making an impressive recovery.

TOP LEFT: DESIGN PICS INC/ALAMY STOCK PHOTO © TOP RIGHT: FRANKAZOIDTRVL/SHUTTERSTOCK © BOTTOM: LUCILAIO/GETTY IMAGES ©

Top left: Wild Horse Sanctuary; Top right: Mill Creek Falls;
Bottom: Bumpass Hell

even if the weather is a bit hazy. Early in the season you'll need snow and ice-climbing equipment to reach the summit.

Near the Kom Yah-mah-nee Visitor Facility, a gentler 2.3-mile trail leads through meadows and forest to **Mill Creek Falls**. Further north on Hwy 89, you'll recognize the roadside sulfur works by its bubbling mud pots, hissing steam vent, fountains and fumaroles.

Bumpass Hell

At Bumpass Hell a moderate 1.5-mile trail and boardwalk lead to an active geothermal area, with bizarrely colored pools and billowing clouds of steam. The road and trails wind through cinder cones, lava and lush alpine glades, with views of Juniper Lake, Snag Lake and the plains beyond. Most of the lakes at higher elevations remain partially and beautifully frozen in summer.

Wild Horse Sanctuary

Since 1978 the **Wild Horse Sanctuary** (☏530-474-5770; www.wildhorsesanctuary.com; 5796 Wilson Hill Rd, Shingletown; ☺10am-4pm Wed & Sat) FREE has been sheltering horses and burros that would otherwise have been destroyed. You can visit its humble visitor center on to see these lovely animals, or even volunteer for a day with advance arrangement. To see them on the open plains, take a two- to three-day weekend pack trip in spring or summer. Shingletown lies 20 miles to the west of the park. ∎

Diverse Landscapes

From snowy peaks to scorching deserts, and golden-sand beaches to misty redwood forests, California is home to a bewildering variety of ecosytems, flora and fauna.

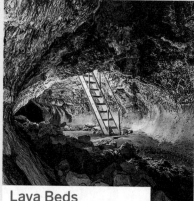

Lava Beds National Monument

Lava flows, cinder and spatter cones, volcanic craters, lava tubes... This was the site of the Modoc War, and ancient Native American petroglyphs are etched into rocks and pictographs painted in caves.

Santa Monica Mountains National Recreation Area

The northwestern-most stretch of the Santa Monica Mountains National Recreation Area is where nature gets bigger and wilder, with jaw-dropping red-rock canyons, and granite outcrops with sublime sea views.

CLOCKWISE FROM TOP-LEFT: ALBERTO LOYO/SHUTTERSTOCK ©; ADONIS VILLANUEVA/SHUTTERSTOCK ©; DOUGLAS KLUG/GETTY IMAGES ©; MNSTUDIO/SHUTTERSTOCK ©; TREKANDSHOOT/ALAMY STOCK PHOTO ©

Channel Islands

The Channel Islands have been California's last outpost of civilization ever since seafaring Chumash people established villages on these remote rocks. Marine life thrives here, from coral reefs to giant elephant seals.

Muir Woods National Monument

Wander among an ancient stand of the world's tallest trees at 550-acre Muir Woods National Monument. Easy hiking trails loop past thousand-year-old coast redwoods at Cathedral Grove.

Point Reyes National Seashore

This windswept peninsula juts 10 miles out to sea on an entirely different tectonic plate than the mainland, protecting over 100 sq miles of beaches, lagoons and forested hills.

CHERI ALGUIRE/SHUTTERSTOCK ©

Pinnacles National Park

Named for the towering rock spires that rise abruptly out of the chaparral-covered hills, Pinnacles National Park preserves forests of oak, sycamore and buckeye, wildflower-strewn meadows, and caves. The rocky spires at the heart of the park are the eroded remnants of a long-extinct volcano.

Great For...

State
California

Entrance Fee
7-day pass per car/motorcycle/person on foot or bicycle $30/25/15

Area
42 sq miles

Hiking

Moderate loops of varying lengths and difficulty ascend into the High Peaks and include thrillingly narrow clifftop sections. In the early morning or late afternoon, you may spot endangered California condors soaring overhead. Get an early start to tackle the 9-mile round-trip trail to the top of **Chalone Peak**.

Rangers lead guided full-moon hikes and stargazing programs on some weekend nights, usually in spring or fall. Call ☎831-389-4485 to reserve or check for last-minute vacancies at the visitor center.

Talus Caves

Among the park's biggest attractions are its two talus caves, formed by piles of boulders. **Balconies Cave** is almost always open for exploration. It's pitch-black inside and not for claustrophobes. A flashlight is essential and be prepared to get lost a bit.

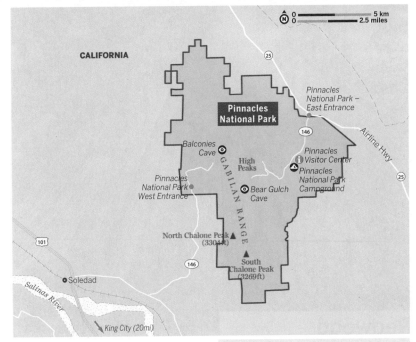

It's along a 2.5-mile hiking loop from the west entrance. Nearer the east entrance, **Bear Gulch Cave** is closed seasonally, so as not to disturb a resident colony of Townsend's big-eared bats.

Climbing

Pinnacles is popular for rock climbing, but has unique conditions due to its relatively soft rock. The most popular areas for climbing are **Bear Gulch**, **Discovery Wall** and the **High Peaks**. Spring and fall are the best seasons, with dry, comfortable weather. Winter climbing can also be good, but expect chilly conditions in the shade. Summer tends to be oppressively hot. For route information, visit the Friends of Pinnacles website (www.pinnacles.org). ∎

Essential Information

There is no road connecting the two sides of the park. To reach the less-developed **west entrance** (⊙7:30am-8pm), exit Hwy 101 at Soledad and follow Hwy 146 northeast for 14 miles. The **east entrance** (⊙24hr), for the visitor center and campground, is accessed via lonely Hwy 25 in San Benito County, southeast of Hollister and northeast of King City.

On the park's east side, the popular, family-oriented **Pinnacles National Park Campground** (✆831-389-4538; www.recreation.gov; 5000 Hwy 146; tent/RV sites $23/36; ⊛) has over 130 sites (some with shade), drinking water, coin-op hot showers, fire pits and an outdoor pool.

WILDNERDPIX/SHUTTERSTOCK ©

Redwood National Park

In the upper reaches of California's northwestern Pacific coast, Redwood National Park houses some of the world's tallest trees, which predate the Roman Empire by over 500 years. Alongside, there's a verdant mix of coastal, riverine and prairie wildlands. Prepare to be impressed.

Great For...

State
California

Entrance Fee
Free

Area
172 sq miles

The national park is seamlessly intertwined with three state parks (Prairie Creek Redwoods, Del Norte Coast Redwoods and Jedediah Smith Redwoods SP), all jointly administered by the National Park Service and the California Department of Parks and Recreation.

Hiking

A network of trails passes through the park's variety of landscapes, offering hiking experiences for all fitness levels.

After picking up a map at the **Thomas H. Kuchel Visitor Center** (☏707-465-7765; www.nps.gov/redw; Hwy 101, Orick; ⏰9am-5pm Apr-Oct, to 4pm Nov-Mar), you'll have a suite of choices for hiking. The 1-mile kid-friendly loop trail at **Lady Bird Johnson Grove** is a good choice, or you might want to get lost in the secluded serenity of **Tall Trees Grove**.

Most popular with hikers is the 0.7-mile loop into **Fern Canyon**, along a creekside

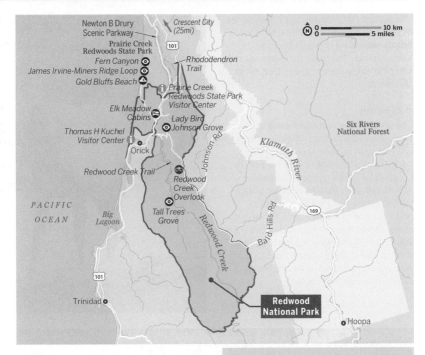

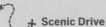

path framed by fern-covered cliff faces. The 6.3-mile **Rhododendron Trail** is especially scenic between mid-May and early June when flamboyant pink and red rhododendrons tower as high as 35ft above the trail. For a classic loop through some of the park's most majestic redwoods, followed by a short jaunt along the Pacific Ocean and a return walk along a 19th-century gold-mining trail, take the 9-mile **James Irvine-Miner's Ridge Loop**.

Stock up on water, muesli bars and similar if you are planning on hiking. Although there are some small towns dotted around, there are very few stores for buying provisions.

Wildlife & Nature

The massive stands of first-growth California coastal redwoods (*Sequoia sempervirens*) here, draped in moss and ferns, tower up to 379ft tall. In among the trees, wildlife-watching opportunities abound,

✤ Scenic Drive

Just north of Orick is the turnoff for the 8-mile **Newton B Drury Scenic Parkway**, which runs parallel to Hwy 101 through untouched ancient redwood forests. The parkway is a not-to-miss short detour off the freeway where you can view the magnificence of these trees. Numerous trails branch off from roadside pullouts, including family-friendly options and trails that fit ADA (American Disabilities Act) requirements, such as Big Tree Wayside and Revelation Trail.

One key attraction is the park's resident population of **Roosevelt elk**, which can be seen grazing in the prairie lands at the heart of Prairie Creek Redwoods and along the coast near Gold Bluffs Beach. The males are especially impressive from late summer into the fall, when they sport massive antlers for the rutting season. **Whale-watching** is excellent at the Klamath River Overlook and other coastal sites within the park between December and March.

Kayaking

The Smith River, part of America's National Wild and Scenic River system, runs through pristine scenery in the park's northern reaches. There are some exceptional kayaking opportunities here. In summer, park rangers lead organized half-day trips along a 3.5-mile, class I and II section of the river, which includes minor rapids interspersed with moving flat water. During the rainy season (December through April), independent boaters can pit their skills against more challenging rapids, rated up to class V.

ROBERT MUTCH/SHUTTERSTOCK ©

Top left: Roosevelt elk; Top right: Fern Canyon;
Bottom: Lady Bird Johnson Grove

TOP LEFT: SEAN WANDZILAK/SHUTTERSTOCK © TOP RIGHT: CHRISTINEMINATO/SHUTTERSTOCK ©

Essential Information

Sleeping

There is an excellent choice of campsites, several with tent pitches beside the pristine Smith River. **Gold Bluffs Beach** (Prairie Creek Redwoods State Park; tent sites $35) sits between 100ft cliffs and wide-open ocean (no reservations). Spotless and bright **Elk Meadow Cabins** (866-733-9637; www. redwoodadventures.com; 7 Valley Green Camp Rd, Orick; cabins $169-299;) has equipped kitchens and all the mod-cons are in a perfect mid-parks location. Expect to see elk on the lawn in the mornings. Cabins sleep six to eight people.

Information

Unlike most national parks, Redwood does not have a main entrance and only charges fees in some sections, most notably the Gold Bluffs Beach and Fern Canyon area. The park's widely dispersed sites of interest are signposted along the main highway, with side roads and parking lots providing access. It's imperative to pick up the free map at the park headquarters in **Crescent City** (707-465-7306; www.nps.gov/redw; 1111 2nd St; 9am-5pm Apr-Oct, to 4pm Nov-Mar) or at the information center in Orick. Rangers here issue permits to visit Tall Trees Grove and loan bear-proof containers to backpackers.

For in-depth redwood ecology, buy the excellent official park handbook. The **Redwood Parks Association** (www.redwood parksassociation.org) provides good information on its website, including detailed descriptions of all the park's hikes.

DJ/DIU HRUBARU/SHUTTERSTOCK ©

Tall Trees Grove

Northern Redwood Coast

Hug a 700-year-old tree, stroll moody coastal bluffs and drop in on roadside attractions of yesteryear on this trip through verdant redwood parks and personality-packed villages.

Duration 3–4 days

Distance 150 miles

Best Time to Go
April to October for usually clear skies and the region's warmest weather.

Essential Photo
Misty redwoods clinging to rocky Pacific cliffs at Del Norte Coast Redwoods State Park.

Best Scenic Drive
Howland Hill Rd through dense old-growth redwood forests.

❶ Samoa Peninsula
Even though this trip is about misty primeval forest, the beginning is a study of opposites: the grassy dunes and wind-swept beaches of the 10-mile long Samoa Peninsula. At the peninsula's south end is **Samoa Dunes Recreation Area**, part of a 34-mile-long dune system that's the largest in Northern California. While it's great for picnicking or fishing, the wildlife viewing is also excellent.

The Drive ›› Head north on Hwy 101 from Eureka, passing myriad views of Humboldt Bay. Fifteen miles north of Arcata, take the first Trinidad exit.

❷ Trinidad
Perched on an ocean bluff, cheery Trinidad somehow manages an off-the-beaten-path feel despite a constant flow of visitors. The free town map at the information kiosk will help you navigate the town's cute little shops and several fantastic hiking trails, most notably the **Trinidad Head Trail** with superb coastal views and excellent whale-watching (December to April). If the weather is nice, stroll the exceptionally beautiful cove at **Trinidad State Beach**; if not, make for the **HSU Telonicher Marine Laboratory** (☑707-826-3671; www.humboldt. edu/marinelab; 570 Ewing St; $1; ◷9am-4:30pm Mon-Fri year-round, plus 10am-5pm Sat & Sun mid-Sep–mid-May) ✿. It has a touch tank, several aquariums (look for the giant Pacific octopus), an enormous whale jaw and a cool three-dimensional map of the ocean floor.

The Drive ›› Head back north of town on Patrick's Point Dr to hug the shore for just over 5 miles.

❸ Patrick's Point State Park
Coastal bluffs jut out to sea at 640-acre Patrick's Point State Park, where sandy beaches abut rocky headlands. Easy access to dramatic coastal bluffs makes this a best bet for families, but visitors of any age will find a feast for the senses as they climb rock formations, search for breaching whales, carefully navigate tide pools and listen to barking sea lions and singing birds. The park also has **Sumêg**, an authentic reproduction of a Yurok village, with hand-hewn redwood buildings. In the native plant garden you'll find species for making tradi-tional baskets and medicines. The 2-mile **Rim Trail**, a former Yurok trail around the bluffs, circles the point with access to huge rocky outcrops. Don't miss **Wedding Rock**, one of the park's most romantic spots, or **Agate Beach**, where lucky visitors spot (but don't take, since that's illegal) bits of jade and sea-polished agate.

The Drive ›› Make your way back out to Hwy 101 through thick stands of redwoods. North another five minutes will bring you

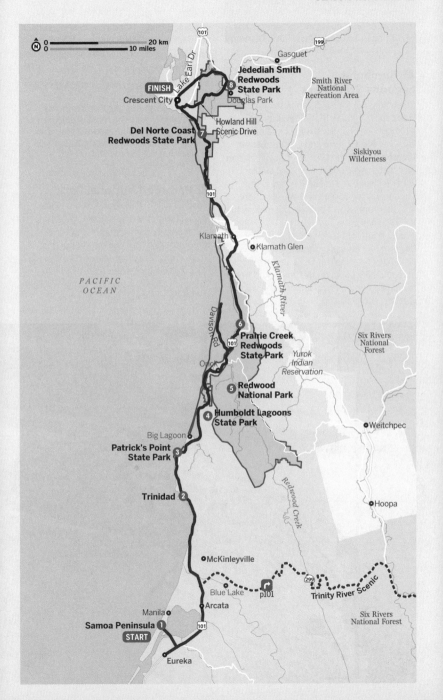

to the sudden clearing of Big Lagoon, part of Humboldt Lagoons State Park. Continue 6 miles north to the visitor center.

❹ Humboldt Lagoons State Park

Stretching out for miles along the coast, Humboldt Lagoons State Park has long, sandy beaches and a string of coastal lagoons. **Big Lagoon** and prettier **Stone Lagoon** are both excellent for kayaking and bird-watching. Sunsets are spectacular, with no structures in sight. At the Stone Lagoon Visitor Center, on Hwy 101, there are restrooms and a bulletin board displaying information.

Just south of Stone Lagoon, tiny **Dry Lagoon** (a freshwater marsh) has a fantastic day hike. Park at Dry Lagoon's picnic area and hike north on the unmarked trail to Stone Lagoon; the trail skirts the southwestern shore and ends up at the ocean,

passing through woods and marshland rich with wildlife. Mostly flat, it's about 2.5 miles one way – and nobody takes it because it's unmarked.

The Drive ≫ Keep driving north on Hwy 101. Now, at last, you'll start to lose all perspective among the world's tallest trees. This is likely the most scenic part of the entire trip; you'll emerge from curvy two-lane roads through redwood groves to stunning mist-shrouded shores dotted with rocky islets.

❺ Redwood National Park

Heading north, Redwood National Park is the first park in the patchwork of state and federally administered lands under the umbrella of Redwood National and State Parks. Grab a map from the Thomas H Kuchel Visitor Center (p90) and take your pick of the hikes on offer. A few miles further north along Hwy 101, a trip inland

RANDY ANDY/SHUTTERSTOCK ©

Top: Sumêg; Bottom left: Wedding Rock; Bottom right: Memorial lighthouse, Trinidad

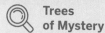

Trees of Mystery

As you pass through Klamath, it's hard to miss the giant statues of Paul Bunyan and Babe the Blue Ox towering over the parking lot at Trees of Mystery – a shameless, if lovable, tourist trap. It has a gondola running through the redwood canopy, and a surprisingly wonderful museum that has an outstanding collection of Native American arts and artifacts.

At Tour Thru Tree, also in Klamath, you can squeeze through a tree and check out the emus.

on Bald Hills Rd will take you to **Lady Bird Johnson Grove**, with its 1-mile kid-friendly loop trail, or get you lost in the secluded serenity of **Tall Trees Grove**. To protect the latter grove, a limited number of cars per day are allowed access; get permits at the visitor center. This can be a half-day trip itself, but you're well rewarded after the challenging approach (a 6-mile rumble on an old logging road behind a locked gate, then a moderately strenuous 4-mile round-trip hike).

The Drive » Back on Hwy 101, less than 2 miles north of Bald Hills Rd, turn left onto Davison Rd, which trundles for 7 miles (mostly unpaved) out to Gold Bluffs Beach.

⑥ Prairie Creek Redwoods State Park

The short stroll to **Gold Bluffs Beach** will lead you to the best spot for a picnic. Past the campground, you can take a longer hike beyond the end of the road into **Fern Canyon**, whose 60ft, fern-covered, sheer rock walls are seen in *The Lost World: Jurassic Park*. This is one of the most photographed spots on the North Coast – damp and lush, all emerald green – and totally worth getting your toes wet to see.

Back on Hwy 101, head two miles further north and exit onto the 8-mile **Newton B Drury Scenic Parkway**, which runs parallel to the highway through magnificent, untouched ancient redwood forests.

Family-friendly nature trails branch off from roadside pullouts, including the wheelchair-accessible Big Tree Wayside, and also start outside the **Prairie Creek Redwoods State Park Visitor Center** (📞707-488-2039; www.parks.ca.gov; Newton B Drury Scenic Pkwy; ⊗9am-5pm May-Sep, to 4pm Wed-Sun Oct-Apr), including the Revelation Trail for visually impaired visitors.

The Drive » Follow the winding Newton B Drury Scenic Pkwy with views of the east and its layers of ridges and valleys. On returning to Hwy 101, head north to Klamath, with its bear bridge. Del Norte Coast Redwoods State Park is just a few minutes further north.

⑦ Del Norte Coast Redwoods State Park

Marked by steep canyons and dense woods, half the 6400 acres of this park are virgin redwood forest, crisscrossed by 15 miles of hiking trails. Even the most jaded of redwood-watchers can't help but be moved. Tall trees cling precipitously to canyon walls that drop to the rocky, timber-strewn coastline. It's almost impossible to get to the water, except via gorgeous but steep **Damnation Creek Trail** or **Footsteps Rock Trail**. The former may be only 4 miles long, but the 1100ft elevation change and cliffside redwoods make it the park's best hike (temporarily closed since mid-2015). The trailhead is at an unmarked parking pullout along Hwy 101 near mile marker 16.

The Drive » Leaving Del Norte Coast Redwoods State Park and continuing on Hwy 101, you'll enter dreary little Crescent City, a fine enough place to gas up or grab a bite, but not worth stopping at for long. About 4 miles northeast of town, Hwy 199 splits off from Hwy 101; follow it northeast for 6 miles to Hiouchi.

⑧ Jedediah Smith Redwoods State Park

The final stop on the trip is loaded with worthy superlatives – the northernmost park has the densest population of redwoods and the last natural undammed, free-flowing river in California, the sparkling

Smith. All in all Jedediah Smith Redwoods State Park is a jewel. The redwood stands here are so dense that few hiking trails penetrate the park, so drive the outstanding 10-mile **Howland Hill Rd**, which cuts through otherwise inaccessible areas, heading back toward Crescent City.

The Drive » It's a rough, unpaved road, and it can close if there are fallen trees or washouts, but you'll feel as if you're visiting from Lilliput as you cruise under the gargantuan trunks. To spend the night, reserve a site at the park's fabulous campground tucked along the banks of the Smith River. ■

Detour: Trinity Scenic Byway

Start: ❶ **Samoa Peninsula**

If you've got an extra couple of days, cut inland on Hwy 299 from Arcata and get lost in the wild country of California's northern mountains.

Cruising this secluded corner of California you'll pass majestic peaks, tranquil inland lakes and historic mountain towns, experiencing both rugged nature and plush hospitality.

LAURENS HODDENBAGH/SHUTTERSTOCK ©

Jedediah Smith Redwoods State Park

SIMON DANNHAUER/SHUTTERSTOCK ©

General Sherman Tree

Sequoia National Park

With trees as high as 20-story buildings and as old as the Bible, this extraordinary park has five-star geological highlights, soul-sustaining forests and wildflower meadows. Gaze at dagger-sized stalactites in a 10,000-year-old cave, climb 350 steps to admire the Great Western Divide or drive through a hole in a 2000-year-old log.

Great For...

State
California

Entrance Fee
7-day pass per car/motorcycle $35/20

Area
631 sq miles

❶ General Sherman Tree

By volume the largest living tree on earth, the massive General Sherman Tree rockets into the sky and waaay out of the camera frame. Pay your respects to this giant (which measures more than 100ft around at its base and 275ft tall) via a paved, wheelchair-accessible path from the upper parking lot off Wolverton Rd. The trail cleverly starts at the height of the tree's tip (14 stories high) and descends 0.5 miles to its base.

❷ Giant Forest

This 3-sq-mile grove protects the park's most gargantuan tree specimens, including the General Sherman. Join the Congress Trail, a paved 2-mile pathway that takes in General Sherman, the Washington Tree (the world's second-biggest sequoia) and the see-through Telescope Tree. Hint: take your time on the steep walk back up from

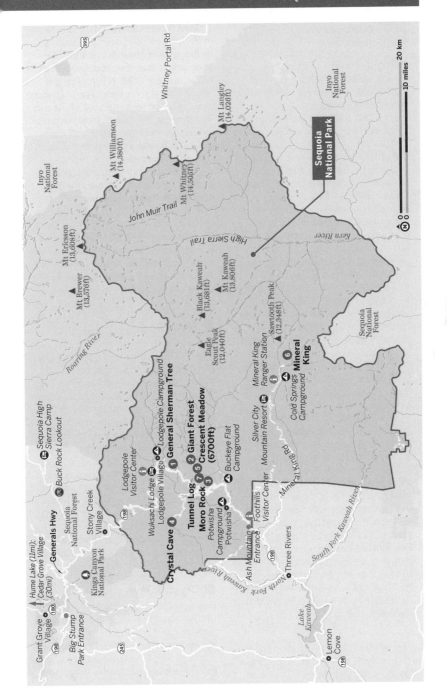

California's Trees

California is a region of superlative trees: the oldest (bristlecone pines of the White Mountains live to nearly 5000 years old), the tallest (coast redwoods reach 380ft) and the largest (giant sequoias of the Sierra Nevada exceed 36ft across). Sequoias are unique to California, adapted to survive in isolated groves on the Sierra Nevada's western slopes in Yosemite, Sequoia and Kings Canyon National Parks.

An astounding 20 native species of oak grow in California, including live (evergreen) oaks with holly-like leaves and scaly acorns. Other common trees include the aromatic California bay laurel, whose long slender leaves turn purple. Rare native trees include Monterey pines and Torrey pines, gnarly species that have adapted to harsh coastal conditions such as high winds, sparse rainfall and sandy, stony soils. Torrey pines only grow at Torrey Pines State Reserve near San Diego and in the Channel Islands, California's hot spot for endemic plant species.

Heading inland, the Sierra Nevada has three distinct eco-zones: the dry western foothills covered with oak and chaparral; conifer forests starting from an elevation of 2000ft; and an alpine zone above 8000ft. Almost two dozen species of conifer grow in the Sierra Nevada, with mid-elevation forests home to massive Douglas firs, ponderosa pines and, biggest of all, the giant sequoia. Deciduous trees include the quaking aspen, a white-trunked tree with shimmering leaves that turn pale yellow in the fall, helping the Golden State live up to its name in the Eastern Sierra.

the grove – it's 7000ft in elevation and the air is thin. The 5-mile Trail of the Sequoias helps you lose the crowds.

Giant Forest was named by John Muir in 1875. At one point over 300 buildings, including campgrounds and a lodge, encroached upon the sequoias' delicate root systems. In 1997, recognizing this adverse impact, the park began to remove structures and resite parking lots. It also introduced a convenient, seasonal visitor shuttle, significantly cutting traffic congestion and reducing the potential harm to these majestic trees.

For a primer on the intriguing ecology and history of giant sequoias, the pint-sized **Giant Forest Museum** (☏559-565-4480; www.nps.gov/seki; 47050 Generals Hwy, cnr Crescent Meadow Rd; ⊙9am-4:30pm winter, 9am-6pm summer) ✔**FREE** has hands-on exhibits about the life stages of these big trees, which can live for more than 3000 years, and the fire cycle that releases their seeds and allows them to sprout on bare soil.

❸ Moro Rock

A quarter-mile staircase climbs 350 steps (over 300ft) to the top of Sequoia's iconic granite dome at an elevation of 6725ft, offering mind-boggling views of the Great Western Divide. This spectacular vantage point is sometimes obscured by thick haze, especially during summer. Historical photos at the trailhead show the rock's original rickety wooden staircase, erected in 1917.

From the Giant Forest Museum, the trailhead is 2 miles up narrow, twisty Moro Rock–Crescent Meadow Rd. The free seasonal shuttle bus (summer only) stops at the small parking lot, which is often full. Alternatively, park at Giant Forest Museum and walk the 1.7 miles along Crescent Meadow Rd to the trailhead.

❹ Crystal Cave

Discovered in 1918 by two park employees who were going fishing, this unique **cave** (www.recreation.gov; Crystal Cave Rd, off Generals Hwy; tours adult/child/youth from $16/5/8; ⊙late May-Sep) ✔ was carved by an underground river and has marble formations estimated to be 10,000 years old. The cave is also a unique biodiverse habitat for spiders, bats and tiny aquatic insects that are found nowhere else on earth.

Tours fill up quickly, especially on weekends, so buy tickets online at least a month before your trip.

⑤ Crescent Meadow

Said to have been described by John Muir as the 'gem of the Sierra,' this lush meadow is buffered by a forest of firs and giant sequoias. High grass and summer wildflowers are good excuses for a leisurely loop hike (1.3 miles), as is watching black bears snack on berries and rip apart logs to feast on insects.

The meadow is almost 3 miles down Moro Rock–Crescent Meadow Rd, best accessed by the free seasonal shuttle bus. The road closes to all traffic after the first snowfall and doesn't reopen until spring, but you can still walk to it – snowshoes or cross-country skiing may be needed.

⑥ Mineral King

A scenic subalpine valley at 7500ft, Mineral King is Sequoia's backpacking mecca and a good place to find solitude. Gorgeous and gigantic, its glacially sculpted valley is ringed by massive mountains, including the jagged 12,348ft Sawtooth Peak. The area is reached via Mineral King Rd – a slinky, steep and narrow 25-mile road not suitable for RVs or speed demons; it's usually open from late May through October. Plan on spending the night unless you don't mind driving the three-hour round-trip.

⑦ Tunnel Log

Visitors can drive through a 2000-year-old tree, which fell naturally in 1937. It once stood 275ft high with a base measuring 21ft in diameter. Regular sedans and small cars fit through the gap, or it's just as fun to walk through the 17ft-wide, 8ft-high arch cut into the tree by the Civilian Conservation Corps (CCC).

Tunnel Log

ELENA PUEYO/GETTY IMAGES ©

Hike Monarch Lakes

HUDSON FLEECE/ALAMY STOCK PHOTO ©

A marmot-lover's paradise! This exceptionally scenic out-and-back high-country route reaches two alpine lakes below jagged Sawtooth Peak. Although it's not very long, the trail can be breathtakingly steep.

A steep climb kicks off this higher-altitude trek. At the Timber Gap Trail junction just over 0.5 miles in, you can see Mineral King Rd back below and snow-brushed peaks looking south. Turn right, following the signs for Sawtooth Pass. Corn lilies and paintbrush speckle **Groundhog Meadow**, named for the whistling marmots that scramble around the granite rocks seemingly everywhere you look during this hike.

Leaving the meadow, rock-hop across burbling **Monarch Creek**. On its far bank, a shady wooded spot is the perfect place for a picnic lunch. From there, begin ascending a stretch of loose and lazy

Duration 4–6 hours

Distance 8.4 miles

Difficulty Hard

Start & Finish Sawtooth/Monarch trailhead parking area

Nearest Town Silver City

switchbacks with goose-bump views. It's a slow, steady climb through red fir and pine forest that won't leave you too winded, though you'll feel the altitude the higher you climb. Blue grouse may be spotted on the hillsides.

At about 2.5 miles, there's a signed junction for the Crystal Lake Trail, which takes a hard and steep right. Bear left and continue straight up toward Sawtooth Pass instead. After flipping to the opposite side of the ridgeline, the trail rounds

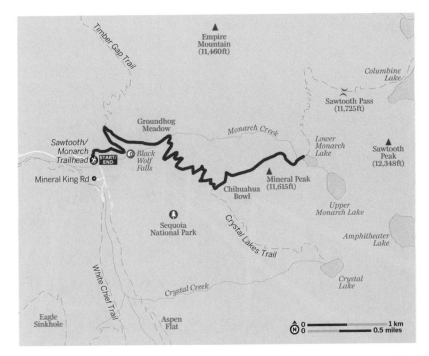

Chihuahua Bowl, an avalanche-prone granite basin named after a Mexican mining region. The tree line wavers and fades away, opening up gorgeous views of Monarch Creek canyon, Timber Gap and the peaks of the Great Western Divide.

The distinctive pitch of Sawtooth Peak (12,348ft) is visible ahead. A walk through a large talus field and some stream crossings brings you to **Lower Monarch Lake** (10,400ft), where round-topped Mineral Peak (11,615ft) points up directly south. The maintained trail stops here, but **Upper Monarch Lake** (10,640ft) can be reached by a steep trail heading up the hillside. Established backpacker campsites are by the lower lake; for overnight camping, a wilderness permit is required.

When you're ready, retrace your steps to return. If you're looking for extremely challenging cross-country treks with some steep drop-offs and rock scrambling required, detour up scree-covered **Sawtooth Pass** (11,725ft) or make an alternate return route via **Crystal Lake** (10,900ft). Ask for route advice and safety tips at the Mineral King Ranger Station first.

Note: Mineral King Rd, the winding route up to the Sawtooth/Monarch trailhead, is closed during winter (usually between October and June). Hardcore hikers with snow gear may attempt to trek the snow-covered road from Three Rivers to the trailhead (around 25 miles), but it's not recommended.

Hike General Sherman Tree to Moro Rock

CHECUBUS/SHUTTERSTOCK ©

A deviation from the popular Congress Trail Loop, this rolling one-way hike takes in huge sequoias, green meadows and the pinnacle of Moro Rock. Expect stretches of blissful solitude and potential black bear sightings.

Keep in mind that hiking this route in one direction is possible only when the free seasonal park shuttle buses are running, usually from late May until late September.

From the General Sherman parking lot and shuttle stop off Wolverton Rd, just east of the Generals Hwy, a paved trail quickly descends through towering sequoias. At an overlook on the way down, you'll get the best view of the **General Sherman Tree**. After walking up to the giant's trunk, turn around and walk downhill on the western branch of the Congress Trail Loop. (If you end up on the eastern branch by mistake, jog right then left

Duration	3–4 hours
Distance	6 miles one way
Difficulty	Moderate
Start	Wolverton Rd parking lot/ shuttle stop
Finish	Moro Rock parking lot/ shuttle stop
Nearest Town	Lodgepole Village

at two minor trail junctions that appear about 0.5 miles south of the General Sherman Tree.)

At a five-way junction by the **McKinley Tree**, continue straight ahead south on the dirt trail toward **Cattle Cabin**. Pass the hollow-bottom **Room Tree** and the pretty cluster of the **Founders Group** as you walk through tufts of ferns and corn lilies. Approaching the bright green strip of

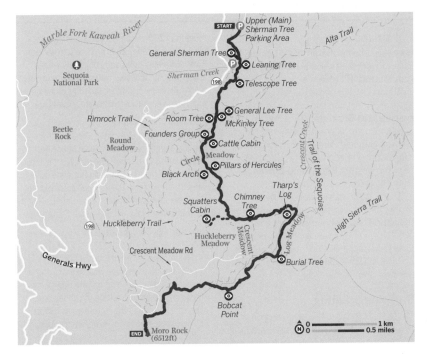

'C'-shaped **Circle Meadow**, there are no more crowds and all you can hear is the breeze and birdsong. Trace the eastern edge of the meadow toward another well-named tree group, the **Pillars of Hercules**. Stand between them and look up for a heroic view.

The trail then passes the huge charred maw of the **Black Arch** tree. Continue south, veering slightly right and then left at the next two trail junctions. At a three-way intersection, lush Crescent Meadow finally comes into view. Go straight at this junction to continue or make a 0.6-mile round-trip detour to the **Squatters Cabin** by going right on the trail marked 'Huckleberry Meadow.' On the north side of Crescent Meadow stands the hollow-bodied **Chimney Tree**. Continue east past **Tharp's Log**, which once was a pioneer cabin, then turn right (south) on

a paved trail along the east side of **Log Meadow**.

Before reaching the Crescent Meadow parking lot, head left then right onto the signed High Sierra Trail, heading west for more marvelous ridge views. Stop at **Bobcat Point** overlook to take in the Great Western Divide and Kaweah Canyon. In 0.2 miles, cross Crescent Creek on a log to join the Sugar Pine Trail. Go left (west) and follow it for 0.9 miles to **Moro Rock** (pictured). Climb the granite dome for some of the park's best views, then return to your starting point via shuttle buses (the gray route leaves from Moro Rock and goes to Giant Forest Museum, from where the green route goes to General Sherman).

Essential Information

Entrances

Hwy 198 runs north from Visalia through Three Rivers past Mineral King Rd to the **Ash Mountain Entrance** (Generals Hwy, via Sierra Dr; car/person (walk-in)/motorcycle $30/15/25). Beyond here, the road continues as the Generals Hwy, a narrow and windy road snaking all the way into Kings Canyon National Park, where it joins the Kings Canyon Scenic Byway (Hwy 180) near the western **Big Stump Entrance** (Hwy 180; entry per car $30).

There are no gas stations in the park proper; fill up your tank before you arrive in the park. Those in need can find **gas** (☑559-305-7770; 64144 Hume Lake Rd; ⊙pumps 24hr (credit card only after hours), market 8am-noon & 1-5pm) at Hume Lake year-round (11 miles north of Grant Grove Village).

Sleeping & Eating

There's one lodge in the main section of the park proper. Two other lodges are in the adjoining Sequoia National Forest and Grant Grove Village in Kings Canyon has a couple of options. Otherwise, camping is the easiest and most inexpensive way to go.

There's a snack bar at Lodgepole Village, plus a market for camping supplies. Basic supplies are also available at the small store in Stony Creek Lodge (closed between November and April). Park restaurants are limited to Wuksachi and Stony Creek. The town of Three Rivers has more variety and quality.

Camping

Lodgepole, Potwisha and Buckeye Flat campgrounds in the national park and both Stony Creek campgrounds in the national forest offer reservations (essential in summer); most other campgrounds are first-come, first-served. Campfires are allowed only in existing fire rings.

Lodgepole Campground (www.nps.gov/seki; Lodgepole Rd; tent & RV sites $22; ⊙mid-Apr–late Nov) Closest to the Giant Forest area, with more than 200 closely packed sites, this place fills quickly because of its proximity to Kaweah River swimming holes and Lodgepole Village amenities. The 16 walk-in sites are more private. Flush toilets, picnic tables, fire rings, drinking water and bear-proof lockers are available.

Potwisha Campground (www.recreation.gov; Generals Hwy; tent & RV sites $22; ⊙year-round) Popular campground with decent shade near swimming spots on the Kaweah River. It's 3 miles northeast of the Ash Mountain Entrance, with 42 sites. There are flush toilets, bear-proof lockers, picnic benches and fire pits. Reservations (highly recommended) taken May through September.

Cold Springs Campground (www.nps.gov/seki; Mineral King Rd; tent sites $12; ⊙late May-late Oct) A short walk from the ranger station, Cold Springs has 40 sites (nine walk-in sites) and is a peaceful, creekside location with ridge views and a gorgeous forest setting of conifers and aspens. If you spend the night here at 7500ft, you'll be well on your way to acclimatizing for high-altitude hikes.

Lodgings

Silver City Mountain Resort (☑559-561-3223; www.silvercityresort.com; Mineral King Rd; cabins with/without bath from $205/165, largest cabin from $495; ⊙late May-late Oct; ☜) The only food-and-lodging option anywhere near these parts, this rustic, old-fashioned place rents everything from cute and cozy 1950s-era cabins to modern chalets sleeping up to eight. It's 3.5 miles west of the ranger station. Minimum two-night booking may be required.

Wuksachi Lodge (☑information 866-807-3598, reservations 317-324-0753; www.visitsequoia. com; 64740 Wuksachi Way; r $220-325; ☜) Built in 1999, Wuksachi Lodge is the park's most upscale option. But don't get too excited: the wood-paneled atrium lobby has an inviting stone fireplace and forest views, and the motel-style rooms are fairly generic, with coffeemakers, minifridges, oak furniture and thin walls. The location near Lodgepole Village, however, can't be beat. ∎

General Sherman Tree

DAVIDHOFFMANN PHOTOGRAPHY/SHUTTERSTOCK ©

MIMI DITCHIE PHOTOGRAPHY/GETTY IMAGES ©

Half Dome

Yosemite National Park

From the emerald-green Yosemite Valley to the giant sequoias catapulting into the air at Mariposa Grove, this place inspires a sense of reverence. Four million visitors wend their way to the country's third-oldest national park annually – and this head-turning park garners the devotion of all who enter.

Great For...

State
California

Entrance Fee
7-day pass per car/motorcycle/person on foot or bicycle $35/30/20

Area
1169 sq miles

❶ Yosemite Valley

The park's crown jewel, spectacular meadow-carpeted Yosemite Valley stretches 7 miles long, bisected by the rippling Merced River and hemmed in by some of the most majestic chunks of granite anywhere on earth. Ribbons of water, including some of the highest waterfalls in the US, fall dramatically before crashing in thunderous displays.

It's also where you'll find amenities in Yosemite and Curry Villages, the visitor center, museum, theater and the Ansel Adams Gallery.

❷ Half Dome

Yosemite's most distinctive natural monument is 87 million years old and has a 93% vertical grade – the sheerest cliff in North America. Climbers come from around the world to grapple with its legendary north face, but good hikers can reach its summit via a 17-mile round-trip trail from Yosemite

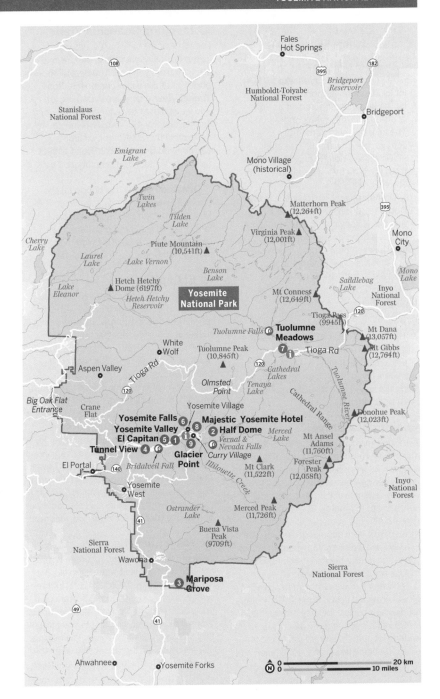

108

395

Fales
Hot Springs

182

*Bridgeport
Reservoir*

Humboldt-Toiyabe
National Forest

Bridgeport

*Stanislaus
National Forest*

*Emigrant
Lake*

Mono Village
(historical)

*Twin
Lakes*

Matterhorn Peak
▲(12,264ft)

395

*Tilden
Lake*

Virginia Peak▲
(12,001ft)

Mono
City

*Cherry
Lake*

*Laurel
Lake*

Lake Vernon

Piute Mountain
(10,541ft) ▲

*Mono
Lake*

*Benson
Lake*

*Saddlebag
Lake*

Inyo
National
Forest

*Lake
Eleanor*

Hetch Hetchy
▲Dome (6197ft)

*Hetch Hetchy
Reservoir*

**Yosemite
National Park**

Mt Conness
(12,649ft)▲

Tioga Pass
(9945ft)

120

Mt Dana
▲(13,057ft)

Tuolumne Falls Ⓡ **Tuolumne
Meadows**

Mt Gibbs
▲(12,764ft)

White
●Wolf

Tuolumne Peak
(10,845ft)
▲

7 ⓘ Tioga Rd

Aspen Valley
Ⓟ

Tioga Rd

120

*Cathedral
Lakes*

120

Olmsted
Point

*Tenaya
Lake*

Tuolumne River

Donohue Peak
(12,023ft)

*Big Oak Flat
Entrance*

Crane
Flat

Yosemite Village

Yosemite Falls **6** **8**

Yosemite West

Majestic Yosemite Hotel

Cathedral Range

*Merced
Lake*

Mt Ansel
Adams
(11,760ft)

Yosemite Valley

2 Half Dome

El Capitan **5 1**

Tunnel View 4 Ⓡ

9

Ⓡ *Vernal &
Nevada Falls*

**Glacier
Point**

Curry Village

El Portal
●

140

Bridalveil Fall

Forester
Peak
(12,058ft)

Illilouette Creek

Mt Clark
(11,522ft)▲

Inyo
National
Forest

Yosemite
West

*Ostrander
Lake*

*Merced Peak
(11,726ft)*▲

41

Sierra
National Forest

Buena Vista
Peak
(9709ft)

Sierra
National Forest

Wawona●

49

3 **Mariposa
Grove**

41

Ahwahnee●

●Yosemite Forks

Ⓝ 0 _____ 20 km
  0 _____ 10 miles

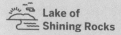

Lake of Shining Rocks

Just east of Olmsted Point, the shiny blue surface of **Tenaya Lake** (8150ft) looks absolutely stunning framed by thick stands of pine and a series of smooth granite cliffs and domes. The lake takes its name from Chief Tenaya, the Ahwahneechee chief who aided white soldiers, only to be driven from the land by white militias in the early 1850s.

Dominating its north side is **Polly Dome** (9806ft). The face nearest the lake is known as Stately Pleasure Dome, a popular spot with climbers – you may see them working their way up from the road. Sloping up from the lake's south shore are Tenaya Peak (10,266ft) and Tresidder Peak (10,600ft).

Valley. The trail gains 4900ft in elevation and has cable handrails for the last 200yd. The hike can be done in a day but is more enjoyable if you break it up by camping along the way (Little Yosemite Valley is the most popular spot).

❸ Mariposa Grove

With their massive stature and multi-millennium maturity, the chunky high-rise sequoias of Mariposa Grove will make you feel rather insignificant. The largest grove of giant sequoias in the park, Mariposa is home to approximately 500 mature trees spread over 250 acres. Walking trails wind through this very popular grove; you can usually have a more solitary experience if you come during the early evening in summer or anytime outside of summer.

Following a major restoration project, the grove reopened in mid-June, 2018. Visitors will see new trails, including accessible boardwalks, and the removal of most of the parking lot, gift shop, tram tours and grove roads, meaning less traffic congestion and a more natural visitor experience.

❹ Inspiring Roadside Views

For some of the very best views over Yosemite Valley, you don't even have to stroll far from your car. The best all-around photo op of the valley can be had from **Tunnel View**, a large, busy parking lot and viewpoint at the east end of Wawona Tunnel, on Hwy 41. From here you can take in much of the valley floor, including El Capitan and Bridalveil Fall. Don't expect a spot for solitary contemplation; it gets extremely crowded.

Olmsted Point is the 'honey, hit the brakes!' viewpoint, midway between the May Lake turnoff and Tenaya Lake: a lunar landscape of glaciated granite with a stunning view down Tenaya Canyon to the back side of Half Dome.

❺ El Capitan

At nearly 3600ft from base to summit, El Capitan ranks as one of the world's largest granite monoliths. Its sheer face makes it a world-class destination for experienced climbers, and one that wasn't 'conquered' until 1958. Since then, it's been inundated.

The road offers several good spots from which to watch climbers reckoning with El Cap's series of cracks and ledges, including the famous 'Nose' – like the Valley View turnout and the pullout along Southside Dr just east of Bridalveil Fall. You can also park on Northside Dr, just below El Capitan. At night, park along the road and dim your headlights; once your eyes adjust, you'll easily make out the pinpricks of headlamps dotting the rock face. Listen, too, for voices.

❻ Yosemite Falls

West of Yosemite Village, Yosemite Falls is considered the tallest waterfall in North America, dropping 740m (2425ft) in three tiers. A slick trail leads to the bottom or, if you prefer solitude, you can clamber up the Yosemite Falls Trail, which puts you atop the falls after a grueling 3.4 miles. The falls are usually mesmerizing, especially when the spring runoff turns them into thunderous cataracts, but are reduced to a trickle by late summer.

❼ Tuolumne Meadows

About 55 miles from Yosemite Valley, 8600ft Tuolumne Meadows is the largest subalpine meadow in the Sierra. Blanketed in snow for most of the year, the meadow explodes to life in summer, when the wildflowers, taking full advantage of the short growing season, fill the grassy expanse with color. Hikers and climbers will find a paradise of options.

The 200ft scramble to the top of Pothole Dome – preferably at sunset – gives you great views of the meadow. Park along Tioga Rd, then follow the trail around the dome's west side and up to its modest summit. It's a fairly quick trip and well worth the effort.

Tuolumne is far less crowded than the valley, though the area around the campground, lodge store and visitor center gets busy, especially on weekends. Altitude can make breathing harder than in the valley, and nights can be nippy, so pack warm clothes.

Tuolumne Meadows sits along Tioga Rd (Hwy 120) west of the park's Tioga Pass Entrance. The **Tuolumne Meadows Hikers' Bus** (☑209-372-1240; www.travelyosemite.com) makes the trip along Tioga Rd once daily in each direction, and can be used for one-way hikes. There's also a free **Tuolumne Meadows Shuttle** (one-way adult/child 5-12yr $9/4.50; ⊙7am-7pm Jun–mid-Sep), which travels between the Tuolumne Meadows Lodge and Olmsted Point, including a stop at Tenaya Lake.

DAN POPOVICI/SHUTTERSTOCK ©

Yosemite Falls

LEFT: KIT LEONG/SHUTTERSTOCK. RIGHT: PIXHOUND/SHUTTERSTOCK ©

Left: Majestic Yosemite Hotel;
Right: Glacier Point

❽ Majestic Yosemite Hotel

The elegant Majestic Yosemite Hotel has drawn well-heeled tourists through its towering doors since 1927. Originally named the Ahwahnee, the hotel was built on the site of a former Ahwahnee–Miwok village. A visit to Yosemite Valley is hardly complete without a stroll through the **Great Lounge** (aka the lobby), which is handsomely decorated with leaded glass, sculpted tile, Native American rugs and Turkish kilims. If the hotel's lobby looks familiar, perhaps it's because it inspired the lobby of the Overlook Hotel, the ill-fated inn from Stanley Kubrick's *The Shining*.

❾ Glacier Point

If you drove, the views from 7214ft Glacier Point might make you feel like you cheated – superstar sights present themselves without your having made barely any physical effort. A quick mosey up from the parking lot and you'll find the entire eastern Yosemite Valley spread out before you, from Yosemite Falls to Half Dome, as well as the distant peaks that ring Tuolumne Meadows. Half Dome looms practically at eye level, and if you look closely you can spot hikers on its summit.

Hike Vernal & Nevada Falls

BAS VERMOLEN/GETTY IMAGES ©

If you can only do a single day hike in Yosemite – and it's springtime – make this the one. Not only are Vernal and Nevada Falls two of Yosemite's most spectacular waterfalls, but Yosemite Falls and Illilouette Fall both make appearances in the distance from select spots on the trail.

There are two ways to hike this loop: up the **Mist Trail** and down the **John Muir Trail** (in a clockwise direction) or vice versa. It's easier on the knees to go for the clockwise route. The granite slabs atop Nevada Fall make for a superb lunch spot (as close to the edge as you want), with the granite dome of **Liberty Cap** (7076ft) towering above.

From the Happy Isles shuttle stop, cross the road bridge over the Merced River, turn right at the trailhead and follow the riverbank upstream. As the trail steepens,

Duration 4–6 hours

Distance 5.4-mile round-trip

Difficulty Moderate–difficult

Start & Finish Vernal & Nevada Falls/ John Muir trailhead

Nearest Junction Happy Isles

Transportation Valley Visitor Shuttle (shuttle stop 16)

watch over your right shoulder for Illilouette Fall (often dry in summer), which peels over a 370ft cliff in the distance. From a lookout, you can gaze west and see Yosemite Falls. After 0.8 miles you arrive at the **Vernal Fall footbridge**, which offers the first view of 317ft Vernal Fall upstream.

Shortly beyond the Vernal Fall footbridge (just past the water fountain and restrooms), you'll reach the junction of the

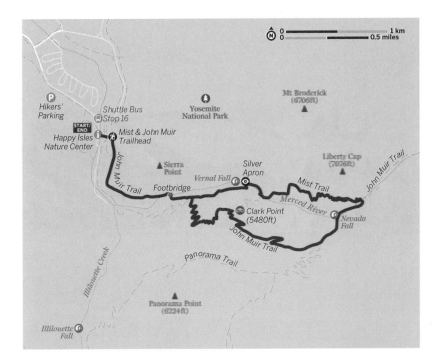

John Muir and Mist Trails. To do the trail clockwise, hang a left and shortly begin the steep 0.3-mile ascent to the top of **Vernal Fall** (pictured) by way of the Mist Trail's granite steps. If it's springtime, prepare to get drenched in spray – wear some waterproof clothing!

Above the falls, the Merced whizzes down a long ramp of granite known as the **Silver Apron** and into the deceptively serene Emerald Pool before plunging over the cliff. *Don't enter the water:* underwater currents in Emerald Pool have whipped many swimmers over the falls.

From above the apron, it's another 1.3 miles via granite steps and steep switchbacks to the top of the Mist Trail, which meets the John Muir Trail, about 0.2 miles northeast of the falls. From this junction, it's 2.5 miles back to Happy Isles via the Mist Trail or 4 miles via the John Muir Trail.

Shortly after joining the John Muir Trail, you'll cross a footbridge (elevation 5907ft) over the Merced. Beneath it, the river whizzes through a chute before plummeting 594ft over the edge of **Nevada Fall**. Nevada Fall is the first of the series of steps in the **Giant Staircase**, a metaphor that becomes clear when viewed from afar at Glacier Point. Plant yourself on a slab of granite for lunch and views, and be prepared to fend off the ballsy Steller's jays and squirrels.

Returning back from Nevada Fall along the John Muir Trail offers a fabulous glimpse of Yosemite Falls. The trail passes the Panorama Trail junction and traverses a cliff, offering awesome views of Nevada Fall. Soon you'll reach **Clark Point** and a junction that leads down to the Mist Trail. From here it's just over 2 miles downhill, through Douglas firs and canyon live oaks to Happy Isles.

Hike Cathedral Lakes

MARKMANDERSONFILMS/SHUTTERSTOCK ©

Easily one of Yosemite's most spectacular hikes, this steady climb through mixed conifer forest ends with glorious views of Cathedral Peak from the shores of two shimmering alpine lakes.

Lower Cathedral Lake (9289ft) sits within a mind-blowing glacial cirque, a perfect amphitheater of granite capped by the iconic spire of nearby **Cathedral Peak** (10,911ft). From the lake's southwest side, the granite drops steeply away, affording views as far as Tenaya Lake, whose blue waters shimmer in the distance. Although it's only about two hours to this lower lake, you could easily spend an entire day exploring the granite slopes, meadows and peaks surrounding it. Continuing to the **Upper Cathedral Lake** (9585ft) adds less than an hour to the hike and puts the round-trip walk at 8 miles, including the stop at Cathedral Lake. Admittedly,

Duration 3–6 hours

Distance 8-mile round-trip (upper lake)

Difficulty Moderate

Start & Finish Cathedral Lakes trailhead

Nearest Town Tuolumne Meadows

Transportation Tuolumne Meadows hikers' bus (shuttle stop 7)

the upper lake is less spectacular when measured against the lower lake, but by all other standards it's utterly sublime.

Parking for the Cathedral Lake trailhead is along the shoulder of Tioga Rd, 0.5 miles west of Tuolumne Meadows Visitor Center. Due to the popularity of this hike, parking spaces fill up fast, so arrive early or take the free shuttle. Camping is allowed at the lower lake (despite what

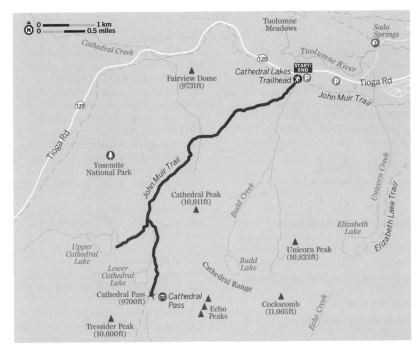

some maps show), but be absolutely certain you're 100ft from the water *and* the trail, and that you choose an already impacted site to prevent further damage. Better yet, camp somewhere near the upper lake or off the pass.

From the Cathedral Lake trailhead on Tioga Rd, the hike heads southwest along the John Muir Trail. Almost immediately, it begins to climb through forest of lodgepole pine, mountain hemlock and the occasional whitebark pine. After ascending over 400ft, the trail levels out and a massive slab of granite – the northern flank of Cathedral Peak – slopes up from the left side of the trail. Soon you'll see Fairview Dome (9731ft) through the trees to your right.

Before long, the trail begins its second ascent, climbing nearly 600ft before leveling off and affording outstanding views of Cathedral Peak. Three miles from the trailhead, you'll hit the junction that leads 0.5 miles southwest to Cathedral Lake. This trail crosses a stunning **meadow** (turn around as you cross it for the head-on view of Cathedral Peak) before arriving at the granite shores of the lake. Be sure to follow the trail around the lake and take in the views from the southwest side.

To visit the upper lake, backtrack to the main trail, turn right (southeast) and, after about 0.5 miles, you'll hit the lake. If you wish to stretch the hike out even further, you can continue past the upper lake to **Cathedral Pass** (9700ft), where you'll be rewarded with a stellar side view of Cathedral Peak and Eichorn Pinnacle (Cathedral's fin-like west peak). This side trip adds about 0.6 miles to the trip.

Essential Information

Access

Yosemite is accessible year-round from the west (via Hwys 120 W and 140) and south (Hwy 41), and in summer from the east (via Hwy 120 E). Roads are plowed in winter, but snow chains may be required at any time. In 2006 a mammoth rockslide buried part of Hwy 140, 6 miles west of the park; traffic there is restricted to vehicles under 45ft.

Visitor Centers

Big Oak Flat Information Station (209-372-0200; 8am-5pm late May-Oct) Has a wilderness permit desk.

Tuolumne Meadows Visitor Center (209-372-0263; 9am-6pm Jun-Sep) Information desk, bookstore and small exhibits on the area's wildlife and history.

Tuolumne Meadows Wilderness Center (209-372-0309; 8am-5pm late May–mid-Oct) Issues wilderness permits.

Yosemite Valley Visitor Center (209-372-0200; 9035 Village Dr, Yosemite Village; 9am-5pm) Park's busiest information desk.

Yosemite Valley Wilderness Center (209-372-0745; Yosemite Village; 8am-5pm May-Oct) Permits, maps and backcountry advice.

Information

Upon entering the park, you'll receive an NPS map and a copy of the seasonal *Yosemite Guide* newspaper. The official NPS website (www.nps.gov/yose) has comprehensive information. For recorded park information, call 209-372-0200.

Stores in Yosemite Village, Half Dome Village and Wawona all have ATMs, as do the Yosemite Valley Lodge and the Majestic Yosemite Hotel.

Fill your tank year-round at Wawona or Crane Flat inside the park (you'll pay dearly), at El Portal on Hwy 140 just outside its western boundary, or at Lee Vining at the junction of Hwys 120 and 395 outside the park in the east.

Safe Travels

Landslides frequently close trails and steep paths get slippery after rains and flooding.

Avoid direct contact and exposure to animal droppings, especially rodents, and never touch a dead one. Avoid sleeping on the ground; always use a cot, hammock, sleeping bag or other surface. Follow park rules on proper food storage and utilize bear-proof food lockers when parked overnight.

Mountain lion sightings are uncommon, but if you see one, do not run; rather, attempt to scare it away by shouting and waving your arms. Do the same for coyotes, which are more frequently seen. Report sightings to park dispatch (209-372-0476).

Sleeping

Reservations for the seven campgrounds within the park that aren't first-come, first-served are handled by Recreation.gov, up to five months in advance. Competition for sites is fierce from May to September. Without a booking, your only chance is to hightail it to an open campground or proceed to one of four campground reservation offices in Yosemite Valley, Wawona, Big Oak Flat and Tuolumne Meadows.

All noncamping reservations within the park are handled by **Aramark/Yosemite Hospitality** (888-413-8869; www.travel yosemite.com) and can be made up to 366 days in advance; reservations are critical from May to early September. Rates – and demand – drop from October to April.

Other park visitors overnight in nearby gateway towns like Fish Camp, Midpines, El Portal, Mariposa and Groveland; however, commute times into the park can be long.

Eating

The **Village Store** (Yosemite Village; 8am-8pm, to 10pm summer) has the best selection (including health-food items and some organic produce), while stores at Half Dome Village, Wawona, Tuolumne Meadows and the Yosemite Valley Lodge are more limited. ■

MELISSAMN/SHUTTERSTOCK/SHUTTERSTOCK ©

Yosemite Valley Visitor Center

CLASSIC ROAD TRIPS

Yosemite, Sequoia & Kings Canyon

Drive up into the lofty Sierra Nevada, where glacial valleys and ancient forests overfill the windshield scenery. Go climb a rock, pitch a tent or photograph wildflowers and wildlife.

Duration 5–7 days

Distance 450 miles

Best Time to Go
April and May for waterfalls; June to September for full access.

Essential Photo
Yosemite Valley from panoramic Tunnel View.

Best Scenic Drive
Kings Canyon Scenic Byway to Cedar Grove.

❶ Tuolumne Meadows
These are the Sierra Nevada's largest sub-alpine meadows, with fields of wildflowers, bubbling streams, ragged granite peaks and cooler temperatures at an elevation of 8600ft. Note that the route crossing the Sierra and passing by the meadows, **Tioga Rd** (a 19th-century wagon road and Native American trading route), is completely closed by snow in winter. It usually reopens in May/June and remains passable until October or November.

Nine miles west of the meadows, a sandy half-moon beach wraps around **Tenaya**

Lake, tempting you to brave some of the park's coldest swimming. A few minutes further west, stop at **Olmsted Point**, overlooking a lunar-type landscape of glaciated granite.

The Drive » From Tuolumne Meadows it's 50 miles to Yosemite Valley, following Tioga Rd (Hwy 120), turning south onto Big Oak Flat Rd, then east onto El Portal Rd.

❷ Tunnel View
For your first, spectacular look into Yosemite Valley, pull over at Tunnel View, a vista that has inspired painters, poets, naturalists and adventurers for centuries. On the right, Bridalveil Fall swells with snowmelt in late spring, but by late summer it's a mere whisper. Spread below you are the pine forests and meadows of the valley floor, with the sheer face of El Capitan rising on the left and, in the distance straight ahead, iconic granite Half Dome.

The Drive » Merge carefully back onto eastbound Wawona Rd, which continues downhill into Yosemite Valley, full of confusingly intersecting one-way roads. Drive east along the Merced River on Southside Dr past the Bridalveil Fall turnoff. Almost 6 miles from Tunnel View, turn left and drive across Sentinel Bridge to Yosemite Village's day-use parking lots. Ride free shuttle buses that circle the valley.

❸ Yosemite Valley
At busy Yosemite Village, start inside the Yosemite Valley Visitor Center (p122), with its thought-provoking history and nature displays and free *Spirit of Yosemite* film screenings. At the nearby **Yosemite Museum** (www.nps.gov/yose; 9037 Village Dr, Yosemite Village; ⊙9am-5pm summer, 10am-4pm rest of year, often closed noon-1pm) 🎫 FREE, Western landscape paintings are hung beside Native American baskets and beaded clothing.

The valley's famous waterfalls are thunderous cataracts in May, but mere trickles by late July. Triple-tiered **Yosemite Falls** is North America's tallest, while **Bridalveil Fall** is hardly less impressive. A strenuous, often slippery staircase beside Vernal Fall

Tuolumne Meadows

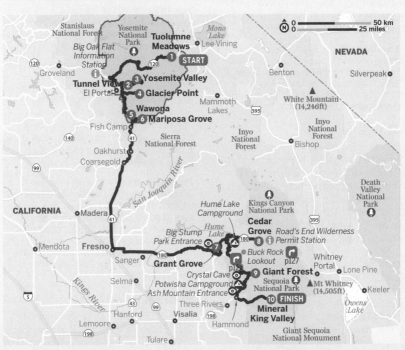

❄ Winter Wonderlands

When the temperature drops and the white stuff falls, there are still tons of fun outdoor activities around the Sierra Nevada's national parks. In Yosemite, strap on some skis or a snowboard and go tubing downhill off Glacier Point Rd; plod around Yosemite Valley on a ranger-led snowshoe tour; or just try to stay upright on ice skates at Half Dome Village. Further south in Sequoia and Kings Canyon National Parks, the whole family can go snowshoeing or cross-country skiing among groves of giant sequoias. Before embarking on a winter trip to the parks, check road conditions on the official park websites or by calling ahead. Don't forget to put snow tires on your car, and always carry tire chains too.

leads you, gasping, right to the top edge of the waterfall, where rainbows pop in clouds of mist. Keep hiking up the same Mist Trail to the top of **Nevada Fall** for a heady 5.5-mile round-trip trek.

The Drive » Use Northside Dr to loop round and join Wawona Rd again. Follow Wawona Rd/Hwy 41 up out of the valley. After 9 miles, turn left onto Glacier Point Rd at the Chinquapin intersection, driving 15 more miles to Glacier Point.

❹ Glacier Point

In just over an hour, you can zip from Yosemite Valley up to head-spinning Glacier Point. Note that the final 10 miles of Glacier Point Rd is closed by snow in winter, usually from November through April or May. During winter, the road remains open as far as the Yosemite Ski & Snowboard Area, but snow tires and tire chains may be required.

Rising over 3000ft above the valley floor, dramatic Glacier Point (7214ft) practically puts you at eye level with Half Dome. On your way back from Glacier Point, take time out for a 2-mile hike up **Sentinel Dome** or out to **Taft Point** for incredible 360-degree valley views.

The Drive » Drive back downhill past Yosemite Ski & Snowboard Area, turning left at the Chinquapin intersection and winding south through thick forest on Wawona Rd/Hwy 41. After almost 13 curvy miles, you'll reach Wawona, with its lodge, visitor center, general store and gas station, all on your left.

❺ Wawona

At Wawona, a 45-minute drive south of the valley, drop by the **Pioneer Yosemite History Center** (☑209-372-0200; www.nps.gov/yose/planyourvisit/upload/pyhc.pdf; rides adult/child $5/4; ⊗24hr, rides 10am-2pm Wed-Sun Jun-Sep) **FREE**, with its covered bridge, pioneer-era buildings and historic Wells Fargo office. On summer evenings, imbibe a civilized cocktail in the lobby lounge of the **Big Trees Lodge** (☑reservations 888-413-8869; www.travelyosemite.com; 8308 Wawona Rd; r with/without bath from $220/150; ⊗mid-Mar–late Nov & mid-Dec–early Jan; ☏☒), where pianist Tom Bopp often plays tunes from Yosemite's bygone days.

The Drive » By car, follow Wawona Rd/Hwy 41 south for 4.5 miles to the park's south entrance, where you must leave your car at the parking lot. A free shuttle will take you to Mariposa Grove.

❻ Mariposa Grove

Wander giddily around the Mariposa Grove, home to 500 giant sequoias. Nature trails wind through this popular grove, but you can only hear yourself think above the noise of vacationing crowds during the early morning or evening.

The Drive » From Yosemite's south entrance station, it's a 115-mile, three-hour trip to Kings Canyon National Park. Follow Hwy 41 south 60 miles to Fresno, then slingshot east on Hwy 180 for another 50 miles, climbing out of the Central Valley back into the mountains. Keep left at the Hwy 198 intersection, staying on Hwy 180 toward Grant Grove.

❼ Grant Grove

North of Big Stump entrance station in Grant Grove Village, turn left and wind

Mariposa Grove

Detour: Buck Rock Lookout

Start: 8 Cedar Grove

To climb one of California's most evocative fire lookouts, drive east of the Generals Hwy on Big Meadows Rd into the Sequoia National Forest between Grant Grove and the Giant Forest. Follow the signs to staffed **Buck Rock Fire Lookout** (☎559-901-8151; www.buckrock.org; ⏰10am-4pm mid–May-Oct). Constructed in 1923, this active fire lookout allows panoramic views from a dollhouse-sized cab lording it over the horizon from 8500ft atop a granite rise, reached by 172 spindly stairs. It's not for anyone with vertigo. Opening hours may vary seasonally, and the lookout closes during lightning storms and fire emergencies.

Glacier Point and Half Dome

Detour: Crystal Cave

Start: ❾ Giant Forest

Off the Generals Hwy, about 2 miles south of the Giant Forest Museum, turn right (west) onto twisting 6.5-mile-long Crystal Cave Rd for a fantastical walk inside 10,000-year-old **Crystal Cave** (www.recreation.gov; ☼late May-Sep; tours adult/child/youth from $16/5/8), carved by an underground river. Stalactites hang like daggers from the ceiling, and milky-white marble formations take the shape of ethereal curtains, domes, columns and shields. Bring a light jacket – it's 50°F (10°C) inside the cave. Buy tour tickets a month or more in advance online at www.recreation.gov; during October and November, tickets are only sold in person at the Giant Forest Museum and Foothills Visitor Center. Tour tickets are not available at the cave itself.

downhill to Grant Grove, where you'll see some of the park's landmark giant sequoia trees. You can walk right through the Fallen Monarch, a massive, fire-hollowed trunk that's done duty as a cabin, hotel, saloon and horse stable.

The Drive » Kings Canyon National Park's main visitor areas, Grant Grove and Cedar Grove, are linked by the narrow, twisting, 30-mile Kings Canyon Scenic Byway (Hwy 180). Hwy 180 from the Hume Lake turnoff to Cedar Grove is closed during winter (usually mid-November through mid-April).

❽ Cedar Grove

Hwy 180 plunges down to the Kings River, where roaring white water ricochets off the granite cliffs of North America's deepest canyon, technically speaking. Pull over part-way down at the **Junction View** overlook for an eyeful, then keep rolling down along the river to **Cedar Grove Village**. East of the village, **Zumwalt Meadow** is the place for spotting birds, mule deer and black

bears. Starting from **Road's End**, a very popular day hike climbs 4 miles each way to **Mist Falls**, which thunders in late spring.

The Drive » Backtrack from Road's End nearly 30 miles up Hwy 180. Turn left onto Hume Lake Rd. Curve around the lake past swimming beaches and campgrounds, turning right onto 10 Mile Rd. At Hwy 198, turn left and follow the Generals Hwy (often closed from January to March) south for about 23 miles to the Wolverton Rd turnoff on your left.

❾ Giant Forest

Park off Wolverton Rd and walk downhill to reach the world's biggest living tree, the **General Sherman Tree**. By car, drive 2.5 miles south along the Generals Hwy to the **Giant Forest Museum**. Starting outside the museum, Crescent Meadow Rd makes a 6-mile loop into the Giant Forest, passing right through **Tunnel Log**. Note: Crescent Meadow Rd is closed to traffic by winter snow; during summer, ride the free shuttle buses around the loop road.

The Drive » Narrowing, the Generals Hwy drops for more than 15 miles into the Sierra Nevada foothills, passing Amphitheater Point and exiting the park beyond Foothills Visitor Center. Before reaching the town of Three Rivers, turn left on Mineral King Rd, a dizzyingly scenic 25-mile road (partly unpaved, no trailers or RVs allowed and closed in winter) that switchbacks up to Mineral King Valley.

❿ Mineral King Valley

Navigating over 700 hairpin turns, it's a winding 1½-hour drive up to the glacially sculpted **Mineral King Valley** (7500ft). Trailheads into the high country begin at the end of Mineral King Rd, where historic private cabins dot the valley floor flanked by massive mountains. Your final destination is just over a mile past the ranger station, where the valley unfolds all of its hidden beauty, and hikes to granite peaks and alpine lakes beckon.

Note that Mineral King Rd is typically open only from late May through late October. ■

Top left: Zumwalt Meadow; Top right: Giant Forest Museum; Bottom: Upper Yosemite Falls

THE SOUTHWEST

In This Chapter

Arches..................................134
Big Bend.............................140
Bryce Canyon....................152
Canyonlands.....................164
Capitol Reef......................170
Carlsbad Caverns.............178
Grand Canyon...................180
Great Basin........................190
Guadalupe Mountains....................192
Mesa Verde.......................198
Petrified Forest................204
Saguaro.............................208
Zion....................................210
White Sands.....................222

The Southwest

The Southwest is America's untamed playground, luring travelers with giant arches, desert mesas, canyons and ancient petroglyphs. Whether you're admiring a giant cactus or the polished walls of a narrow slot canyon, one thing's clear: water rules all here.

Trace the Colorado River to find a string of desert jewels: Arches, Canyonlands and the Grand Canyon. Further west are neck-craning Zion and Bryce's surreal hoodoos. A network of scenic drives links the most beautiful sites.

Don't Miss

○ Feeling minuscule in front of the Grand Canyon (p180)

○ Driving Big Bend's scenic roads (p146)

○ Witnessing Island in the Sky's enthralling views (p164)

○ Rambling to rock formations in Arches National Park (p134)

○ River-splashed hiking in Zion's fabled Narrows (p210)

○ Delving into Mesa Verde's ancient mysteries (p198)

When to Go

In summer (June to August), temperatures soar well above 100°F and national parks are at maximum capacity; higher elevations bring cool relief. Fall is the best time to go, with colorful scenes, cooler temperatures and lighter crowds on the Grand Canyon South Rim.

National parks in Utah and northern Arizona clear out as the snow arrives from December to March, though it's busy on the slopes in Utah, Colorado and New Mexico.

Previous page: Grand Canyon National Park (p180)
AMINEAH/SHUTTERSTOCK ©

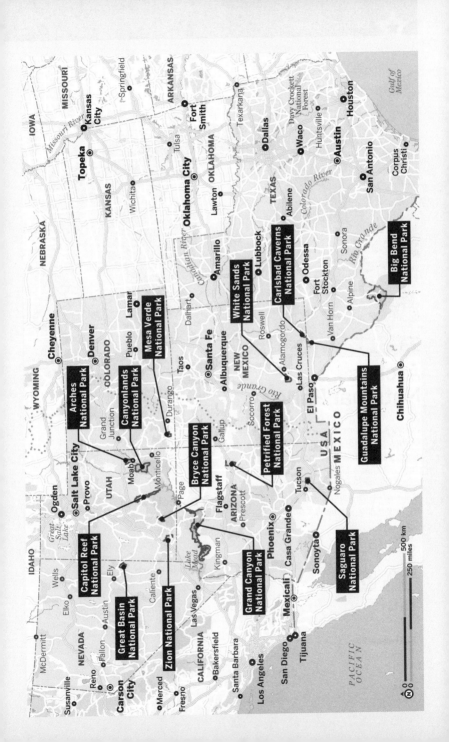

CHECUBUS/SHUTTERSTOCK ©

Double Arch

Arches National Park

Giant sweeping arcs of sandstone frame snowy peaks and desert landscapes at Arches National Park. It's the highest density of rock arches on earth: more than 2500 in a 119-sq-mile area. You'll lose perspective on size at some, such as 290ft-wide Landscape Arch. Others are tiny – the smallest is only 3ft across.

Great For...

State
Utah

Entrance Fee
7-day pass per car/motorcycle/person on foot or bicycle $30/25/15

Area
119 sq miles

To hit all the highlights, follow the paved **Arches Scenic Drive**. It's packed with photo ops and short walks to arches and iconic landmarks. The full 43-mile drive (including spurs) takes two to three hours if you're not taking any hikes.

❶ Delicate Arch

You've seen this arch before: it's the unofficial state symbol, stamping nearly every Utah tourist brochure. The best way to experience it is from beneath. Park near **Wolfe Ranch**, a well-preserved 1908 pioneer cabin. From there a footbridge crosses **Salt Wash** (near Native American rock art) and marks the beginning of the moderate-to-strenuous, 3-mile round-trip trail to the arch itself. The trail ascends slickrock, culminating in a wall-hugging ledge before reaching the arch.

Ditch the crowds by passing beneath the arch and continuing down the rock by several yards to where there's a great

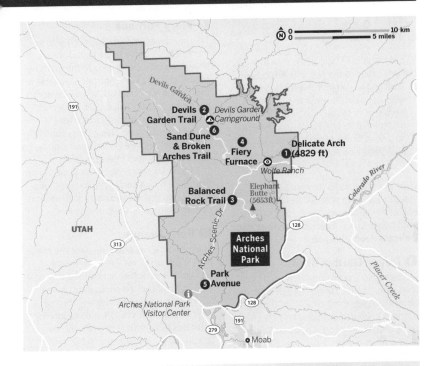

Delicate Arch

Quick Walk

Tight on time? Do part or all of this easy 1-mile round-trip. The **Windows Trail** brings you up to North Window, where you can look out to the canyon beyond. Continue on to South Window and the castle-like Turret Arch. You can also see Double Arch via an easy 0.5-mile path, just across the parking lot.

view, but fewer folks (bring a picnic). If instead you drive past the ranch to the end of the spur road, there's a 50yd paved path (wheelchair accessible) to the **Lower Delicate Arch Viewpoint**.

② Devils Garden Trail

At the paved road's end, 19 miles from the visitor center, Devils Garden trailhead marks the beginning of a 2- to 7.7-mile round-trip hike that passes eight arches. Most people only go 1.3 miles to **Landscape Arch**, a gravity-defying, 290ft-long behemoth. Further along, the trail gets less crowded, growing rougher and steeper toward **Double O Arch** and **Dark Angel Spire**.

The optional, difficult **Devils Garden Primitive Loop** has narrow-ledge walking and serious slickrock hiking. Ask rangers about conditions before attempting it.

③ Balanced Rock Trail

A 3577-ton boulder atop a leaning pedestal, Balanced Rock shoots from the earth like a fist. The pedestal is made of soft Dewey Bridge mudstone, which erodes faster than the rock above. Eventually, this pedestal will snap, and the boulder will come crashing down.

While you can see the formation clearly from the trailhead, the easy, 0.3-mile loop allows you to grasp its actual size (55ft to the top of the pedestal, 128ft to the top of the rock). There is wheelchair access to the viewpoint.

④ Fiery Furnace

This narrow sandstone labyrinth with no marked trails provides an extra level of adventure for visitors. Due to the extreme nature of hiking here, permits (available at the Arches National Park Visitor Center) are required. Otherwise, paid ranger-led walking tours are offered from April through September. These tours run 2½ to three hours and are generally offered twice daily (morning and afternoon).

Tickets for ranger-led tours (adult/child from $10/5) are sold in person only on a first-come, first-served basis at the visitor center up to seven days in advance.

⑤ Park Avenue

Many short hikes originate near the main park road. Just over 2 miles from the entrance is Park Ave, a mile-long trail past a giant fin of rock reminiscent of a New York skyline. Kids love running through the Sand Dune Arch (0.4-mile round-trip); from the same trailhead, walk across grassland for 1 mile to reach 60ft Broken Arch.

⑥ Sand Dune & Broken Arches Trail

From the Sand Dune Arch parking area, follow the trail through deep sand between narrow stone walls that are the backmost fins of **Fiery Furnace**. In less than 0.25 miles you'll arrive at **Sand Dune Arch**, which looks something like a poodle kissing a polar bear. Resist the temptation to climb or jump off the 8ft arch. From here you can bear left to return to your car or bear right across open grassland en route to Broken Arch. At the next fork (the start of the loop trail), grasses give way to piñon pines and junipers along a gentle climb to **Broken Arch**. The treat here is the walk *through* the arch atop a slickrock ledge. Wear rubber-soled shoes or boots, or you may have trouble climbing to the arch.

This 2.4-mile loop is a good trail for kids, especially the first section.

BLAZG/SHUTTERSTOCK ©

Devils Garden trail

Essential Information

Sleeping & Eating

There's stiff competition for camping in the park but there are plenty of campgrounds throughout the region and lodging galore in Moab. No food is available in the park; Moab is the place to stock up or dine out.

Devils Garden Campground (☑877-444-6777; www.recreation.gov; Arches National Park; tent & RV sites $25) Surrounded by red rock and scrubby piñons, the park's only campground is 19 miles from the Arches National Park Visitor Center. From March to October, sites are available by reservation. Book months ahead.

Information

In summer arrive by 9am, when crowds are sparse and temperatures bearable, or visit after 7pm and enjoy a moonlight stroll. July highs average 100°F (38°C); carry at least one gallon of water per person if hiking. Two rugged back roads lead into semi-solitude, but 4WD is recommended – ask at the visitor center. Cell phones do not work in most of the park.

Arches National Park Visitor Center (☑435-719-2299; www.nps.gov/arch/planyourvisit/hours.htm; Arches National Park; ⊙7:30am-5pm) Has Arches canyoneering and climbing permits (also available at archespermits.nps.gov). You can watch an informative video, check ranger-led activity schedules and pick up your Fiery Furnace tickets.

Getting There & Around

As yet the park has no shuttle system and no public buses so most visitors arrive in cars. Ongoing road-widening efforts mean delays are possible.

Several outfitters in Moab run motorized park tours. **Moab Adventure Center** (☑866-904-1163, 435-259-7019; www.moab adventurecenter.com; 225 S Main St; half-day tours from $85) and **Adrift Adventures** (☑800-874-4483, 435-259-8594; www.adrift.net; 378 N Main St; half-day tours from $90) have scenic-drive van tours. ∎

Top left: Broken Arch; Top right: Long-nosed leopard lizard; Bottom: Balanced Rock

ERIC FOLTZ/SHUTTERSTOCK ©

Balanced Rock

Big Bend National Park

When you're traversing Big Bend's 1252 sq miles, you come to appreciate what 'big' really means. It's a land of incredible diversity, vast enough to allow a lifetime of discovery, yet laced with enough well-placed roads and trails to permit short-term visitors to see a lot in two to three days.

Great For...

State
Texas

Entrance Fee
7-day pass per car/motorcycle/person on foot or bicycle $25/20/12

Area
1252 sq miles

Scenic Drives

With 110 miles of paved road and 150 miles of dirt road, scenic driving is easily the park's most popular activity.

Old Maverick Road

The 23-mile stretch between the west entrance and park headquarters is notable for its desert scenery and wildlife. Just west of Basin Junction, a side trip on the gravel Grapevine Hills Rd leads to fields of oddly shaped, highly eroded boulders.

Ross Maxwell Scenic Drive

This 30-mile route leaves Maverick Dr midway between the west entrance and park headquarters. The Chisos Mountains provide a grand panorama, and the big payoff is the view of Santa Elena Canyon and its 1500ft sheer rock walls.

Rio Grande Village Drive

This 21-mile drive leads from park head-quarters toward the Sierra del Carmen

Santa Elena Canyon

CAT SPARKS/SHUTTERSTOCK ©

Starry Nights

Big Bend has taken major steps to reduce light pollution in the last few years, installing LED lights and retrofitting outdoor light sources on more than 280 buildings and in other developed areas. These steps make it easier to see stars in the night sky. The International Dark Sky Association awarded the park a gold-tier certification in 2012, and the park shares the honor with only a dozen or so other parks worldwide.

Check the *Paisano*, the park's seasonal newspaper, for a list of celestial events, from solstices to meteor showers, that may occur during your visit. Evening ranger talks may cover night skies, with a telescope provided for celestial viewing.

range, running through the park toward Mexico. The best time to take this drive is at sunrise or sunset, when the mountains glow brilliantly with different hues.

Hiking

With more than 150 miles of trails to explore, it's no wonder hiking is big in Big Bend. The **Chisos Basin Loop Trail** (1.8 miles) offers nice views of the basin and a relatively large amount of shade, while the popular **Lost Mine Trail** (4.8 miles) has views that just get better and better as you climb over 1000ft in elevation.

The **Hot Springs Historic Walk** (0.75 miles) passes historic buildings and Native American pictographs painted on rock walls on its way to a stone tub brimming with 105°F (41°C) water.

The fascinating desert **Grapevine Hills Trail** (2.2 miles), near Panther Junction, accesses Balanced Rock, a much-photographed formation of three acrobatic boulders that form an inverted-triangle 'window.'

River Trips

The Rio Grande has earned its place among the top North American river trips for both rafting and canoeing. Rapids up to class IV alternate with calm stretches that are perfect for wildlife-viewing, photography and just plain relaxation.

Trips on the river can range from several hours to several days. **Boquillas Canyon** is the longest and most tranquil of the park's three canyons and is best for intermediate to advanced boaters and canoeists with camping skills. **Colorado Canyon** is just upriver from the park and, depending on the water level, has lots of white water. **Mariscal Canyon** is noted for its beauty and isolation, and **Santa Elena Canyon** is a classic float featuring the class IV Rock Slide rapid.

Guided floats cost about $145 per person per day ($79 for a half-day), including all meals and gear (except a sleeping bag for overnighters). **Big Bend River Tours** (☑432-371-3033, 800-545-4240; www.bigbendrivertours.com; 23331 FM 170; half-/full day river trip $75/135) offers saddle-paddle tours with half a day each rowing and horseback riding.

Bird-Watching

Over 450 bird species have been spotted in the park; prime sites include Rio Grande Valley, the Sam Nail Ranch, the Chisos Basin and Castolon near Santa Elena Canyon. The Big Bend region may be best known for its peregrine falcons, which, while still endangered, have been making a comeback. The current number of falcon nests is not known, but there are some within the park.

The **Rio Grande Village Nature Trail** (0.75 miles) is a good short trail for birding and photography. Beginning at campsite 18 at the Rio Grande Village campground, the trail passes through dense vegetation before emerging in the desert for a view of the Rio Grande.

Canoeing, Rio Grande

MARK TAYLOR CUNNINGHAM/SHUTTERSTOCK ©

Essential Information

Sleeping & Eating

Tent campers or smaller RVs that don't require hookups can use the three main campgrounds; some take reservations but some are first-come, first-served.

Chisos Lodge Restaurant (Lodge Dining Room; www.chisosmountainslodge.com; Chisos Mountain Lodge; lunch $7-12, dinner $10-22; ⊘7-10am, 11am-4pm & 5-8pm) Run by concessionaire Forever Resorts, this is the only full-service restaurant in the park. It offers breakfast, lunch and dinner and has a small bar. Otherwise, bring your own food or buy snacks and basic groceries at one of the park's convenience stores.

Cottonwood Campground (www.nps.gov/ bibe; tent sites $14) Set beneath cottonwood trees near Castolon, the 24-site Cottonwood Campground provides a subdued and shady environment along the river with no generators or idling vehicles to ruin the ambience. No hookups and no dump station. Pit toilets and water are available. No reservations.

Maps

Readily available at the entrances and visitor centers, the free National Park Service (NPS) *Big Bend* map is adequate for most visitors to the park. You'll also find summaries and mileage information about popular trails in the *Paisano,* the free park newspaper. The visitor centers also sell trail guides. Serious backpackers or anyone looking to hike the less-developed trails will want to pick up a topographic map.

Visitor Centers

In addition to the park headquarters and visitor center at **Panther Junction** (Main Visitor Center; ✆432-477-1158; www.nps. gov/bibe; ⊘9am-5pm), visitor centers are found in **Chisos Basin** (✆432-477-2264; ⊘8:30am-noon & 1-4pm) and at **Persimmon Gap** (✆432-477-2393; ⊘9:30-11:30am & 12:30-4pm).

Safety

Don't underestimate the heat; this is the desert, after all. Drink lots of water, and take plenty with you when you hike.

Most snakes keep a low profile in daylight, when you're unlikely to see them. Night hikers should stay on the trail and carry a flashlight. Big Bend's scorpions are not deadly, but you should still get prompt attention if you're stung. Shake out boots or shoes before putting them on.

Getting There & Away

There is no public transportation to, from or within the park. The closest buses and trains run through Alpine, 108 miles northwest of Panther Junction. The nearest major airports are 230 miles northeast in Midland and 325 miles northwest in El Paso.

You'll find gas at the service stations at **Panther Junction** (✆432-477-2294; ⊘convenience store 7am-6:30pm May-Sep, 8am-5:30pm Jun-Aug. pumps 24hr) and **Rio Grande Village** (✆432-477-2293; ⊘8am-7pm Oct-May, to 5pm Jun-Sep).

Note that the border patrol has checkpoints for vehicles coming from Big Bend. If you're not a US citizen, presenting your passport will help avoid delays (ie prove you're not coming from Mexico).

Top left: Painted bunting; Top right: Claret cup cactus; Bottom: Stargazing at Balanced Rock

CLASSIC ROAD TRIPS

Big Bend Scenic Loop

Big Bend National Park and the endless vistas straight out of an old Western are reason enough to make this trip. But you'll also have plenty of fun along the way, exploring quirky small towns, minimalist art and astronomy parties.

Duration 5–7 days

Distance 690 miles

Best Time to Go

Best between February and April – before the heat sets in.

Essential Photo

Prada Marfa, a quirky roadside art installation.

Best for Outdoors

McDonald Observatory's nighttime star parties.

❶ El Paso

Start your trip in El Paso, a border city that's wedged into a remote corner of west Texas. While here, take advantage of the great Mexican food you can find all over the city – it's right across the river from Mexico – and enjoy El Paso's many free museums. Downtown, the **El Paso Museum of Art** (☏915-212-0300; www.epma. art; 1 Arts Festival Plaza; ☉9am-5pm Tue-Sat, to 9pm Thu, noon-5pm Sun) **FREE** has a terrific Southwestern collection, and the engaging modern pieces round out the display nicely.

Another one you shouldn't miss is the **El Paso Holocaust Museum** (☏915-351-0048; www.elpasoholocaustmuseum.org; 715 N Oregon St; ☉9am-5pm Tue-Fri, 1-5pm Sat & Sun) **FREE**. It may seem a little anachronistic in a predominately Hispanic town, but it hosts amazingly thoughtful and moving exhibits that are imaginatively presented for maximum impact.

To the west, you'll find several good restaurants and watering holes in the developing Montecillo commercial and residential district.

The Drive » Head east on I-10 for two hours, then turn onto TX 118 toward Fort Davis. The area is part of both the Chihuahuan Desert and the Davis Mountains, giving it a unique setting where the endless horizons are suddenly interrupted by rock formations springing from the earth.

❷ Fort Davis

Here's why you'll want to plan on being in Fort Davis on either a Tuesday, Friday or Saturday: to go to an evening star party at **McDonald Observatory** (☏432-426-3640; www.mcdonaldobservatory.org; 3640 Dark Sky Dr; day pass adult/child 6-12yr/under 6yr $8/7/free; ☉visitor center 10am-5:30pm). The observatory has some of the clearest and darkest skies in North America, not to mention some of the most powerful telescopes – a perfect combination for gazing at stars, planets and assorted celestial bodies, with astronomers on hand to explain it all.

Besides that, nature lovers will enjoy **Davis Mountains State Park**, and history buffs can immerse themselves at the 1854 **Fort Davis National Historic Site** (☏432-426-3224; www.nps.gov/foda; Hwy 17; adult/child under 16yr $7/free; ☉8am-5pm), a well-preserved frontier military post that's impressively situated at the foot of Sleeping Lion Mountain.

The Drive » Marfa is just 20 minutes south on TX 17, a two-lane country road where tumbleweeds bounce slowly by and congregate around the barbed-wire fences.

McDonald Observatory

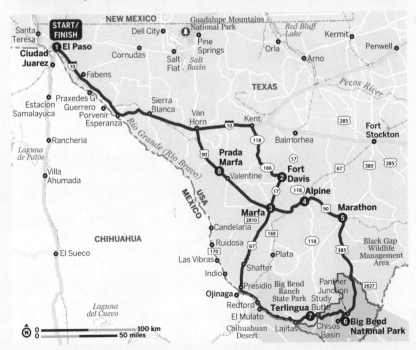

❸ Marfa

Marfa got its first taste of fame when Rock Hudson, Elizabeth Taylor and James Dean came to town to film the 1956 film *Giant*. It's since served as a film location for movies like *There Will Be Blood* and *No Country for Old Men*.

But these days, this tiny town with one stoplight draws visitors from around the world for a different reason: its art scene. Donald Judd single-handedly put Marfa on the art-world map in the 1980s when he used a bunch of abandoned military buildings to create one of the world's largest permanent installations of minimalist art at the **Chinati Foundation** (☏432-729-4362; www.chinati.org; 1 Calvary Row; adult/student Full Collection Tour $25/10, Selections Tour $20/10; ⊗9am-4:30pm Wed-Sun, tours 10am, 10:30am, 11am, 11:30am).

Art galleries are sprinkled around town, exploring everything from photography to sculpture to modern art. **Ballroom Marfa** (☏432-729-3600; www.ballroommarfa.org; 108 E San Antonio St; suggested donation $5; ⊗10am-6pm Wed-Sat, to 3pm Sun) is a great gallery to catch the vibe. Try not to visit on a Monday or Tuesday, when many businesses are closed.

The Drive » Alpine is about 30 minutes east of Marfa on Hwy 90/67.

❹ Alpine

The biggest little town in the area, Alpine is the county seat, a college town (Sul Ross University is here) and the best place to stock up on whatever you need before you head down into the Chihuahuan Desert.

Stop by the **Museum of the Big Bend** (☏432-837-8143; www.museumofthebigbend.com;

Top: Prada Marfa; Bottom left: Cemetery, Terlingua; Bottom right: Wagon, Fort Davis

ARTISTS:ELMGREEN & DRAGSET.PHOTO:KRIS DAVIDSON/LONELY PLANET ©

JEN MCCORMACK/SHUTTERSTOCK ©

VINCENT K. HO/SHUTTERSTOCK ©

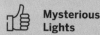
Mysterious Lights

The Marfa Lights that flicker beneath the Chinati Mountains have captured the imagination of many a traveler over the decades, with accounts of mysterious lights that appear and disappear on the horizon that go all the way back to the 1800s. Numerous studies have been conducted to explain the phenomenon, but the only thing scientists all agree on is that they have no idea what causes the apparition.

Catch the show at the Marfa Lights Viewing Area, on the south side of the road between Marfa and Alpine. From the platform, look south and find the red blinking light (that one's real). Just to the right is where you will (or won't) see the Marfa Lights doing their ghostly thing.

---

400 N Harrison St; donations accepted; ⊘9am-5pm Tue-Sat, 1-5pm Sun) **FREE** to brush up on the history of the Big Bend region. But don't expect it to be dry and dusty. The multimedia exhibits are big and eye-catching, and display-reading is kept to a minimum. Most impressive? The enormous replica wing bone of the Texas pterosaur found in Big Bend – the largest flying creature ever found, with an estimated wing span of more than 50ft – along with the intimidatingly large re-creation of the whole bird that's big enough to snatch up a fully grown human to carry off for dinner.

The Drive » Keep heading east. In 15 miles, look south for the the guerrilla art installation *Target Marathon,* a fun nod to Prada Marfa. In another 15 miles you'll reach the seriously tiny town of Marathon (*mar*-a-thun). The views aren't much during this stretch of the drive, but Big Bend will make up for all that.

❺ Marathon

This tiny railroad town has two claims to fame. It's the closest town to Big Bend's north entrance – providing a last chance to fill up your car and your stomach – and it's got the **Gage Hotel** (☑432-386-4205; www.gagehotel.com; 102 NW 1st St/Hwy 90; r $229-279; ❄@☎☎), a true Texas treasure that's worth a peek, if not an overnight stay.

The Drive » Heading south on US-385, it's 40 miles to the northern edge of Big Bend, and 40 more to get to the Chisos Basin, the heart of the park. The flat road affords miles and miles of views for most of the drive.

❻ Big Bend National Park

Talk about big. At 1252 sq miles, this national park (p140) is almost as big as the state of Rhode Island. Some people duck in for an afternoon, hike a quick trail and leave, but we recommend staying at least two nights to hit the highlights.

Seventeen miles south of the Persimmon Gap Visitor Center, pull over for the **Fossil Discovery Exhibit**, which spotlights the dinosaurs and other creatures that inhabited this region beginning 130 million years ago.

The Drive » From the west park entrance, turn left after 3 miles then follow the signs for Terlingua Ghost Town, just past Terlingua proper. It's about a 45-minute drive from the middle of the park.

❼ Terlingua

Quirky Terlingua is a unique combination: it's both a ghost town and a social hub. When the local cinnabar mines closed down in the 1940s, the town dried up and blew away like a tumbleweed, leaving buildings that fell into ruins.

But the area has slowly repopulated, businesses have been built on top of the ruins, and locals gather here for two daily rituals. In the late afternoon, everyone drinks beer on the porch of **Terlingua Trading Company** (☑432-371-2234; http://terlinguatradingco.homestead.com; 100 Ivey St; ⊘10am-9pm). And after the sun goes down, the party moves next door to **Starlight Theatre** (☑432-371-3400; www.thestarlighttheatre.com; 631 Ivey Rd; mains

$10-27; ⊘5pm–midnight Sun-Fri, to 1am Sat), where there's live music every night.

Come early enough to check out the fascinating **stone ruins** (from the road – they're private property) and the old **cemetery**, which you're welcome to explore.

The Drive » Continue west on Rte 170, also known as the River Road, for a gorgeous drive along the Rio Grande inside Big Bend Ranch State Park. In 60 miles or so you'll reach Presidio. Head north on US-67 to return to Marfa, then cut west on US-90.

❽ Prada Marfa

So you're driving along a two-lane highway out in the middle of nowhere, when suddenly a small building appears in the distance like a mirage. You glance over and see...a Prada store? Known as the 'Prada Marfa' (although it's really closer to Valentine) this art installation set against the backdrop of dusty west Texas is a tongue-in-cheek commentary on consumerism. You can't go in, but you're encouraged to window shop or snap a photo. ∎

Starlight Theatre

Thor's Hammer

Bryce Canyon National Park

The high altitude of Bryce Canyon National Park, which hugs the eastern edge of an 18-mile plateau, sets it apart from southern Utah's other national parks. Famous for its otherworldly sunset-coloured spires punctuated by tracts of evergreen forest, this is one of the planet's most exquisite geological wonders.

Great For...

State
Utah

Entrance Fee
7-day pass per car/motorcycle/person on foot or bicycle $35/30/20

Area
56 sq miles

❶ Bryce Point

If you stop nowhere else along the scenic drive, be sure to catch the stunning views from Bryce Point. You can walk the rim above Bryce Amphitheater for awesome views of the Silent City, an assemblage of hoodoos so dense, gigantic and hypnotic that you'll surely begin to see shapes of figures frozen in the rock. Be sure to follow the path to the actual point, a fenced-in promontory that juts out over the forested canyon floor, 1000ft below. The extension allows a broad view of the hoodoos. This rivals any overlook in the park for splendor and eye-popping color. An interpretive panel tells the story of Ebenezer Bryce, the Mormon pioneer for whom the canyon was named, and his wife Mary.

❷ Natural Bridge

Natural Bridge is an extremely popular stop, and with good reason: a stunning span of eroded, red-hued limestone juts

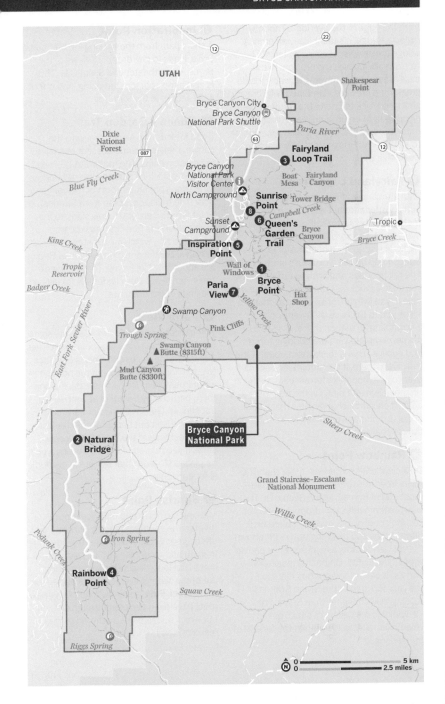

UTAH

Shakespear
Point

Bryce Canyon City
*Bryce Canyon
National Park Shuttle*

Dixie
National
Forest

Paria River

**Fairyland
Loop Trail** **3**

Fairyland
Canyon

Blue Fly Creek

Boat
Mesa

Bryce Canyon
National Park
Visitor Center
North Campground

**Sunrise
Point**

Tower Bridge

Tropic

Campbell Creek

8

6 **Queen's
Garden
Trail**

Bryce
Canyon

Bryce Creek

Sunset
Campground

King Creek

Inspiration **5**
Point

Tropic
Reservoir

Wall of
Windows

1

Badger Creek

Paria **7**
View

**Bryce
Point**

Hat
Shop

Swamp Canyon

Yellow Creek

Pink Cliffs

Trough Spring

Swamp Canyon
▲ Butte (8315ft)

▲

Mud Canyon
Butte (8330ft)

**Bryce Canyon
National Park**

Sheep Creek

2 **Natural
Bridge**

Grand Staircase-Escalante
National Monument

Willis Creek

Iron Spring

Squaw Creek

Rainbow **4**
Point

Riggs Spring

N 0 ———————————— 5 km
   0 ———————————— 2.5 miles

from the edge of the overlook. Though called a bridge, it's technically an arch. A bridge forms when running water, such as a stream, causes the erosion. In this case, freezing and thawing of water inside cracks and crevices, combined with gravity, shattered rock to create the window. Even if you're tight on time, squeeze this stop onto your agenda. There is also a viewpoint to see Natural Bridge from above at Scenic Drive Mile 12.5.

❸ Fairyland Loop Trail

With a trailhead at Fairyland Point north of the visitor center, this 8-mile round-trip makes for a beautiful half-day hike (four to five hours). The sorbet-colored, sand-castle-like spires and hoodoos of Bryce Canyon pop up like a Dr Seuss landscape. The tall hoodoos and bridges unfold best if you go in a clockwise direction. At around mile 4, you will run into a side trail that takes you to the base of Tower Bridge, a crumbling formation that looks like a castle, complete with drawbridge, turrets and goblins. This is the bottom point of the trail. From there, it's a rather long ascent over rolling moon-like terrain back to the rim near Sunset Point. On the trail there's a 700ft elevation change, plus many additional ups and downs, making this a good fitness challenge.

❹ Rainbow Point

On a clear day you can see more than 100 miles from this overlook at the southern-most end of Bryce Canyon Scenic Dr. The viewpoint provides jaw-dropping views of canyon country. Giant sloping plateaus, tilted mesas and towering buttes jut above the vast landscape, and interpretive panels explain the sights. On the northeastern horizon look for the Aquarius Plateau – the very top step of the Grand Staircase – rising 2000ft higher than Bryce. The viewpoint is reached on a short, paved, wheelchair-accessible path at the far end of the parking lot.

❺ Inspiration Point

A short path from the parking lot, off Scenic Drive, leads to jaw-dropping views of the Bryce Amphitheater and Silent City. This is also a top spot for stargazing, and offers easy access to the Rim Trail.

❻ Queen's Garden Trail

Good for kids, the easiest trail into the canyon makes a gentle descent over slop-ing erosional fins. The moderate 1.8-mile out-and-back hike passes elegant hoodoo formations but stops short of the canyon floor. The trail is accessed from Sunrise Point, from where you follow signs to the trailhead off the Rim Trail. As you drop below the rim, watch for the stark and primitive bristlecone pines, which at Bryce are about 1600 years old. These ancient trees' dense needles cluster like foxtails on the ends of the branches.

❼ Paria View

Three miles north of Swamp Canyon, signs point to the Paria View viewpoint, which lies 2 miles off the main road. This is *the* place to come for sunsets. Most of the hoodoo amphitheaters at Bryce face east, making them particularly beautiful at sunrise, but not sunset. The amphitheater here, small by comparison but beautiful nonetheless, faces west toward the Paria River water-shed. If you're tired of RVs and buses, you'll be pleased to learn that this small overlook is for cars only.

❽ Sunrise Point

Marking the north end of Bryce Amphi-theater, the southeast-facing Sunrise Point offers great views of hoodoos, the Aquarius Plateau and the Sinking Ship, a sloping mesa that looks like a ship's stern rising out of the water. Keep your eyes peeled for the **Limber Pine**, a spindly pine tree whose roots have been exposed through erosion, but which still remains anchored to the receding sand.

BLAZG/SHUTTERSTOCK ©

Natural Bridge

Drive Scenic Bryce Canyon

CARLOS BRUZOS/SHUTTERSTOCK ©

The scenic drive winds south for 17 miles and roughly parallels the canyon rim, climbing from 7894ft at the visitor center to 9115ft at Rainbow Point, the plateau's southern tip at road's end. Snowstorms may close the road in winter. Check at the visitor center for current road conditions.

Duration 2 hours

Distance 34 miles

Start & Finish Bryce Canyon National Park Visitor Center

Nearest Town/Junction Bryce

Head directly to **Rainbow Point** (a 35-minute drive; pictured), then stop at the scenic overlooks as you return to avoid left-hand turns into the turnouts. Visit Rainbow Point via a short, paved, wheelchair-accessible path at the far end of the parking lot.

At the other end of the parking lot another short, paved, wheelchair-accessible trail leads to **Yovimpa Point**, one of the park's windiest spots. The southwest-facing view reveals more forested slopes and less eroding rock.

Just north of Mile 16, at 8750ft, the small **Black Birch Canyon** overlook shows precipitous cliffs roadside.

Higher than the previous stop, **Ponderosa Canyon** offers long vistas like those at Rainbow Point. One of the best stops at this end of the park, the **Agua Canyon** viewpoint overlooks two large formations of precariously balanced, top-heavy hoodoos. Park at **Natural Bridge** to view a stunning span of eroded, red-hued limestone. The stop at **Farview Point** offers a grand view of giant plateaus,

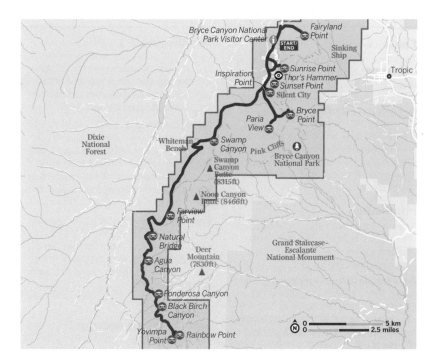

blue-hued mesas and buttes. The over-look at **Swamp Canyon** sits in a forested dip between two ridgelines. Three miles north, turn right and follow signs to **Paria View** (p154),

At **Bryce Point** (p152), you can wonder at the natural architecture of Bryce Amphitheater and take in the hoodoos the **Silent City**, standing like melting sandcastles in shades of coral, magenta, ocher and white against a deep-green pine forest background.

At **Inspiration Point** a short ascent up a paved path takes you to another overlook into Bryce Amphitheater. The Silent City is most compelling from here. The hoodoos feel closer, and you can make out more details on the canyon floor.

Views at **Sunset Point** are as good as they get, but don't expect solitude. This point is known for **Thor's Hammer**, a big square-capped rock balanced atop a spindly hoodoo. Don't be fooled by the name of this point. Because it faces east, sunrises are better here than sunsets.

At the north end of Bryce Amphitheater, **Sunrise Point** (p154) offers great views.

End your driving tour at the visitor center or head to **Fairyland Point**. To reach the point, drive a mile north of the entrance gate, then a mile east of the main road. Fairyland Point is a less-visited spot with wooded views north toward the Aquarius Plateau. Here you can see hoodoos at all stages of evolution, from fin to crumbling tower, and start the Fairyland Loop Trail.

Essential Information

Entrance

The nearest town is Bryce Canyon City, just 3 miles north of the park. Tropic is 11 miles northeast on Hwy 12.

Take advantage of the **Bryce Canyon National Park Shuttle** (☏435-834-5290; www.nps.gov/brca/planyourvisit/shuttle.htm; ☺hours vary) **FREE**, a free service between Ruby's Inn and Bryce Point, with buses every 15 minutes between 8am and 8pm in high season. Parking at the visitor center is limited to one hour.

Information

A booth at the park's sole entrance distributes a park brochure with a driving map and facilities information as well as the park newspaper, the *Hoodoo*.

Bryce Canyon National Park Visitor Center (☏435-834-5322; www.nps.gov/brca; Hwy 63; ☺8am-8pm May-Sep, 8am-6pm Oct & Apr, 8am-4:30pm Nov-Mar; ☎) Issues backcountry permits for overnight travel on a first-come, first-served basis.

Safety

Hydration stations throughout the park offer free water bottle refills (rangers recommend a gallon of water per person per day in summer).

If there is lightning, crouch low to the ground and avoid stand-alone trees. If there's flooding, head to higher ground.

Backcountry travelers can get free bear-proof cans at the visitor center. Never cook or store food in your tent, especially in the backcountry. Never leave designated trails.

Sleeping

The park has one lodge and two campgrounds. Most travelers stay just north of the park in Bryce Canyon City, near the Hwy 12/63 junction, or 11 miles east in Tropic.

There are limited vacation rentals near the park, but extend your search by about 20 miles and you'll find plenty of options.

North Campground (☏877-444-6777; www.recreation.gov; Bryce Canyon Rd; tent/RV sites $20/30) Near the visitor center, the 101 sites at this enormous trail-side campground all have campfire rings. A short walk takes you to showers, a coin laundry and a general store.

Sunset Campground (☏877-444-6777; www.recreation.gov; Bryce Canyon Rd; tent/RV site $20/30; ☺Apr-Sep) Just south of Sunset Point, this 102-site campground offers more shade than North Campground but has few amenities beyond flush toilets. Inquire about availability at the visitor center, and secure your site early.

Bryce Canyon Resort (☏800-834-0043; www.brycecanyonresort.com; cnr Hwys 12 & 63; r $189, cabins $250; ✳☎✉) Four miles from the park, this is a great option. While the grounds leave much to be desired, there's a modernist-kitsch appeal to the rooms.

Eating

Bryce Canyon Lodge Restaurant (☏435-834-5361; Bryce Canyon Rd; breakfast & lunch $10-20, dinner $10-35; ☺7am-10pm Apr-Oct) ✿ While service may lag, meals deliver, with the excellent regional cuisine ranging from fresh green salads to bison burgers, braised portobellos and steak. All food is made on-site and the certified green menu offers only sustainable seafood.

Ebenezer's Barn & Grill (☏800-468-8660; www.ebenezersbarnandgrill.com; 1000 S Hwy 63; dinner show $32-38; ☺7pm mid-May–Oct) A big BBQ dinner here comes with a kitschy but good-natured evening of country and western music (drinks not included). Options include salmon, steak, pulled pork or chicken served with beans and cornbread. Reservations are necessary.

Travelers with Disabilities

The national park's multi-use trail is a paved trail perfect for visitors with restricted mobility, though a few sections may be too steep for solo wheelchair users. The visitor center is wheelchair accessible.

Top left: Bryce Canyon Motel; Top right: Squirrel; Bottom: Sunset Campground

SILKY/SHUTTERSTOCK ©

Under the Rim Trail

This hike skirts beneath cliffs, through amphitheaters and amid pines and aspens. Rangers prefer visitors hike south to north, but you can do it either way. Permits ($5 per person) are obtained at the visitor center. This is a one-way hike, so consider leaving a car at one or both ends.

Duration 3 days

Distance 22.9 miles

Difficulty Moderate–hard

Start Rainbow Point

Finish Bryce Point

Nearest Towns Tropic, Panguitch

DAY 1: Bryce Point to Right Fork Swamp Canyon Campsite (4–6 hours, 10.5 miles)

From **Bryce Point** the trail descends steeply almost due east, then swings south. After 0.5 miles you'll wind down to a ridge and over the next 0.5 miles **Rainbow Point** comes into view. Two miles in you'll pass the **Hat Shop**, its gray boulder caps perched atop spindly conglomerate stands.

At the base of this descent, 2.8 miles from Bryce Point, is the **Right Fork Yellow Creek campsite**. Follow the left (east) bank of the creek for half a mile, then cross it and bear south. As the trail turns

west, you'll pass the **Yellow Creek group campsite**.

A quarter-mile further, you'll reach **Yellow Creek**. The trail climbs toward the Pink Cliffs and Paria View, 1000ft above, and soon crosses the creek; cairns point the way. Another 0.25 miles brings you to the **Yellow Creek campsite**. It's a great spot to watch the sunset.

From here you'll turn southwest up a short, steep hill. The trail undulates for about 2 miles, crossing a slope between two amphitheaters. After 1.5 miles the trail drops into Pasture Wash. Follow cairns to the south edge of the wash and look for a sharp uphill turn. The view will reward your effort.

Descend into the valley to the junction with the **Sheep Creek Connecting Trail**, which climbs 2 miles to the scenic drive. A well-marked spur leads 0.5 miles south to the **Sheep Creek campsite** (closed when we last visited due to bear activity); you can usually find water here.

From the junction, the trail climbs 150ft – crossing from the Sheep Creek amphitheater to the Swamp Canyon amphitheater – then descends into Swamp Canyon. On the left (southeast), in a clearing among large ponderosa pines, is the **Right Fork Swamp Canyon campsite**; water is sometimes available in upper Swamp Canyon, 100yd west of the campsite.

DAY 2: Right Fork Swamp Canyon Campsite to Natural Bridge Campsite (1½–2½ hours, 4.6 miles)

Three hundred feet past the campsite is the junction with the mile-long Swamp Canyon Connecting Trail. From the connecting trail junction, you'll climb steadily south, then turn west up switchbacks. Just beyond, at 8200ft, is the **Swamp Canyon campsite**. You'll sometimes find water 0.25 miles up the Whiteman Connecting Trail.

Beyond camp, the trail descends to the base of Farview Cliffs. From here you'll skirt **Willis Creek** for a mile until it turns southeast. Bear south and west.

The trail ducks into Dixie National Forest for 0.25 miles, then curves sharply east to climb an eroded sandstone slope southwest of Willis Creek. At the top, the sandy trail offers gorgeous views of the **Pink Cliffs**.

Descend to a southern tributary of Willis Creek and continue 0.5 miles to the **Natural Bridge campsite**, which lacks water.

DAY 3: Natural Bridge Campsite to Rainbow Point (3–5 hours, 7.8 miles)

Half a mile out of camp, the trail traverses a sage meadow toward Agua Canyon. Due to floods you now need to hike up the canyon 0.75 miles, then switchback up the canyon's south ridge. When in doubt, follow the cairns. Atop this ridge, the Agua Canyon Connecting Trail climbs 1.6 miles to the scenic drive. This is one of the hardest stretches of the trail, with fallen trees and washouts.

From the connecting trail junction, you'll descend into Ponderosa Canyon, then zigzag to South Fork Canyon. Past the head of the canyon, you'll reach the **Iron Spring campsite**. Amid a grove of aspens 600ft up canyon (southwest) from the campsite, **Iron Spring** supplies year-round water. The turnoff for the spring lies 100yd north of the campsite.

The trail dips to cross both arms of Black Birch Canyon. After clambering over the lower slopes of a northwest-jutting promontory, you'll enter the southernmost amphitheater of Bryce Canyon's Pink Cliffs.

The trail traces the hammer-shaped ridge below Rainbow Point. Ascend the final 1.5 miles up the back (south) side of the amphitheater to the rim. You'll cross the Riggs Spring Loop Trail, 100yd east of the **Rainbow Point** parking lot. ∎

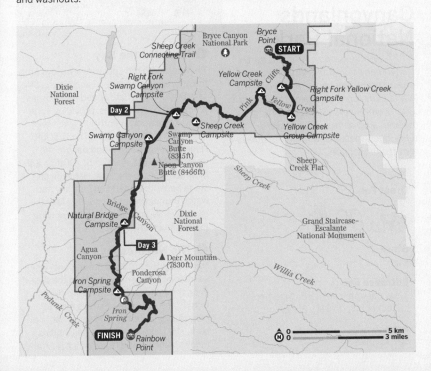

ED REINSEL/SHUTTERSTOCK ©

Mesa Arch

Canyonlands National Park

A 527-sq-mile vision of ancient earth, Canyonlands is Utah's largest national park. Serpentine canyons tipped with white cliffs loom high over the Colorado and Green Rivers. Skyward-jutting needles and spires, deep craters, blue-hued mesas and majestic buttes dot the landscape.

Great For...

State
Utah

Entrance Fee
7-day pass per car/motorcycle/person on foot or bicycle $30/25/15

Area
527 sq miles

❶ Island in the Sky

You'll comprehend space in new ways atop the appropriately named Island in the Sky. This 6000ft-high flat-topped mesa drops precipitously on all sides, providing some of the longest, most enthralling vistas of any park in southern Utah. The 11,500ft Henry Mountains bookend panoramic views in the west, and the 12,700ft La Sal Mountains are to the east. Here you can stand beneath a sparkling blue sky and watch thunderheads inundating far-off regions while you contemplate applying more sunscreen.

❷ The Needles

Named for the spires of orange-and-white sandstone jutting skyward from the desert floor, the Needles District is so different from Island in the Sky that it's hard to believe they're both in the same national park. The Needles receives only half as many visitors as the Island since it's more

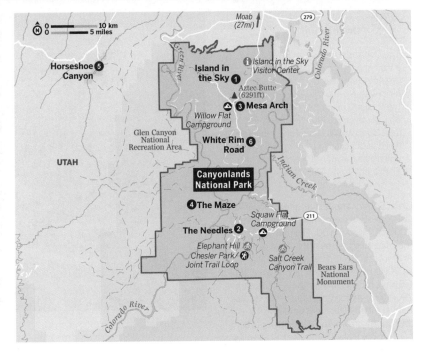

remote – though only 90 minutes from Moab – and there are fewer roadside attractions (but most are well worth the hike). The payoff is huge: peaceful solitude and the opportunity to participate in, not just observe, the vastness of canyon country. Morning light is best for viewing the rock spires.

Get among them on the **Chesler Park/ Joint Trail Loop**, an awesome 11-mile route across desert grasslands, past towering red-and-white-striped pinnacles and between deep, narrow slot canyons, some only 2ft across. Elevation changes are mild, but the distance makes it an advanced day hike.

❸ Mesa Arch

Canyonlands' most photographed arch is one of the best places to watch the sunrise – though don't expect to be alone. A moderately easy walk up a gentle rise brings you to the arch, an elegant sweep of Navajo sandstone that dramatically frames

the La Sal Mountains. A thousand feet below, the basin extends in layers of red, brown, green and tan.

❹ The Maze

A 30-sq-mile jumble of high-walled canyons, the Maze is a rare preserve of true wilderness for hardy backcountry veterans. The colorful canyons are rugged, deep and sometimes completely inaccessible. Many of them look alike and it's easy to get turned around – hence the district's name. (Think topographic maps and GPS.) Rocky roads absolutely necessitate reliable, high-clearance 4WD vehicles. Plan on spending at least three days. If you're at all inexperienced with four-wheel driving, stay away.

❺ Horseshoe Canyon

Far west of Island in the Sky, Horseshoe Canyon shelters one of the most impressive collections of millennia-old rock art in the Southwest. The centerpiece is the

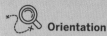 **Orientation**

The Colorado and Green Rivers form a Y dividing the park into separate districts, inaccessible to one another from within the park. Cradled atop the Y, Island in the Sky (30 miles, 45 minutes from Moab) is the most developed and visited district due to its ease of access. Its viewpoints look down into the incredible canyons of The Needles and The Maze.

Great Gallery and its haunting Barrier Canyon–style pictographs from between 2000 BC and AD 500. The heroic, bigger-than-life-size figures are magnificent. Artifacts recovered here date back as far as 9000 BC. The gallery lies at the end of a 6.5-mile round-trip hiking trail descending 750ft from a dirt road. Plan on six hours. Rangers lead hikes here on Saturday and Sunday from April through October; contact the Hans Flat Ranger Station for times.

❻ Mountain Biking on White Rim Road

Blazed by uranium prospectors in the 1950s, primitive **White Rim Road** encircling Island in the Sky is the top choice for mountain-biking trips. This 70-mile route is accessed near the visitor center via steeply descending Shafer Trail Rd. It generally takes three to four days by bike. Since the route lacks any water sources, cyclists should team up with a 4WD support vehicle or travel with a Moab outfitter.

Other trails include the moderate-level 27-mile **Salt Creek Canyon Trail** loop, a favorite for archaeology junkies for its rock art, and the 32-mile **Elephant Hill** round trip. This route is the most well-known and technically challenging in the state, with steep grades and tight turns – smell the burning brakes and clutches. (Don't try this as your first mountain-bike adventure.)

Top left: Island in the Sky; Top right: Narrow canyons, Needles District; Bottom: Mountain biking White Rim Rd

TOP LEFT: NATALI GLADO/SHUTTERSTOCK © TOP RIGHT: ROBIN RUNCK/SHUTTERSTOCK ©

KYLE T PERRY/SHUTTERSTOCK ©

Essential Information

Sleeping & Eating

Many visitors sleep in nearby Moab. Canyonlands' campgrounds in the Needles and Island in the Sky districts are extremely popular.

At Island in the Sky sites are first-come, first-served. Backcountry camping in the Island is mostly open-zone (not in prescribed areas), but is still permit-limited. Visitors can reserve some campsites and all group sites at the Needles. Backcountry camping, in prescribed areas only, is quite popular, so it's hard to secure an overnight permit without advance reservation.

There are no restaurants in the park. Bring your own provisions and plenty of water.

Squaw Flat Campground (☏435-719-2313; www.nps.gov/cany/planyourvisit/camping.htm; tent & RV sites $20; ☺year-round) This first-come, first-served, 26-site campground 3 miles west of the Needles Visitor Center fills up every day from spring to fall. It has flush toilets and running water, but no showers and no hookups. Opt for side A, where many sites (12 and 14, for example) are shaded by juniper trees and cliffs.

Willow Flat Campground (☏435-719-2313; tent & RV sites $15; ☺year-round) Seven miles from the Island in the Sky Visitor Center, the first-come, first-served, 12-site Willow Flat Campground has vault toilets but no water or hookups. Bring firewood and don't expect shade.

Information

Island in the Sky (☏435-259-4712; www.nps.gov/cany; Hwy 313; ☺8am-6pm Mar-Oct, 9am-4:30pm Nov-Feb) and the **Needles** (☏435-259-4711; Hwy 211; ☺8am-6pm Mar-Oct, 9am-4:30pm Nov-Feb) have visitor centers. The information center in **Moab** (☏435-259-8825; http://discovermoab.com/visitor-center/; 25 E Center St; ☺8am-7pm; ☏) also covers the park.

The easiest way to tour Canyonlands is by car. Traveling between districts takes two to six hours, so plan to visit no more than one per day. ∎

Top left: Island in the Sky; Top right: Shafer Canyon Overlook; Bottom: Needles District

LAURENS HODDENBAGH/SHUTTERSTOCK ©

Hickman Bridge Trail

Capitol Reef National Park

Native Americans once called this colorful landscape the Land of the Sleeping Rainbow. The park's center-piece is Waterpocket Fold, a 100-mile-long buckle in the earth's crust, and it's known for enormous domes – one of which echoes Washington, DC's Capitol Dome.

Capitol Reef harbors fantastic hiking trails, rugged 4WD roads and 1000-year-old Fremont petroglyph panels. At the park's heart grow the shady orchards of the Fruita Rural Historic District, a Mormon settlement dating back to the 1870s. Most services, including food, gas and medical aid, are in the town of Torrey, 11 miles west.

Scenic Drives

The rolling, mostly paved **Capitol Reef Scenic Drive** follows the Waterpocket Fold. It's a geology diorama come to life, with arches, hoodoos, canyon narrows and other unique features easily within view, plus day-hiking opportunities, too. The best of the route is its last 2 miles between the narrow sandstone walls of Capitol Gorge. It'll knock your socks off. Pay admission at the visitor center or self-service kiosk. The 9.3-mile road starts at the Scenic Dr fee station, just south of Fruita Campground.

Great For...

State
Utah

Entrance Fee
7-day pass per car/motorcycle/person on foot or bicycle $15/10/7

Area
378 sq miles

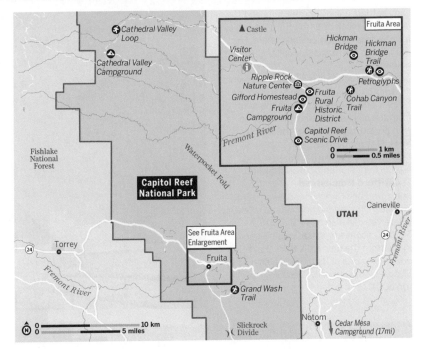

To continue south past Pleasant Creek, a 4WD vehicle is advised.

Long-distance mountain bikers and 4WDers love the 58-mile **Cathedral Valley Loop**, starting 18.6 miles east of the visitor center. The bumpy, roughshod backcountry road explores the remote northern area of the park and its alien desert landscapes, pierced by giant sandstone monoliths eroded into fantastic shapes. Before starting, check conditions at the visitor center and purchase an interpretive route guide.

Hiking

Along Scenic Dr, a good dirt road leads to the **Grand Wash Trail** (2.25 miles, easy), a flat hike between canyon walls that, at one point, tower 80 stories high but are only 15ft apart. You can follow an offshoot of level slickrock to the cool Cassidy Arch (2 miles) or continue further to link with other trails.

Often overlooked, the moderate 1.7-mile **Cohab Canyon Trail** deters crowds with a

steep climb at the beginning, but exploring a hidden canyon and the views from atop Capitol Reef are worth every sweaty step. Starting across the road from Fruita Campground, the trail makes a 0.25-mile ascent atop a rocky cliff. From there it levels out through a desert wash, beside small slot canyons.

The popular **Hickman Bridge Trail** (1 mile, moderate) includes a canyon stretch, a stunning natural bridge and wildflowers in spring. Mornings are coolest; it starts about 2 miles east of the visitor center off Hwy 24.

Fruita Rural Historic District

Fruita (*froo*-tuh) is a cool, green oasis, where shade-giving cottonwoods and fruit-bearing trees line the Fremont River's banks. The first Mormon homesteaders arrived here in 1880; Fruita's final resident left in 1969. Among the historic buildings, the NPS maintains 2700 cherry, apricot, peach, pear and apple trees planted by early settlers. Visit between June and October to pluck ripe fruit from the trees, for free, from any unlocked orchard. For availability, ask rangers or call the fruit hotline.

Near the orchards is a wonderful picnic area, with roaming deer and birds in the trees – a desert rarity. Across the road from the blacksmith shop (just a shed with period equipment) is the **Ripple Rock Nature Center** (☎435-425-2233; 281 Scenic Dr; ⊙1-5pm late May–mid-Aug) **FREE**, a family-oriented learning center. The **Gifford Homestead** (☎435-425-3791; Scenic Dr, Capitol Reef National Park; ⊙8am-5pm Mar-Oct) is an old homestead museum where you can also buy ice cream, Scottish scones or salsas and preserves made from the orchard's fruit. Don't skip purchasing one of its famous pies – up to 13 dozen are sold daily (and they usually run out!).

BARBARA ASH/SHUTTERSTOCK ©

Top left: Gifford Homestead; Top right: Rock climbing;
Bottom: Petroglyphs

TOP LEFT: OLOS/SHUTTERSTOCK © TOP RIGHT: LEE COHEN/GETTY IMAGES ©

Petroglyphs

East of the visitor center on Hwy 24, look for the roadside petroglyphs; these are the carvings that convinced archaeologists that the Fremont Indians were a distinct group. Follow the roadside boardwalk to see several panels.

Rock Climbing

Technical rock climbing is allowed without permits. Note that Wingate Sandstone can flake unpredictably. Follow clean-climbing guidelines, and take all safety precautions. For details, check with rangers or see www. nps.gov/care.

Drive Highway 24

EDMUND LOWE PHOTOGRAPHY/SHUTTERSTOCK ©

This easy, winding route gives you a taste of everything that Capitol Reef offers: striking geology, dramatic desert overlooks, ancient Native American petroglyphs, early Western settlers' sites and hiking trails for stretching your legs.

Duration 1–4 hours

Distance 22 miles

Start Torrey

Finish Orientation pullout

From Torrey, head east into Capitol Reef on Hwy 24. There is no entrance station; driving this route is free. Be sure to stop at turnouts along the way to read interesting geologic interpretive panels. Then pull over at **Chimney Rock** (pictured), the towering reddish-brown rock formation 7 miles east of Torrey. If you're in great shape, consider hiking the strenuous 3.6-mile loop for wide-open clifftop views of Capitol Reef.

A half-mile east of Chimney Rock, turn right toward Panorama Point and drive 0.8 miles along a graded dirt road to the **Gooseneck Overlook**. An easy 0.1-mile walk from the parking area over rock slabs

takes you to this viewpoint above Sulphur Creek, which twists through the canyon in elegant S-curves. Though the observation platform is fenced in, much of the area around it is open – watch your little ones! From the parking area it's an easy 0.4-mile stroll to **Sunset Point**, where the ambient light on the cliffs and domes is best for photographers in the late afternoon.

Another 2.4 miles further east on Hwy 24, you'll arrive at the well-signed turnoff to Capitol Reef's visitor center (p176), just north of the Fruita Rural Historic District and the paved **Scenic Drive**. Rising

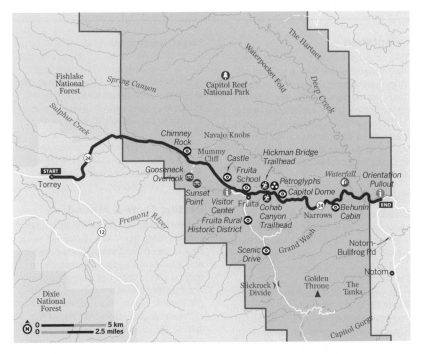

majestically just north of this junction is the snaggle-toothed **Castle**; an interpretive panel details its geologic history.

East of the visitor center, Hwy 24 skirts the Fremont River, the surrounding rock growing paler and more yellow as you approach the park's Navajo sandstone domes. Peer through the windows of the historic **Fruita school**, 0.8 miles east of the visitor center, before stopping at the **ancient petroglyphs** 0.2 miles further east. Created by the Fremont Culture, these carvings helped convince archaeologists that the Fremont culture was distinct from that of Ancestral Puebloans. The boardwalk is wheelchair-accessible. Bring binoculars or a camera with a zoom lens.

Stop at the turnout 0.8 miles east of the petroglyphs for views of **Capitol Dome**, a giant sandstone dome that vaguely resembles the US Capitol, as it appeared in 1850. This parking area beside the Fremont River is where you'll find the trailheads for **Hickman Bridge** and the more strenuous Rim Overlook and Navajo Knobs route. On the south side of Hwy 24 is an alternate trailhead for **Cohab Canyon**, while 2.7 miles further east is the end of the Grand Wash.

About 4 miles east of Hickman Bridge, on your right, stop to peer through the window of the one-room 1882 **Behunin Cabin**, once home to a Mormon settler's family of 13. On the north side of the highway, 0.7 miles east of the cabin, you'll pass a waterfall. Swimming is not allowed here; numerous accidents and even drownings have occurred. At the park's eastern orientation pullout, just over 9 miles from the visitor center, are restrooms and an information kiosk. It's on the north side of the intersection with Notom-Bullfrog Rd.

Essential Information

Orientation

The narrow park runs north–south following the Waterpocket Fold. A little over 100 miles southwest of Green River, Hwy 24 traverses the park. Capitol Reef's central region is the Fruita Rural Historic District. To the far north lies Cathedral Valley, the least-visited section; toward the south you can cross over into Grand Staircase–Escalante National Monument on the Burr Trail Rd.

Safe Travel

Occasional summer thunderstorms pose a serious risk of flash flooding. Always check weather with rangers at the **Visitor Center** (📞435-425-3791; www.nps.gov/care; cnr Hwy 24 & Scenic Dr; ⊗8am-6pm Jun-Aug, 8am-4:30pm Sep-May).

Remember that Capitol Reef has little shade. Drink at least one quart of water for every two hours of hiking and wear a hat. Summer temperatures can exceed 100°F (38°C) at the visitor center (5400ft), but it's cooler than Moab. If it's too hot, ascend to Torrey (10°F/6°C cooler) or Boulder Mountain (30°F/17°C cooler). Bugs bite in May and June.

Sleeping & Eating

The nearest motel lodgings are in Torrey.

The park has one large campground and several small ones. Free primitive camping is possible year-round at **Cathedral Valley Campground** (📞435-425-3791; www.nps.gov/care/planyourvisit/primitivecampsites.htm; cnr Hartnet & Cathedral Rds; ⊗year-round) FREE, at the end of River Ford Rd, and at **Cedar**

Mesa Campground (📞435-425-3791; www.nps.gov/care/planyourvisit/primitivecampsites.htm; Notom-Bullfrog Rd;⊗year-round) FREE, where five first-come, first-served free sites lack water, but have pit toilets, fire grates and picnic tables, as well as great views east along the fold. It's 30 miles south of Hwy 24.

Visitors can get a slice of pie or ice cream at the general store in the park; otherwise head east toward Torrey for multiple dining options.

Getting There & Around

Capitol Reef has no public transportation system. Aside from Hwy 24 and Scenic Dr, park routes are dirt roads that are bladed only a few times a year. In summer you may be able to drive Notom-Bullfrog Rd and the Burr Trail in a regular passenger car. Remote regions like Cathedral Valley will likely require a high-clearance 4WD vehicle. Bicycles are allowed on all park roads but not trails. Check weather and road conditions with rangers before heading out.

Inquire about ranger-led programs, watch the short film, then ooh and aah over the 64-sq-ft park relief map at the visitor center. The bookstore sells several interpretive trail and driving tour maps as well as area-interest books and guides. ■

Top left: Capitol Reef NP entrance; Top right: Capitol Dome; Bottom: Grand Staircase–Escalante National Monument

DOUG MEEK/SHUTTERSTOCK ©

Carlsbad Caverns National Park

Elaborately carved by the slow hand of time, the magnificent underground rooms and passageways of Carlsbad Caverns feel like they belong in another realm. The portals to this magical place? An elevator that drops the length of the Empire State Building or, more enjoyably, a spooky 1.25-mile subterranean walk.

Great For...

State
New Mexico

Entrance Fee
3-day pass adult/child $12/free

Area
73 sq miles

While a cave might not sound quite as sexy as redwoods, geysers or the Grand Canyon, there's no question that this one measures up on the national parks' jaw-droppingly ginormous scale. The Big Room is an underground room 1800ft long (that's the equivalent of 11 American football fields), 255ft high and over 800ft below the surface, where you're free to walk an intricate loop trail (1.25 miles) past a pick of amazing sights, including the world's largest stalagmite and the ever-popular Bottomless Pit. Wear a sweatshirt: the temperature is 56°F year-round.

Cave Tours

Self-guided and guided ($7 to $20, reserve ahead) tours are available. For a look at the wilder side of Carlsbad, sign up for the moderately challenging 5½-hour **Slaughter Canyon** guided tour. Among the highlights: the 89ft-high Monarch, one of the world's tallest limestone columns. Adventurers will

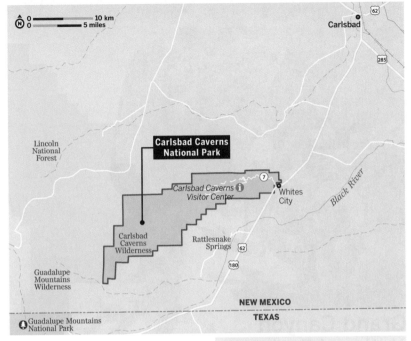

enjoy the three-hour **Lower Cave** ranger-led tour, which takes in an amazing array of formations, including the stalactite-filled 'Texas toothpick.' Descent is by 60ft of ladders and a knotted rope at the cave's entrance. The 1-mile ranger-led tour of **Kings Palace**, which lasts 90 minutes, takes you through three underground chambers, including the Big Room and some of the deepest caverns open to the public.

Bat Watching

From May through October, hundreds of thousands of Brazilian free-tailed bats roost in the caves. Their nightly exodus happens just after dusk when the bats take to the Chihuahuan Desert in search of food. You can watch them set off from the amphitheater near the cave entrance. Around sunset from late May through October you can attend the **Bat Flight Program**, a short and free ranger talk describing these fascinating mammals.

Essential Information

The park is in the southeastern corner of New Mexico. The closest major airport is El Paso (145 miles southwest). From Roswell, NM, about 100 miles north, follow US 285 south to US 62/180 west. From El Paso, the **visitor center** (☉8am-7pm late May-early Sep, to 5pm rest of year) is 155 miles to the northeast via US 62/180 east.

Stargazing

The night sky is exceptionally dark in this remote corner of New Mexico – seeing the Milky Way and hundreds of stars and constellations is not to be missed. The park schedules ranger-led Night Sky programs on select dates each month from June through October. The walks are free but limited to 25 people. Registration is required. Check the park calendar for other stargazing events. ■

STUDIO BARCELONA/SHUTTERSTOCK ©

Grand Canyon National Park

There is nothing like arriving at the edge of the Grand Canyon and taking it all in – the immensity, the depth, the light. The canyon embodies the scale and splendor of the American West, captured in dramatic vistas, dusty trails and stories of exploration, preservation and exploitation.

Great For...

State
Arizona

Entrance Fee
7-day pass per car/motorcycle/person on foot or bicycle $35/30/20

Area
1904 sq miles

❶ Hiking Rim to Rim

There's no better way to fully appreciate the grand of Grand Canyon than hiking through it, rim to rim. The classic corridor route descends the North Rim on the North Kaibab Trail, includes a night at Phantom Ranch or Bright Angel Campground at the bottom of the canyon, crosses the Colorado River and ascends to the South Rim on Bright Angel Trail. A popular alternative rim-to-rim route is to descend from the South Rim on the South Kaibab Trail and ascend via the North Kaibab Trail.

❷ Rafting the Colorado River

Considered the trip of a lifetime by many river enthusiasts, rafting the Colorado is a wild ride down a storied river, through burly rapids, past a stratified record of geologic time and up secretive side canyons. Though riding the river is the initial attraction, the profound appeals of the trip reveal themselves each day and night in

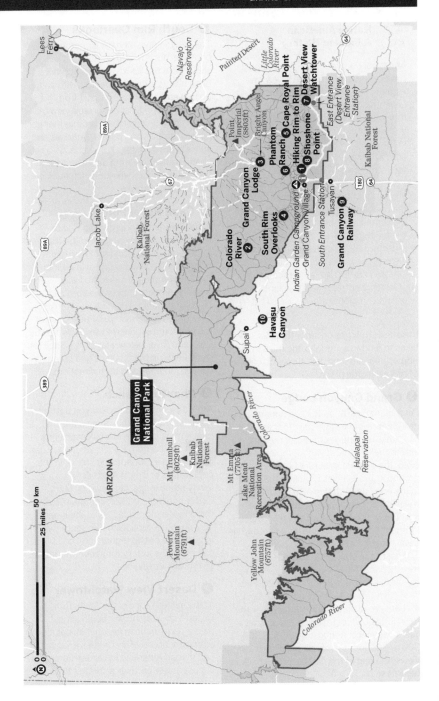

Native American & Pioneer History

Ancestral Puebloans lived in and near the Grand Canyon for centuries, and its pioneer history is full of wild and eccentric characters who wrangled this intimidating expanse for profit and adventure. Their stories echo in the weathered trails they built to access terraced fields; the iconic mule-train traditions that lured 18th-century tourists; and the stone and timber buildings constructed by the railroads in their effort to codify the romance of the American Southwest. Ranger talks and South Rim museums explore the park's native history, showcase indigenous dwellings and crafts, and tell inspiring tales of intrepid entrepreneurs, scientists, artists and pioneer tourists.

the quiet stretches on smooth water, side hikes to hidden waterfalls, the musicality of ripples and birdsong, and the vast solitude of this awesome place.

❸ Grand Canyon Lodge

Perched at 8000ft on the canyon rim, this granddaddy of national park lodges promises a high-country retreat like nothing else in the Grand Canyon. Completed in 1928, the original structure burned to the ground in 1932. It was rebuilt in 1937, and in the early days staff greeted guests with a welcome song and sang farewell as they left. Today, you'll find that same sense of intimate camaraderie, and it's easy to while away the days at a North Rim pace.

Guests can stay in the **cabins** (📋advance reservations 877-386-4383, same-day reservations 928-638-2611; www.grandcanyonforever. com; r/cabins from $141/155; 🕙May 15–Oct 15) 🖉 that spread across the plateau near the main lodge building. Book them at least a year in advance. Request cabin 301, 305, 306 or 309 for mesmerizing Western Rim views; the rest of the cabins are set back in the forest.

❹ South Rim Overlooks

The canyon doesn't have a photographic bad side, but it has to be said that the views from the South Rim are stunners. Each has its individual beauty, with some unique angle that sets it apart from the rest – a dizzyingly sheer drop, a view of river rapids or a felicitous arrangement of jagged temples and buttes. Sunrises and sunsets are particularly sublime, with the changing light creating depth and painting the features in unbelievably rich hues of vermilion and purple.

❺ Cape Royal Point

A pleasant drive through woods with teasing canyon views leads to the trailhead for this most spectacular of North Rim overlooks. It's an easy 0.5-mile walk to Cape Royal along a paved trail with signs pointing out facts about the flora and fauna of the area. The walk is suitable for folks of all ages and capabilities. Once at the point, the expansive view includes the Colorado River below, Flagstaff's San Francisco Peaks in the distance and stunning canyon landmarks in both directions.

❻ Phantom Ranch

After descending to the canyon bottom, it's a delight to ramble along a flat trail, past a mule corral and a few scattered cabins to Phantom Ranch, where you can relax with a lemonade and splash in the cool waters of Bright Angel Creek. This lovely stone lodge, designed by Mary Colter and built in 1922, continues to be the only developed facility in the inner canyon. Mule trips from the South Rim include one or two nights here, and hikers can enter the lottery for accommodations 15 months in advance.

❼ Desert View Watchtower

At the eastern edge of the South Rim, Desert View Watchtower could almost pass as an American Indian ruin, but it's an amalgamation of Mary Colter's imagination and myriad American Indian elements. This circular tower encases a spiral stairway that winds five stories to the top floor, with walls featuring a Hopi mural and graphic symbols from various American Indian tribes. From its many windows on all sides, you can see mile upon magnificent mile of canyon ridges, desert expanse, river and sky.

8 Shoshone Point

For a leisurely walk away from the South Rim circus, hiking through the ponderosa to Shoshone Point does the trick. The soundtrack to this mostly flat 1-mile walk is that of pine needles crunching underfoot and birdsong trilling overhead, and lacy shadows provide cover from the sun. Upon reaching the rim, you'll trace the edge for a short while to the stone point jutting out over the canyon depths. Shoshone Point, or the picnic area at the end of the trail, is perfect for a peaceful lunch.

9 Grand Canyon Railway

Things start out with a bang at the Wild West shootout in Williams, and then the 'sheriff' boards the train to make sure

everything's in its place. Is it hokey? Maybe a little. Fun? Absolutely. Riding the historic Grand Canyon Railway to the South Rim takes a bit longer than if you were to drive, but you avoid traffic and disembark relaxed and ready to explore the canyon. The train drops you off a few minutes from the historic El Tovar and canyon rim.

10 Havasu Canyon

The people of the blue-green waters, as the Havasupai call themselves, take their name from the otherworldly turquoise-colored waterfalls and creek that run through the canyon. Due to limestone deposits on the creekbed, the water appears sky-blue, a gorgeous contrast to the deep red of the canyon walls. The only ways into and out of Havasu Canyon are by foot, horse or helicopter, but those who make the 10-mile trek are richly rewarded by the magic of this place, epitomized by spectacular **Havasu Falls**.

Grand Canyon Railway

Geological Wonders

One look at the russet hues of the canyon walls and the park's spires and buttes, and you can't help but wonder about the hows and whys of the canyon's formation. Luckily for laypeople with rock-related questions, the South Rim has answers, primarily at **Yavapai Point and Geology Museum** (☎928-638-7890; www.nps.gov/grca/planyour visit/yavapai-geo.htm; Rim Trail, Grand Canyon Village Historic District; ⊗8am-7pm Mar-May & Sep-Nov, to 6pm Dec-Feb, to 8pm Jun-Aug; 🚌Kaibab/Rim) **FREE** and the **Trail of Time installation** (Rim Trail, Grand Canyon Village Historic District; 🚌Village), and both rims offer geology talks and walks given by the park's knowledgeable rangers. For a more DIY experience, hike into the canyon with a careful eye for fossilized marine creatures, animal tracks and ferns.

RONNYBAS FRIMAGE/SHUTTERSTOCK ©

Top left: Phantom Ranch; Top right: Grand Canyon rafting; Bottom: Havasu Falls

TOP LEFT: FREDLYFISH4/SHUTTERSTOCK TOP RIGHT: PACIFIC NORTHWEST PHOTO/SHUTTERSTOCK ©

Hike Widforss Trail

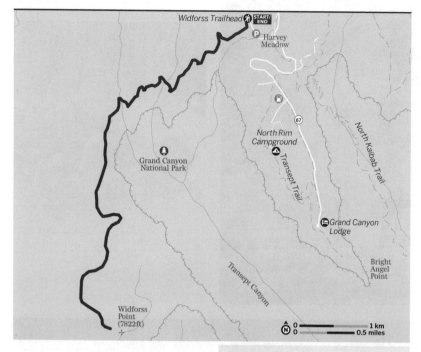

Meandering through shady forests of mixed conifer, old-growth ponderosa pine and quaking aspen punctuated by carpets of lupine, the Widforss Trail rolls past the head of The Transept and out to Widforss Point. Although it's a relatively popular day hike, people disperse quickly, and you likely won't see more than a few other explorers.

To reach the trailhead, turn onto the dirt road just south of the Cape Royal Rd turnoff, continuing a mile to the Widforss Trail parking area. After a 15-minute climb, the **Transept** comes into view. For the next 2 miles, enjoy wide views of the canyon to one side and meadows and woods to the other.

Halfway into the hike, the trail veers away from the rim and dips into gullies of lupines and ferns. The canyon doesn't come into view again until the end. Stops

Duration 6 hours

Distance 10 miles

Difficulty Moderate

Start & Finish Widforss trailhead

along the self-guided trail (brochures are often available at the trailhead, but get one at the visitor center just in case) end at mile 2.5, and many turn around here for a shorter option. Though any given hill is slight, the rolling terrain adds up, and you'll climb and descend about 1100ft over the course of the full 10-mile round-trip. Bring plenty of water.

The trail is named for Gunnar Widforss, an early-20th-century artist who painted many of America's national parks. He spent his final years living at the Grand Canyon and is buried on the South Rim.

Hike Hermit Trail

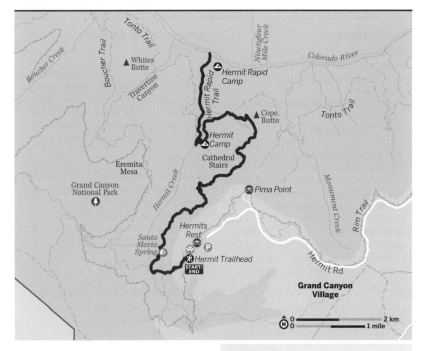

Tracing the path of the Hermit, this steep but rewarding out-and-back hike leads to a backcountry campground on the site of one of the park's earliest tourist accommodations.

Duration 2 days

Distance 18.4 miles

Difficulty Hard

Start & Finish Hermit trailhead

From the trailhead, a steep, rocky path descends 2 miles to **Santa Maria Spring**. The trail levels for a mile or so before zigzagging over loose rocks. The trail hasn't seen a maintenance crew in over 80 years; at the Supai section, hikers will need to scramble over rocks.

After descending the Redwall via extremely steep, compressed switchbacks, the **Cathedral Stairs**, the Hermit eventually hits the cross-canyon Tonto Trail (6.4 miles from the trailhead, at 3210ft).

Turn left (west) to merge with the Tonto; in 1 mile you'll reach the stone remnants of the old Hermit Camp (2800ft). Beyond the ruins, the cliff-rimmed backcountry campground (with pit toilets and seasonal water)

makes a glorious place to sleep. It's another 1.5 miles to the Colorado River; follow your nose down the creek.

At the river, the canyon walls are exquisite black Vishnu schist shot through with veins of pink Zoroaster granite. **Hermit Rapid**, a major Colorado River rapid, marks the confluence of Hermit Creek and the Colorado. There's a backcountry campground, but no facilities.

On day two, to return to Hermits Rest, retrace your steps for the arduous climb back to the trailhead. For a longer wilderness excursion, with advanced backcountry permits, you can pick up the eastbound Tonto and intercept the Bright Angel.

Essential Information

Park Entrances

South Rim

The most accessible area of the park is the South Rim, an easy 60-mile drive north of I-40 at Williams.

From the **South Entrance Station**, the main park entrance, it is a few miles north to Grand Canyon Visitor Center, from where free park shuttles service sights and lodges within Grand Canyon Village year-round and overlooks on Hermit Rd seasonally. Free park shuttles run from Tusayan, just outside the park, to the visitor center every 20 minutes March 1 to September 30.

The Desert View Entrance Station or **East Entrance** has a gas station, general store, seasonal campground and historic overlook. From here, it is a 25-mile drive west to Grand Canyon Village; no public transportation.

North Rim

Getting to the North Rim is more of a challenge. A shuttle (mid-May to mid-November) runs from rim to rim, but otherwise the only way to reach the North Rim is by car, foot or bicycle. It's about 12 miles to North Rim services from the **North Rim Entrance Gate**.

Sleeping

South Rim

Lodges and campgrounds mostly cluster in the tourist hub of Grand Canyon Village, with the best are along the rim in the Historic District. The common areas at the **El Tovar** (☑advanced reservations 888-297-2757, reservations within 48hr 928-638-3283; www. grandcanyonlodges.com; r/ste from $228/461) ooze old-world national park glamor.

Below the rim, there is one lodge, three designated campgrounds, and multiple backcountry primitive campsites.

Phantom Ranch (contact as per El Tovar; dm $49, cabin d $142, available by lottery; ✸) Bunks at this camp-like complex on the canyon floor are in cabins sleeping two to 10 people. Meals must be reserved when booking. Phantom is accessible by mule trip, on foot or via raft on the Colorado River.

Indian Garden Campground (☑Backcountry Information Center 928-638-7875; www.nps.gov/ grca; backcountry permit $10, plus per person per night $8; ☺year-round) ✿ Located 3040ft below the South Rim, and a 4.6-mile hike along the Bright Angel Trail, lovely Indian Garden sits along a creek, with a ranger station, toilets and year-round drinking water (though pipeline breaks regularly result in closed water supplies).

North Rim

Accommodations are limited to one lodge and one campground. If these two options are fully booked, try snagging a cabin or campsite at the Kaibab National Forest. Otherwise, you'll find more options another 60 miles north in Kanab, UT.

Eating & Drinking

South Rim

Grand Canyon Village has all the eating options you'll need. Bright Angel Lodge's **Arizona Room** (☑928-638-2631; www.grand canyonlodges.com; lunch $13-16, dinner $22-28; ☺11:30am-3pm & 4:30-10pm Feb-Oct, dinner only Nov-Jan; ☐Village) and **Harvey House Cafe** (mains $13-21; ☺6am-4:30pm & 5-10pm; ☐Village westbound) are among the few table-service restaurants on the South Rim, though several bars serve small plates and snacks.

North Rim

Food options are limited to the Grand Canyon Lodge dining room, takeout from Deli in the Pines, or the paltry offerings at the general store. Bring your own groceries and plan on picnics or cookouts.

Visitor Centers

Grand Canyon Visitor Center (South Rim; ☑park headquarters 928-638-7888; www.nps. gov/grca; Grand Canyon Village; ☺9am-5pm; ☐Village, ☐Kaibab/Rim, ☐Tusayan Mar 1-Sep 30) The South Rim's main visitor center; on the plaza here, bulletin boards and kiosks display information about ranger programs, the weather, tours and hikes. ■

El Tovar Hotel

PHILLIP B. ESPINASSE/SHUTTERSTOCK ©

Bristlecone pine

Great Basin National Park

With rugged mountain slopes and ancient trees, Great Basin is a gorgeous place to ponder your insignificance. Its bristlecone pines began growing when Egypt's Great Pyramid was still under construction. You'll also find stone arches, thousand-year-old wall paintings and an underground cavern.

Great For...

State
Nevada

Entrance Fee
Free

Area
121 sq miles

Perched 1 mile above sea level in the craggy Snake Range, the park marks the eastern endpoint of the Loneliest Road, which stretches across the white-hot center of Nevada along US 50.

Lehman Caves

This colossal marble cavern features a staggering collection of formations, including stalactites, stalagmites, helictites, flowstone, popcorn and more than 300 rare shields. Local rancher Absalom Lehman is credited with discovering the caves in 1865. The only way to view them today is by guided tour. Take your pick of two tours: the 60-minute **Lodge Tour** (adult/child $9/5) or the slightly more demanding 90-minute **Grand Palace Tour** (adult/child $11/6), which takes in the famous Parachute Shield. Advance reservations recommended. Note that the temperature inside the caves is a constant 50°F (10°C): bring a sweater.

PAMELA MARCELIN/SHUTTERSTOCK ©

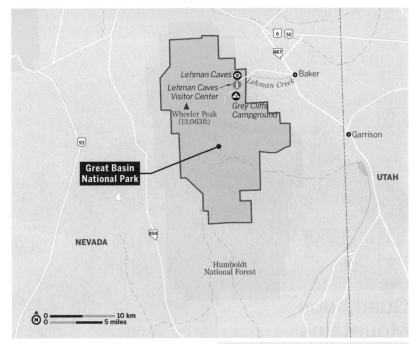

Wheeler Peak Scenic Drive

Rising abruptly from the desert floor to a height of 13,063ft, Wheeler Peak is the tallest mountain in the Snake Range. Its slopes can be explored along the paved 12-mile Wheeler Peak Scenic Drive. Starting at the Lehman Caves Visitor Center, the sinuous road climbs past pinyon pines, a mountain mahogany wilderness and a mixed-conifer forest. At Mile 11 it passes white-barked aspens in a subalpine forest. It's said to be the same ecological diversity as driving from Baker, NV, to Canada's frozen Yukon thousands of miles north.

Stargazing

Cloudless nights in Great Basin offer an extravaganza of stars, and these exceptional stargazing conditions earned the park an International Dark Sky Park designation in 2016. Five planets can be seen with the naked eye, plus the Andromeda Galaxy, the Milky Way and meteor showers. In early September the park hosts its

Essential Information

The park is in eastern Nevada, near the Utah border. The closest major airport is Salt Lake International Airport (235 miles northeast). There is no public transportation to the park.

With the exception of campsites at Grey Cliffs Campground, campgrounds are all first-come, first served. Lower Lehman Creek Campground is the only one open year-round.

Lehman Caves Visitor Center (775-234-7331; www.nps.gov/grba; 5500 NV-488, Baker; 8am-4:30pm, tours 8:30am-4pm) Caves tour bookings and national park information; 5 miles outside the town of Baker, which is 63 miles east of Ely.

annual three-day **Astronomy Festival**, with volunteer astronomers, evening programs, loads of telescopes for star viewing and a night-sky photography workshop. ∎

CHRISTOPHER DINH/SHUTTERSTOCK ©

Guadalupe Mountains National Park

This is a Texas high spot, both literally and figuratively. At 8749ft, Guadalupe Peak is the highest point in the Lone Star State. More than half the park is a federally designated wilderness area and the fall foliage in McKittrick Canyon is the best in west Texas.

Great For...

State
Texas

Entrance Fee
7-day pass per adult/child $5/free

Area
135 sq miles

We won't go so far as to call it Texas' best-kept secret, but even many Texans aren't aware of the Guadalupe Mountains National Park. It's just this side of the Texas–New Mexico state line and a long drive from practically everywhere in the state.

The NPS has deliberately curbed development to keep the park wild. There are no restaurants or indoor accommodations and only a smattering of services and programs (so plan ahead to keep your gas tank full and your cooler stocked).

McKittrick Canyon Trail

Deservedly one of the park's most popular walks, this 3.4-mile one-way hike on a mostly level day-use trail ends at a scenic grotto. You'll pass the historic **Pratt Cabin** along the way. The cabin was built in 1932 by petroleum geologist Wallace Pratt, who later donated the land to the NPS; it

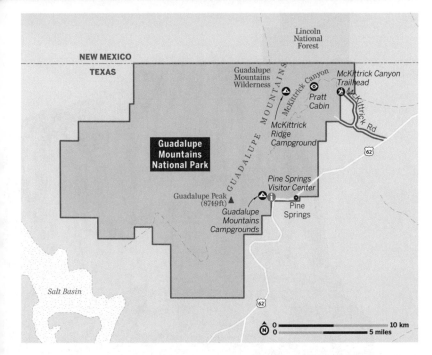

remains furnished as the Pratt family left it. Surrounded by colorful leaves, it's at its most scenic in the fall.

The hike is 15.2 miles round-trip if you climb to the McKittrick Ridge Campground, with a gain of about 2700ft. The entrance road to the trailhead is 7 miles east of the Pine Springs Visitor Center on Hwy 62/180.

Fossil Reef

A geologist's dream, the park sits amid the world's most extensive exposed fossil reef. In fact, the mountains contain the world's best example of a 260- to 270-million-year-old exposed rock layer, the Guadalupian Global Stratotype.

The reef began to grow 250 million years ago, when an immense tropical ocean covered parts of Texas, New Mexico and Mexico. Over a period of five million years, lime-secreting marine organisms built the horseshoe-shaped reef to a length of 400 miles. After the sea evaporated, the reef was buried in sediment for millions more years, until a mountain-building geological uplift revealed part of it as the Guadalupe Mountains.

Fall Colors

McKittrick Canyon's fall colors are glorious from early October through mid-November, and while nights can be chilly, daytime is warmly sublime. But be aware that autumn weekends are by far the busiest time and there may be a wait of several hours to enter the canyon.

Left: El Capitan peak; Right: Sage thrasher

MICHAEL J THOMPSON/SHUTTERSTOCK ©

SHUPHOTOGRAPHY/SHUTTERSTOCK ©

Park History

Until the mid-19th century, the Guadalupe Mountains were used exclusively by Mescalero Apaches, who hunted and camped in the area. Members of this tribe, who called themselves Nde, became the hunted starting in 1849, when the US Army began a ruthless 30-year campaign to drive them from the area. The mid-19th century also marked the brief tenure of the Butterfield Overland Mail Route, a revolution in American communications and transportation whereby a letter could move 2700 miles from St Louis to San Francisco via El Paso, Tucson and Los Angeles in a then-breathtaking 25 days. Guadalupe Mountains National Park was established in 1972.

Essential Information

Time

Unlike most of the rest of Texas, the park is in Mountain Time Zone, as are El Paso and Carlsbad Caverns National Park.

Sleeping & Eating

If you want to stay in the area, there aren't a lot of options. Camp in the park, bring your own food, and...that's it.

If camping doesn't appeal and you want to spend more than a day exploring the park, you can drive 45 minutes to Whites City, NM, a resort town with over 100 motel rooms and two RV parks.

There are even fewer eating options than sleeping options here – in other words, zero. Plan on bringing food, either to tide you over till you can get to Whites City (which has a couple of mediocre restaurants), or to sustain you throughout your stay without having to cross state lines.

Note that no wood or charcoal fires are allowed within the park; propane stoves or grills are permitted, however.

Guadalupe Mountains Campgrounds (☑915-828-3251; www.nps.gov/gumo; tent & RV sites $8) The park's campgrounds are first-come, first-served – unless you have a group of 10 or more, in which case you can reserve a group camping spot up to 60 days in advance (for $3 per person). Campsites fill up during spring break, and several nights a week in the summer, although visitors arriving by early afternoon will usually find a site. The most convenient campgrounds are at Pine Springs, right along Hwy 62/180 near the visitor center; if it looks full, look for the 'campground host' sign for directions to overflow spots. If all the sites are full, RVs are permitted to park overnight at the nearby state highway picnic areas.

Visitor Center

Information, restrooms and drinking water are available at the **Pine Springs Visitor Center** (☑915-828-3251; www.nps.

gov/gumo; ⊙8am-4:30pm). You'll also find water, restrooms and outdoor exhibits in McKittrick Canyon; the Dog Canyon Ranger Station has information, restrooms and water. Visit the park website to download a map of the park before you visit.

Getting There & Away

Guadalupe Mountains National Park is on Hwy 62/180, 110 miles east of El Paso and 55 miles southwest of Carlsbad, NM. The closest gas stations are 35 miles in either direction on Hwy 62/180 and the closest services are in Whites City, NM, 45 minutes northeast of the park entrance on Hwy 62/180. ∎

WITOLD SKRYPCZAK/ALAMY STOCK ©

HIDEAKI OKADA/SHUTTERSTOCK ©

G B HART/SHUTTERSTOCK ©

Top left: Pratt Cabin; Top right: Yucca; Bottom: McKittrick Canyon

SOPOTNICKY/SHUTTERSTOCK ©

Mesa Verde National Park

More than 700 years after its inhabitants disappeared, Mesa Verde retains an air of mystery. It's a wonderland for adventurers of all sizes, who can clamber up ladders to carved-out dwellings, see rock art and delve into the secrets of ancient America.

Great For...

State
Colorado

Entrance Fee
7-day pass per car $15–20, per motorcycle $10–15, per person on foot or bicycle $7–10

Area
81 sq miles

---

❶ Cliff Palace

This grand engineering achievement provided shelter for 250 to 300 people. Springs across the canyon, below Sun Temple, were most likely their primary water sources. The use of small 'chinking' stones between the large blocks is strikingly similar to Ancestral Puebloan construction at distant Chaco Canyon.

The only way to see it is to take the hourlong ranger-led tour ($5), retracing the steps taken by the Ancestral Puebloans – visitors must climb down a stone stairway and five 10ft ladders.

❷ Balcony House

On the east side of the Cliff Palace Loop is an adventure that will challenge anyone's fear of heights or small places. You'll be rewarded with outstanding views of Soda Canyon, 600ft below the sandstone overhang that once served as the ceiling for

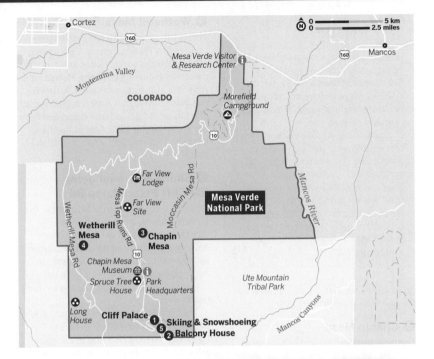

Balcony House

Trail Safety

Given the historical nature of the park, backcountry access is specifically forbidden and fines are imposed on anyone caught wandering off designated trails or entering cliff dwellings without a ranger.

When hiking in Mesa Verde always carry water and avoid cliff edges. Trails can be muddy and slippery after summer rains and winter snows, so wear appropriate footwear. Most park trails, except the Soda Canyon Trail, are strenuous and involve steep elevation changes. Hikers must register at the respective trailheads before venturing out.

35 to 40 rooms. Tickets are required for the one-hour guided tours ($5).

❸ Chapin Mesa

The largest concentration of Ancestral Puebloan sites is at Chapin Mesa, where you'll see the densely clustered **Far View Site** and the large **Spruce Tree House** – check ahead, as the latter may be closed due to safety concerns about rockfalls. It's worth touring the **Chapin Mesa Museum** (☑970-529-4475; www.nps.gov/meve; Chapin Mesa Rd; admission incl with park entry; ⊙8am-6:30pm Apr–mid-Oct, to 5pm mid-Oct–Apr); staff here provide information on weekends when the park headquarters is closed.

❹ Wetherill Mesa

This is the second-largest concentration of Ancestral Puebloan sites. Visitors may enter stabilized surface sites and two cliff dwellings, including the **Long House**, open from late May through August. A strenuous place to visit, it is only reached as part of a ranger-led guided tour organized from the visitor center ($5). Access involves climbing three ladders – two at 15ft and one at 4ft.

❺ Skiing & Snowshoeing the Cliff Palace Loop Rd

Winter is a special time in Mesa Verde. The crowds disperse and the cliff dwellings sparkle in the snow. Certain park roads have been designated for cross-country skiing and snowshoeing when weather permits. Before setting out, check the current snow conditions by calling the park headquarters.

The Cliff Palace Loop Rd is a relatively flat 6-mile loop located off the Mesa Top Loop Rd. The road is closed to vehicles after the first snowfall, so you won't have to worry about vehicular traffic. Park at the closed gate and glide 1 mile to the Cliff Palace overlook, continuing on past numerous other scenic stopping points.

In addition to the Cliff Palace Loop Rd, the Morefield Campground Loop Rds offer multiple miles of relatively flat terrain. The campground itself is closed in winter, but skiers and snowshoers can park at the gate and explore to their heart's content.

ROB CRANDALL/SHUTTERSTOCK ©

Long House

Essential Information

Sleeping

There are plenty of accommodations options in nearby Cortez and Mancos, and Mesa Verde can be easily visited as a day trip from Durango.

Morefield Campground (☎970-529-4465; www.visitmesaverde.com; Mile 4; tent/RV sites $30/40; ☺May-early Oct) ✐ The park's camping option, located 4 miles from the entrance gate, has hundreds of regular tent sites on grassy grounds conveniently located near Morefield Village. The village has a general store, a gas station, a restaurant, showers and a laundry. It's managed by Aramark. Dry RV campsites (without hookup) cost the same as tent sites.

Far View Lodge (☎970-529-4421, toll-free 800-449-2288; www.visitmesaverde.com; Mile 15; r $124-177; ☺mid-Apr–Oct; ❋ 🛜) Perched on a mesa top 15 miles inside the park entrance, this tasteful Pueblo-style lodge has 150 Southwestern-style rooms, some with kiva fireplaces. Don't miss sunset over the mesa from your private balcony. Standard rooms don't have air-con (or TV) and summer daytimes can be hot. You can even bring your dog for an extra $10 per night.

Eating

There's fine dining, a small market and a cafe in the park, but campers will be happiest if they come stocked with provisions.

Metate Room (☎800-449-2288; www.visit mesaverde.com; Mile 15, Far View Lodge; mains $20-36; ☺7-10am & 5:30-9:30pm Apr–mid-Oct, 5-7:30pm mid-Oct–Mar) ✐ With an award in culinary excellence, this upscale restaurant in the Far View Lodge offers an innovative menu inspired by Native American food and flavors.

Visitor Centers

The huge **Mesa Verde Visitor & Research Center** (☎970-529-4465; www.nps.gov/meve; ☺7:30am-7pm Jun-early Sep, 8am-5pm early Sep–mid-Oct & mid-Apr–May, closed mid-Oct–mid-Apr; 🛜) has water, wi-fi and bathrooms, in addition to information desks selling tickets for tours of Cliff Palace, Balcony House or Long House. It also displays museum-quality artifacts.

Getting There & Around

The Mesa Verde National Park entrance is off US 160, midway between Cortez and Mancos. Most people visit with a private car or motorcycle but there are some operators running tours to and around the national park from Durango, 36 miles to the east.

Vehicular transport is necessary to get to the sites from the front park gate as well as to travel between them. ∎

Top left: petroglyph, Mesa Verde National Park; Top right: Anasazi pottery; Bottom: Kiva (ceremonial room)

Painted Desert

EKATERINA POKROVSKY/SHUTTERSTOCK ©

Petrified Forest National Park

This national park is an extraordinary sight: the Painted Desert here is strewn with fossilized logs predating the dinosaurs. Up to 6ft in diameter, they're strikingly beautiful, with extravagantly patterned cross-sections of wood glinting in ethereal pinks, blues and greens.

Great For...

State
Arizona

Entrance Fee
7-day pass per car/person on foot, motorcycle or bicycle $20/10

Area
170 sq miles

Ancient Trees

The 225-million-year-old 'trees' of Petrified Forest National Park are fossilized logs scattered over a vast area of semidesert grassland. Trees arrived in this area via major floods, only to be buried beneath silica-rich volcanic ash before they could decompose. Groundwater dissolved the silica, carried it through the logs and crystallized into solid, sparkly quartz mashed up with iron, carbon, manganese and other minerals. Uplift and erosion eventually exposed the logs.

Souvenir hunters filched thousands of tons of petrified wood before Teddy Roosevelt made the forest a national monument in 1906 (it became a national park in 1962). Scavenge today and you'll be looking at fines and even jail time.

Scenic Drive

Straddling the I-40, the park has an entrance at exit 311 off I-40 in the north,

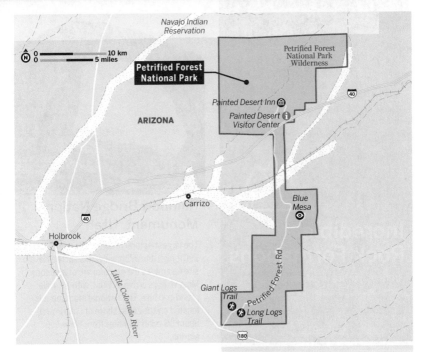

and another off Hwy 180 in the south. A 28-mile, paved scenic road links the two. To avoid backtracking, westbound travelers should start in the north, eastbound ones in the south.

The drive has about 15 pullouts, some with short trails. Two trails near the southern entrance allow close-ups of the petrified logs: the 0.6-mile **Long Logs Trail**, which has the largest concentration, and the 0.4-mile **Giant Logs Trail**, which sports the park's largest log. A highlight in the center section is the 3-mile loop drive (Blue Mesa Scenic Rd) out to **Blue Mesa**, where you'll be treated to 360-degree views of spectacular badlands, log falls and logs balancing atop hills with the leathery texture of elephant skin.

Painted Desert Inn

Redesigned in the 1940s by Mary Colter, the architect behind similar Hopi-style buildings in Grand Canyon Village, this

Essential Information

The 28-mile road through the park runs between I-40 in the north and Hwy 180 in the south.

Camping requires a free permit. The closest lodging is in Holbrook. Food service is very limited.

Painted Desert Visitor Center (☏928-524-6228; www.nps.gov; 1 Park Rd, Petrified Forest National Park; ☉8am-5pm) Good for information and access/camping permits, with a video describing how the logs were fossilized.

1930s adobe lodge is now a **museum** (☏928-524-6228; www.nps.gov; 1 Park Rd; ☉9am-4pm) FREE, decorated with murals by Hopi artist Fred Kabotie. After narrowly avoiding demolition, it was made a National Historic Landmark in 1987. ∎

Incredible Rock Formations

Grottoes, arches, a palette of red, rust and orange... The spellbinding rock formations at the heart of desert national parks transform adventure travelers into budding geologists.

Rainbow Bridge National Monument, Utah

The largest natural bridge in the world, at 290ft high and 275ft wide, this sacred Navajo site resembles the graceful arc of a rainbow. Most visitors arrive by boat, with a 2-mile round-trip hike. The national monument is located on the south shore of Lake Powell, about 50 miles by water from Wahweap Marina.

CLOCKWISE FROM TOP LEFT OSCITY/SHUTTERSTOCK ©, SUMIKOPHOTO/SHUTTERSTOCK ©, A/CAT/ SHUTTERSTOCK ©, JENIFOTO/SHUTTERSTOCK ©, DANNY XU/SHUTTERSTOCK ©

Glen Canyon National Recreation Area, Arizona–Utah

In the 1960s, the construction of a massive dam flooded Glen Canyon, forming Lake Powell, a recreational playground. Fifty years later this is still an environmental hot-button topic, but generations of Western families have grown up boating here. Water laps against stunning, multihued cliffs that rise hundreds of feet; narrow channels and tributary canyons twist off in every direction.

Natural Bridges National Monument, Utah

Forty miles west of Blanding via Hwy 95, this monument became Utah's first NPS land in 1908. The highlight is a dark-stained, white-sandstone canyon containing three easily accessible natural bridges. The oldest, the Owachomo Bridge, spans 180ft but is only 9ft thick. The flat 9-mile Scenic Drive loop is ideal for biking.

Hoodoos, Bryce Canyon

Hoodoos are freestanding pinnacles that have developed from side-eroding fins; layers disintegrate at different rates, creating an irregular profile. The bizarre formations are shaped as runoff over the canyon rim carves parallel gullies with narrow rock walls, the fins. Siltstone layers alternating with resilient limestone bands give them strength as they erode into towering hoodoos.

Chiricahua National Monument, Arizona

Rain, thunder and wind have chiseled volcanic rocks into fluted pinnacles, natural bridges, gravity-defying balancing boulders and soaring spires reaching skyward like totem poles carved in stone. The remoteness made Chiricahua a favorite hiding place of Apache warrior Cochise and his men. Today it attracts birds and wildlife, including bobcats, bears, deer, coatis and javelinas.

DMITRY VINOGRADOV/500PX ©

Saguaro National Park

Saguaros are an iconic symbol of the American Southwest, and an entire army of these majestic cactus plants is protected in this two-part desert playground. Established in 1933, Saguaro National Monument was the first federal monument created to protect a specific plant.

Great For...

State
Arizona

Entrance Fee
7-day pass per vehicle/motorcycle/person on foot or bicycle $15/10/5

Area
143 sq miles

The park is divided into two distinct sections. Petroglyphs, nature trails and saguaro groves grab the spotlight in the **Tucson Mountain District** on the western edge of Tucson. Thirty miles east, the **Rincon Mountain District** unfurls across six eco-zones, stretching from low-lying desert to the summits of isolated mountain ranges known as 'sky islands.'

Hiking
More than 165 miles of hiking trails crisscross the park. In the eastern district, the 1-mile round-trip **Freeman Homestead Trail** leads to a grove of massive saguaros. The 5.6-mile round-trip **Douglas Spring Trail** ascends from saguaros to desert grasslands and a seasonal waterfall in the Rincon Mountain foothills. For a full-fledged desert adventure, tackle the steep and rocky **Tanque Verde Ridge Trail**, which climbs to the summit of Tanque Verde peak (7049ft) and returns, for an 18-mile adventure.

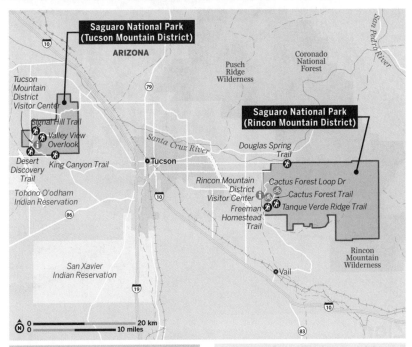

ARIZONA

Tucson
Mountain
District
Visitor Center

Signal Hill Trail

Valley View
Overlook

Desert
Discovery   King Canyon Trail
Trail

Tohono O'odham
Indian Reservation

San Xavier
Indian Reservation

Pusch
Ridge
Wilderness

Coronado
National
Forest

Santa Cruz River

Tucson

Saguaro National Park
(Rincon Mountain District)

Douglas Spring
Trail

Rincon Mountain
District
Visitor Center

Cactus Forest Loop Dr
Cactus Forest Trail

Freeman
Homestead
Trail

Tanque Verde Ridge Trail

Rincon
Mountain
Wilderness

Vail

San Pedro River

0   20 km
0   10 miles

Cactus Facts

Saguaros (sah-wah-ros) grow slowly,
taking almost a century before they
begin to assume their typical many-
armed appearance. The best time
to visit is April, when the cacti begin
blossoming with lovely white blooms.

Don't refer to the limbs of the
saguaro as branches. As park docents
will quickly tell you, the mighty saguaro
grows arms, not lowly branches.

Two easy but rewarding hikes in the western district are the 0.8-mile sunset-worthy
Valley View Overlook and the almost half-
mile **Signal Hill Trail**, which leads to scores
of ancient petroglyphs. For a more strenuous
trek, try the 7-mile **King Canyon Trail**, beginning 2 miles south of the visitor center.

The 0.5-mile informative **Desert Discovery Trail** is wheelchair accessible.

Essential Information

Tucson, a short drive from the park,
sits at the junction of the I-10, I-19 and
Hwy 86.

Rincon Mountain District Visitor Center
(520-733-5153; www.nps.gov/sagu; 3693
S Old Spanish Trail; 9am-5pm) Stop by
this eastern visitor center for permits for
backcountry camping ($8 per site per day).
Camping is allowed at six hike-in campsites.

Cycling

The 8-mile **Cactus Forest Loop Drive**
in the eastern district is an invigorating
introduction to the park. Scenic overlooks
line the ride, which begins just beyond the
Rincon Mountain District Visitor Center.
For off-road cycling, jump onto the **Cactus
Forest Trail**, which divides Cactus Forest
Loop Dr and rolls past historic lime kilns.
There is no drinking water on either loop, so
bring plenty with you. ■

SWMC/SHUTTERSTOCK ©

The Narrows

Zion National Park

The soaring red-and-white cliffs of Zion Canyon, one of southern Utah's most dramatic natural wonders, rise high over the Virgin River. Lush vegetation and low elevation give these magnificent rock formations a different feel from the barren parks in the east. Get ready for an overdose of awesome.

Great For...

State
Utah

Entrance Fee
7-day pass per vehicle/motorcycle/
person on foot or bicycle $35/30/20

Area
229 sq miles

❶ The Narrows

Zion's most famous backcountry route is the unforgettable Narrows, a strenuous 16-mile journey through the towering canyon along the Virgin River's north fork (p220). Plan on getting wet: most of the hike is in the river.

Overnight camping is by far and away the best experience, though you can hike from the top in one very strenuous, long day (90 minutes driving from Springdale to Chamberlain's Ranch, up to 12 hours hiking). Remember that the most difficult sections are at the end of the hike, when you'll be the most tired; we don't recommend this unless you have exceptional stamina and have done the hike before. You can also day hike the Narrows from the bottom, the most popular approach and the only one that doesn't require a permit.

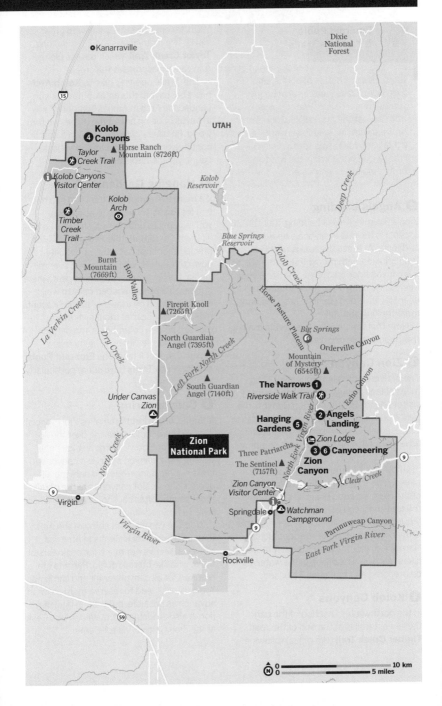

Emerald Pools & Kayenta Trails

This extremely popular sequence of trails links to a series of ponds, photogenic cascades and a surprisingly verdant desert oasis. Water seeps from sandstone and colorful pools are rimmed with life; wildflowers spring up in May and fall leaves turn in October. From Zion Lodge, cross the road and bridge to get to the trailhead.

❷ Angels Landing

Zion's 5.4-mile Angels Landing Trail (1488ft ascent) is the one everyone's heard of – and fears. At times the trail is no more than 5ft wide, with precipitous drop-offs to the canyon floor on both sides. Steel your nerves and hang on to those chains for dear life, and soon you'll be atop the park's most thrilling summit.

Note that the park is considering making this popular hike permit-only.

❸ Zion Canyon

The park encompasses roughly 229 sq miles of land, though the vast majority of visitors head straight for Zion Canyon, the park's crème de la crème: sheer sandstone cliffs, secret hanging gardens, leg-busting adventure-filled hikes and heart-stopping scenery.

Of the easy-to-moderate trails, the paved, mile-long **Riverside Walk** at the end of the road is a good place to start. When the trail ends, you can continue along in the Virgin River for 5 miles to Big Springs; this is the bottom portion of the spectacular Narrows, one of the park's most famous hikes. Yes, you'll be hiking in the water, so be prepared and rent gear if advised.

❹ Kolob Canyons

In the northwestern section of the park, the easiest trail is at the end of the road: **Timber Creek Trail** (0.5 miles) follows a 100ft ascent to a small peak with great views. The main hike is the 2.7-mile-long **Taylor Creek Trail**, which passes pioneer ruins and crisscrosses the creek.

The 7-mile one-way hike to **Kolob Arch** has a big payoff: this arch competes with Landscape Arch in Arches National Park in terms of being one of the biggest in the world. Fit hikers can manage it in a day, or continue on to make it a multiday backcountry trans-park connector.

❺ Hanging Gardens

If a mere five minutes in the Utah sun has you feeling as shriveled up as a raisin, you're going to find these lush desert oases all the more remarkable. Fed by mesa-top precipitation that has slowly percolated down through Navajo sandstone over millennia, these vertical gardens appear where dripping seeps exit shaded canyon walls, forced outward by a layer of harder Kayenta rock. Look for scarlet monkey flowers, mosses, golden columbines, maidenhair ferns and purple violets clinging marvelously to the rock face. The **Emerald Pools and Kayenta Trails** have some particularly lovely examples.

❻ Canyoneering

If there's one sport that makes Zion special, it's canyoneering. Rappelling over the lip of a sandstone bowl, swimming icy pools, tracing a slot canyon's curves…canyoneering is daring, dangerous and sublime all at once. Zion's slot canyons are the park's most sought-after backcountry experience; reserve far in advance.

Zion Canyon also has some of the most famous big-wall rock climbs in America. However, there's not much for beginners or those who like bolted routes. Permits are required for all canyoneering and climbing. You'll usually need to reserve them as far in advance as possible, but walk-in information is also available at the Wilderness Desk at the Zion Canyon Visitor Center.

JONATHAN ASH/SHUTTERSTOCK ©

Left: Angels Landing Trail; Right: Bighorn sheep

ALASKAPHOTO/SHUTTERSTOCK ©

FRANK BACH/GETTY IMAGES ©

⚠ Tortoise Crossing

A desert tortoise can live for up to 80 years, munching on wildflowers and grasses. With its canteen-like bladder, it can go up to a year without drinking. Using its strong hind legs, it burrows to escape the summer heat and freezing winter temperatures, and also to lay eggs.

Disease, predation and shrinking habitat have decimated the desert tortoise population. They like to rest in the shade, including under parked cars, so take a quick look around before driving away. They are often hit by high-speed and/or off-road drivers. If you see a tortoise in trouble, call a ranger. Do not pick it up, as a frightened tortoise may often pee on what it perceives to be an attacker, possibly leading to it dying of dehydration before the next rains come.

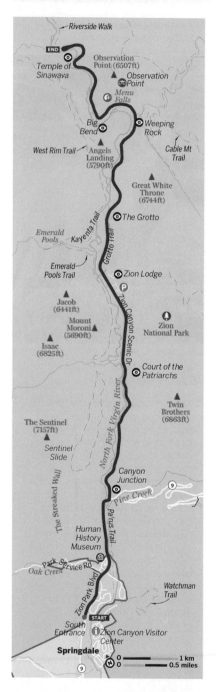

Drive Scenic Zion Canyon

The premier drive in the park leads between the towering red-rock cliffs of Zion's incredible main canyon and accesses all the major front-country trailheads. Note that most of the road is actually closed to private cars from March through October; you'll be traveling aboard the excellent park shuttle instead.

Duration 45 minutes

Distance 6.2 miles

Start South entrance

Finish Temple of Sinawava

Leaving from the visitor center, the first stop is the **Human History Museum** (◷9am-7pm late May-early Sep, shorter hours rest of year) FREE. Just past the museum on Hwy 9 are a few turnouts that overlook the Streaked Wall. In spring, with binoculars, scan the rim for nesting peregrine falcons. Officially, the scenic drive begins where you turn north, and cars are restricted, at **Canyon Junction**.

Continuing up the canyon, you'll pass the **Sentinel Slide** on the left. About 7000 years ago, a big chunk of the cliff face sloughed off and blocked the water flow, turning the canyon into a big lake. The water eventually carved its way through the blockage and carried on.

Next, the **Court of the Patriarchs** stop fronts the shortest trail in the park, a 50yd, staircase of a walk uphill to a view of the namesake peaks. Named by a Methodist minister in 1916, from left to right are Abraham, Isaac and Jacob, while crouching in front of Jacob is Mt Moroni (named for a Mormon angel).

Ahead on your right, **Zion Lodge** houses the park's only cafe and restaurant. The lodge was first built in the 1920s, but burned down in 1966.

The **Grotto**, barely a half-mile north, is a large, cottonwood-shaded picnic area with plenty of tables, restrooms and drinking water. Across the road from the picnic area, the West Rim Trail leads north toward Angels Landing. Those who'd rather admire Angels Landing than climb it should stroll the first flat quarter-mile of the West Rim Trail to a stone bench for the perfect vantage.

Make sure you spend some time at **Weeping Rock**. Pause to admire Angels Landing, the Organ, Cable Mountain, the Great White Throne and looming Observation Point. A short detour up the bucolic Weeping Rock Trail to a sheltered alcove and hanging garden is worthwhile.

There are no trailheads at **Big Bend**, but rock climbers get out here on their way to some of Zion's famous walls. It's a good place to bring binoculars and scan the skies for California condors.

If you're using the shuttle, the only way to the next two sights is to walk. As you continue north, on a ledge up to the right look for a reconstructed granary. Although ancient Native American in origin, it was rebuilt in the 1930s by the Boy Scouts. After about a half-mile, you get to **Menu Falls**, so-named because it was pictured on Zion Lodge's first menu cover. From there, it's easier to backtrack to Big Bend shuttle than to hoof it all the way up to the last stop. The canyon narrows near the cliff face that forms a natural amphi-theater known as the **Temple of Sina-wava**, at the road's end. Across the road the rock called the Pulpit does indeed look a bit like a giant lectern. From here you can take the popular Riverside Walk to the ultimate Zion experience, the Narrows.

Temple of Sinawava

ERIC URQUHART/SHUTTERSTOCK ©

Essential Information

Entrances

Arriving via the south entrance, expect traffic jams of 30 minutes or more just to pass the kiosk – arrive well before 8am (or after 4pm) to avoid the worst of it.

Arriving from the east on Hwy 9, you have to pass through the Zion–Mt Carmel Tunnel.

If your RV or trailer is 7ft 10in wide or 11ft 4in high or larger, it must be escorted through ($15).

Visitor Centers

Kolob Canyons Visitor Center (☎435-586-0895; www.nps.gov/zion; Kolob Canyons Rd; ⊗8am-6pm late May-Sep, shorter hours rest of year) Small visitor center in Kolob Canyons.

Zion Canyon Visitor Center (☎435-772-3256; www.nps.gov/zion; Hwy 9, Zion National Park; ⊗8am-7pm Jun-Aug, shorter hours rest of year) Main visitor center by the south entrance. Contains the **Wilderness Desk** (☎435-772-0170), which issues all permits.

Safety

If you plan on entering a slot canyon or the Narrows, make sure you check the daily flash-flood forecast at the visitor center or www.weather.gov. Late summer is the primary season for floods, but they can happen at any time of the year. If necessary call **National Park Rangers Emergency** (☎435-772-3322).

Sleeping

Both of the park's large, established campgrounds are near the Zion Canyon Visitor Center at the south entrance. Both sites are tops for location, but must be reserved.

Watchman Campground (☎877-444-6777; www.recreation.gov; Hwy 9; tent sites $20, RV sites with hookups $30) Towering cottonwoods provide fairly good shade for the 184 well-spaced sites at Watchman, located south of the visitor center. Sites are by reservation (six months in advance; 14-day maximum stay) and you should book as far in advance as possible. Flush toilets; no showers.

Zion Lodge (☎888-297-2757, 435-772-7700; www.zionlodge.com; Zion Canyon Scenic Dr; cabins/r $260/225; ❄@ ⒮) We love the stunning surrounding red-rock cliffs and the location in the middle of Zion Canyon. But be warned: today's reconstructed lodge is not as grand as other national park lodges (the 1920s original burned down in 1966). Reserve months ahead.

Under Canvas Zion (☎435-359-2911; www.undercanvas.com; 3955 Kolob Terrace Rd; tents $239-549) If you love the idea of camping but are less enthused about actually sleeping on the ground, Under Canvas could be for you. Ringed by red mesas and distant sandstone peaks, these secluded luxury tents off Kolob Terrace Rd sleep up to four and come equipped with woodburning stoves and private bathrooms – some have stargazing windows, too!

Eating

Most visitors pack their own lunch. Zion Lodge has the only in-park dining; otherwise head to Springdale, just outside the park.

Red Rock Grill (☎435-772-7760; Zion Canyon Scenic Dr, Zion Lodge; breakfast & sandwiches $6-17, dinner $16.50-30; ⊗6:30-10am & 11:30am-9pm Mar-Oct, hours vary Nov-Feb) Settle into your replica log chair or relax on the big deck with magnificent canyon views. The dinner menu touts its sustainable-cuisine stance, the results are hit-or-miss. Dinner reservations recommended.

Getting Around

The **Zion Park Shuttle** makes nine stops along the canyon, from the main visitor center to the Temple of Sinawava (a 45-minute round-trip). The **Springdale Shuttle** also makes nine stops along Hwy 9 between the park's south entrance and the Majestic View Lodge in Springdale.

The propane-burning shuttle buses are wheelchair-accessible, can accommodate large backpacks and carry up to two bicycles or one baby stroller. Generally high-season shuttles (mid-May to September) operate from 6am to 9:15pm, every five to 15 minutes.

Great White Throne

BRECK P. KENT/SHUTTERSTOCK ©

CLASSIC HIKES

The Narrows: Top Down

If there's one route that's made Zion famous, it's the wade down the Virgin River through a 1000ft sheer gorge known as the Narrows. Soaring walls, scalloped alcoves and wading through chest deep pools with your backpack lifted over your head make it truly memorable.

Duration 2 days

Distance 16 miles

Difficulty Hard

Start Chamberlain's Ranch (East Zion)

Finish Temple of Sinawava

DAY 1: Chamberlain's Ranch to Kolob Creek (6 hours, 9 miles)

The trail begins at Chamberlain's Ranch, on the east side of the park, 90 minutes' drive from the south entrance. This is a one-way hike, so make reservations for a hiker shuttle, unless you have two cars and drivers. Shuttles usually leave Springdale at 6:15am; a second may leave around 9am if there are enough people. Past the ranch gate, a dirt road leads to the river, where you'll find an NPS trailhead marker.

The first day is the quietest, the flowing water and undulating walls casting a mesmerizing spell. The first 3 miles are out of the river and the least interesting – power through so you can spend more time with the fun stuff, exploring side canyons and taking photographs. Once you see

Bulloch's Cabin, an old homestead about an hour from the trailhead, you'll know that soon enough the trail becomes the river. The **First Narrows**, about 3½ hours into the hike and near the park boundary, is an early highlight and provides a taste of what's to come.

From here the hike is quite photogenic, with the canyon walls gradually coming closer together. A little over four hours from the trailhead, you'll reach a log-jam **waterfall** that appears impassable. Upon closer inspection you'll soon pick out the trail that skirts around to the left. Depending on what time you started, this could be a good lunch spot.

Deep Creek is the first major confluence, doubling the river's volume. In the subsequent 2-mile stretch, expect secretive side canyons and faster water, sometimes waist deep and involving swims. Almost six hours from the trailhead is **Kolob Creek** (generally dry), an interesting side canyon to explore. This area is the location of the 12 overnight campsites, each on a sandy outcrop far from the others.

DAY 2: Kolob Creek to Temple of Sinawava (4.5 hours, 7 miles)

On day 2 you'll pass **Big Springs**, a good place to fill water bottles. After this are the 5 miles open to day hikers and plenty of deep pools and fast-moving water. In 2 miles you'll reach well-known **Wall Street**, certainly one of the most memorable parts of all of Zion. Save some energy for **Orderville Canyon**, a narrow side canyon that is lots of fun to explore. Orderville is about three hours downstream from Big Springs; you can follow it upstream for a half-mile. From here your company will steadily increase until you're just one of the crowd on the **Riverside Walk**.

Practicalities & Permits

The Narrows permits are some of the most sought-after in the park and are attached to campsites, except for through hikers. Only 40 permits per day are issued: six campsites are available online; the other six are reserved for walk-ins at the Wilderness Desk (p218).

Permits are not issued any time the river is flowing more than 120 cubic feet per second, so this hike may be closed at times between March and June. The optimum time to hike is late June through September. Flash floods are not uncommon in late summer when, again, the park may close the route. Outside of summer, wet or dry suits are often necessary, as hypothermia is a real danger. The Wilderness Desk carefully tracks weather, and Springdale outfitters rent all the appropriate gear.

A summer-season checklist includes a walking stick or trekking poles, synthetic clothing (no cotton!), extra fleece layers and at least one dry bag, in addition to all the usual camping gear. Canyoneering shoes and neoprene socks are useful, but not necessary outside spring. Overnight hikers are required to use human-waste disposal (WAG) bags, which are given free to permit holders. ■

CHECUBUS/SHUTTERSTOCK ©

SUMIKOPHOTO/SHUTTERSTOCK ©

White Sands National Park

Undulating through the Tularosa Basin like something out of a dream, these ethereal dunes are a highlight of any trip to New Mexico, and a must on every landscape photographer's itinerary. Try to time a visit to White Sands with sunrise or sunset (or both), when the dazzlingly white sea of sand is at its most magical.

Great For...

State
New Mexico

Entrance Fee
$25/20 per vehicle/motorcycle, or $15 per person on foot

Area
115 sq miles

Scenic Drive

From the visitor center drive the 16-mile scenic route, which loops into the heart of the world's largest gypsum dune field, covering 275 sq miles. Along the way, get out of the car and romp around, or escape the crowds by hiking either the Alkali Flat, a 5-mile (round-trip) backcountry trail through the heart of the dunes, or the simple mile-loop nature trail.

Don't forget your sunglasses – the sand's as bright as snow.

A Day at the Beach

It's a long, long way to the ocean from here, so don't be surprised to find locals picnicking, playing, sunbathing and generally enjoying the full-on beach experience. Join them by springing for a plastic saucer at the visitor center gift shop, and sledding the back dunes.

Check the park calendar for sunset strolls and full-moon hikes.

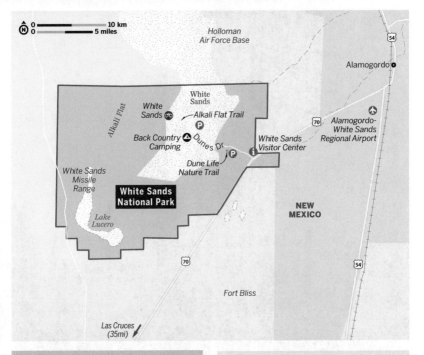

Rocket History

If military history is your thing, consider adding a visit to the **White Sands Missile Test Center Museum** (575-678-3358; history.army.mil/museums/IMCOM/whiteSands/index.html; museum 8am-4:30pm Mon-Fri, 10am-3pm Sat & Sun, missile park sunrise-sunset), 25 miles east of Las Cruces along Hwy 70. It represents the heart of the White Sands Missile Range, a major testing site since 1945. There's a missile garden, a real V-2 rocket and a museum with lots of defense-related artifacts. Visitors have to park outside the Test Center gate and check in with identification at the office before walking in.

Essential Information

To reach the park, drive Hwy 70 either 50 miles northeast of Las Cruces or 16 miles southwest of Alamogordo – and bear in mind that the road occasionally closes at very short notice for up to three hours, during missile tests. Visitors must enter one hour before close.

Camping

Backcountry campsites, with no water or toilet facilities, stand a mile from the scenic drive. At time of research the campsites were closed for renovation; check for availability and permit pricing at the visitor center at least one hour before sunset. Car campers should ask the rangers for a list of other nearby campsites. ∎

Sunset, Yosemite National Park

ALINAMEN/GETTY IMAGES ©

In Focus

The Parks Today 226
One-hundred-plus years old and count-
ing, the National Park Service still faces
an ongoing battle with outside threats.

History 228
Since Yellowstone became the world's
first national park, the foresight of a
few has created a legacy for millions to
enjoy.

Outdoor Activities 234
There's more to the national parks
than spectacular hiking. Wildly diverse
landscapes offer activities to suit every
taste.

Wildlife 240
National parks have helped some of
America's most iconic animals – grizzly
bear, mountain lion and bison – back
from the brink of extinction.

Conservation 245
Safeguarding the parks' treasures has
always been a struggle, and today conservationists are facing new challenges.

Landscapes & Geology 248
California and the Southwest's parks
are a testament to its violent and spectacular geological history.

Tuolumne Meadows, Yosemite National Park

DNY59/GETTY IMAGES ©

The Parks Today

Following a 2016 anniversary celebrating a century in which the US National Park Service grew from 12 parks to 60, 2017 brought new challenges. The Trump administration's downsizing of several national monuments left many reflecting on the precarious nature of these great natural landscapes. While some of those measures were overturned by President Biden, the future remains anything but secure.

Cutbacks in Utah

When President Trump took office in January 2017, the National Park System protected 417 areas comprising 84 million acres across every state of the continental US, DC, Hawaii, American Samoa, Guam, Puerto Rico and the US Virgin Islands. Between 2009 and 2016, President Obama had been proactive in expanding the park network, overseeing the creation of one new national park (Pinnacles) and establishing or expanding 34 equally spectacular national monuments.

However, following a wide-ranging Interior Department review of more recent monument designations, and at the request of the Utah State Legislature, the Trump administration took aim at Utah's Bears Ears National Monument, which protected land sacred to the Pueblo Indians, the Navajo and the Ute. Bears Ears shrank by around 85%, from 1.35 million acres to

160,000 acres, and 1996-designated Grand Staircase–Escalante National Monument, also in Utah, was almost halved in size. The move was unprecedented. While presidents have shrunk national monuments in the past, it has never been undertaken on such a significant scale.

Legal challenges prevented the boundary redrawing from going ahead, and the cases remained unresolved when Trump left office. If the restructures had gone ahead, millions of formerly protected acres would have become available for commercial use, potentially generating billions of dollars of revenue through extraction leases of natural resources. Fears of irreversible damage to these pristine, culturally significant lands prompted large-scale protests from Native American and environmental groups.

On his first day in the Oval Office, President Joe Biden signed an executive order ordering a review to be undertaken by Deb Haaland, America's first-ever Native American Secretary of the Interior. On October 8, 2021, Biden restored the original boundaries of both Bears Ears and Grand Staircase–Escalante monuments.

Paring Back & Other Threats

A number of federally enforced environmental regulations were also pared back under the incoming Trump administration. Affected were laws concerning air and water pollution (emissions control), toxic waste management, infrastructure, public safety and wildlife protection.

Despite record-breaking park visitor numbers in 2016, the 2018 federal budget contained cuts of around $300 million to the NPS's operating budget, prompting the NPS to warn of possible staff cuts, campground closures, reduced operating hours and otherwise reduced services in up to 90% of its parks. After winning the 2020 election, Biden restored much of the NPS's budget funding. In 2022, the Biden administration announced a 2023 budget of US$3.6 billion for the NPS, an increase of US$492.2 million compared with the previous year.

Climate Change

Climate change is another existential threat to the national parks, whether it be in the form of more intense and frequent wildfires in the west or devastating hurricanes in the southeast. The most obvious consequences can already be seen in Glacier National Park, where rapidly melting glaciers may necessitate a name change by 2030.

Wildfires blamed on climate change and rising temperatures threaten many parks in California and the Southwest. According to the *New York Times*, for example, summers in northern California are now 2.5 degrees hotter than they were in the early 1970s, and nine out of the 10 biggest fires in California's history have occurred in the past 18 years. It has also been suggested that rising temperatures might make Joshua Tree National Park too hot for its famous trees before the end of the century.

To complicate matters further, a conservative majority on the US Supreme Court ruled against the Environmental Protection Agency (EPA) and severely restricted its ability to limit carbon and other emissions from the fossil-fuel industry. Seen as a major blow to any attempts by the Federal Government to tackle climate change, the court's ruling could have devastating impacts upon the health of the nation's ecosystems and its national parks.

Good News?

It wasn't all bad news for national parks under Trump (although it mostly was). In 2019, he also created five new national monuments, expanded several national park boundaries, and protected 1.3 million acres of wilderness. National parks created by the Trump Administration were Gateway Arch (Missouri; 2018), Indiana Dunes (Indiana; 2019), White Sands (New Mexico; 2019), and New River Gorge (West Virginia; 2020). New Mexico's White Sands National Park covers 275 square miles of white sand and gypsum dunes in the state's Tularosa Basin.

Vernal Fall, Yosemite National Park

BJORN ALBERTS/GETTY IMAGES ©

History

Few things are as quintessentially American as national parks. Their genesis, implementation and growth since 1872 is a work of genius. A handful of people once had the foresight to pull the reins in on rampant hunting, logging, mining and tourist development, so that some magnificent treasures might be saved for future generations – their actions constitute one of the greatest chapters in US history.

1864
President Lincoln designates Yosemite Valley and the Mariposa Grove a protected state park.

1872
President Ulysses S Grant designates Yellowstone the world's first national park.

1890
Yosemite National Park is established, but the State of California retains control of Yosemite Valley and Mariposa Grove.

Muir Woods National Monument

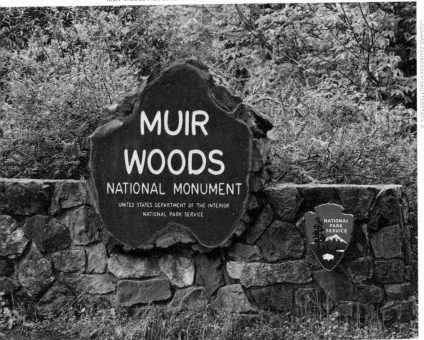

LEONARD ZHUKOVSKY/SHUTTERSTOCK ©

A Magnificent Park

American portrait artist George Catlin (1796–1872) is credited with being the first person to conceptualize a 'nation's park.' He envisioned a 'magnificent park' to protect the country's remaining indigenous people, buffalo and wilderness from the onslaught of western expansion. But over three decades would pass before anything remotely resembling that vision existed.

In 1851, members of an armed militia accidentally rode into a massive granite valley in the Sierra Nevada and decided to call it 'Yosemity,' possibly a corruption of the Miwok word *Oo-hoo'-ma-te* or *uzumatel*, meaning 'grizzly bear.' The name stuck, and soon word of the valley and its waterfalls got out. Within no time, entrepreneurs were divvying up the land in hopes of profiting from tourists.

Thanks to a handful of outspoken writers, artists, naturalists and – most importantly – the efforts of the great landscape architect Frederick Law Olmstead, Yosemite Valley was spared privatization. In 1864 President Abraham Lincoln signed a bill into law that put

1894
After a poacher is caught killing bison in Yellowstone, Congress grants the park the power to enforce conservation laws.

1906
Mesa Verde becomes the seventh national park and the first dedicated to protecting cultural heritage.

1916
Stephen Mather convinces the Department of the Interior to create the National Park Service.

The Father of US National Parks

Often considered the 'father of the US National Park System,' Scottish-born John Muir (1838–1914) was an eloquent writer, naturalist and arguably the greatest defender of wilderness areas in the late-19th century. It should be noted, however, that he has recently become a more controversial figure as people have become increasingly aware of his racist views on Native Americans and African Americans. Nonetheless, his writings were pivotal in the creation not just of Yosemite, but of Sequoia, Mt Rainier, Petrified Forest and Grand Canyon National Parks. Famously – but unsuccessfully – Muir fought to save Yosemite's Hetch Hetchy Valley, which he believed rivaled Yosemite Valley in beauty and grandeur. Although he couldn't stop the damming of the river, his writings on the issue cemented the now widely held belief that national parks should remain as close as possible to their natural state.

Yosemite Valley, and the nearby Mariposa Grove of giant sequoias, under the control of California. Although it wasn't a national park, it was the first time *any* government had mandated the protection of a natural area for public use.

Birth of a National Park

Four years later, a group of men bankrolled by Northern Pacific Railroad headed into the Wyoming wilderness to investigate reports of thermal pools and geysers. Among their discoveries were the Great Fountain Geyser and another geyser they would name Old Faithful. Soon, lobbyists at Northern Pacific, with their eyes on tourist dollars, rallied alongside conservationists for a public park like Yosemite. In 1872 Ulysses S Grant signed the landmark Yellowstone National Park Act, creating the country's first national park.

Meanwhile, in Yosemite, the famed naturalist John Muir lamented the destruction that logging companies, miners and sheep – which he famously deemed 'hoofed locusts' – were wreaking upon the park. In 1890 Yosemite became the country's second national park, but it wasn't until 1905 that Muir convinced Congress to expand the boundaries to include all of Yosemite Valley and the Mariposa Grove.

In 1906, Mesa Verde, in southwestern Colorado, became the country's sixth national park.

Theodore Roosevelt: The Conservation President

In 1903, President Theodore Roosevelt undertook a two-month-long campaign tour of the United States. In between giving 263 speeches in 25 states, he still managed to spend two weeks exploring Yellowstone and three nights camping out with John Muir in Yosemite. But the greatest legacy of that trip – which was to have a lasting impact on the degree of protection afforded to national parks – arose from the time he spent at the Grand

1923	1926	1933
Yosemite's Hetch Hetchy Valley is dammed, the first shot in a continuing battle between conservationists and developers.	Yellowstone's last wolves are killed in the federal predator control program, which also targets mountain lions, bears and coyotes.	FDR creates the Civilian Conservation Corps; CCC workers improve infrastructure in national parks and plant over 3 billion trees.

Canyon. Upon seeing the canyon for the first time, Roosevelt famously opined that the mystical natural wonder could not be improved by any human intervention – it should be left exactly as it was. A nascent conservationist movement had just gained an influential new member.

Muir may have provided the philosophical underpinnings of the national parks, but it was Roosevelt who transformed the vision into reality. An avid hunter, birder, far-sighted thinker and lover of the outdoors, Roosevelt's time out West – before he became president – profoundly shaped his life and legacy. By the time he left office in 1909, he had signed off on five national parks, 18 national monuments, 51 federal bird sanctuaries and 100 million acres of national forest.

Grand Canyon National Park

In 1908 Theodore Roosevelt declared the Grand Canyon a national monument. The act was met with utter outrage from Arizona politicians, mining claim holders and ranchers, who believed he overstepped his bounds as president – a theme that continues to this day concerning the designation of federal lands.

Mather & the National Park Service

Still, there existed no effective protection or management of the new parks until the creation of the National Park Service (NPS) in 1916. The NPS was the brainchild of an industrialist and conservationist named Stephen Mather, who convinced the Department of Interior that a single governing body was precisely what the parks needed. When President Woodrow Wilson signed the National Park Service Act into law, Mather became the first director.

Mather believed that the best way to promote and improve the parks was to get people into them. A public relations guru, Mather encouraged park superintendents to run publicity campaigns, created the park ranger system, initiated campfire talks and opened the first park museums. His efforts – always coupled with media outreach – were so successful that by 1928 he had tripled the number of park visitors to three million.

While Mather was extremely successful in developing the parks, some felt he'd gone too far. Conservation groups such as the National Parks Association and the Sierra Club felt that Mather's emphasis on development came at the expense of the parks themselves. Mather's successor and protégé, Horace Albright, partially addressed these concerns by creating a national wildlife division within the NPS.

FDR & the CCC

With the Great Depression, the parks went through significant changes. President Franklin Delano Roosevelt created the Civilian Conservation Corps (CCC) and put thousands of young men to work improving national park roads, visitors' shelters, campsites and trails.

1941–49
Ansel Adams photographs every national park in the US, bar the Everglades, for the NPS.

1956–66
Mission 66 improves park facilities and creates the first national park visitor centers.

1995
Fourteen grey wolves are reintroduced to Yellowstone nearly 70 years after they disappeared from the park ecosystem.

NPS Logo

The National Park Service adopted its official logo in 1951. Shaped like an arrowhead, it features a bison and sequoia tree set against a snow-capped peak in the background.

During his presidency, FDR also created Joshua Tree, Capitol Reef, and Channel Islands National Monuments (all of which would become national parks), and Olympic and Kings Canyon National Parks.

With the beginning of WWII, the country's greatest public relief program came to an end, CCC workers went off to war, and the national park budget was slashed. Postwar prosperity allowed more Americans to travel – and hordes of them headed to the parks. By 1950 some 32 million people visited America's national parks. Within five years the number topped 60 million.

Mission 66

The number of travelers descending on the parks put tremendous pressure on them. In 1956 NPS director Conrad Wirth created Mission 66, a 10-year plan to improve park infrastructure and dramatically increase visitor services. The plan established the first park visitor centers, more staff and improved facilities. Over the course of Mission 66, Congress also added more than 50 new protected areas to the National Park System.

In 1964 George Hartzog succeeded Wirth as director of the NPS and continued to add new acquisitions. During his tenure nearly 70 new parks came under the jurisdiction of the NPS. In 1972 President Nixon replaced Hartzog with his own appointee, and expansions to the park service were halted.

Doubling Down

Little was added to the National Parks System until 1980, when President Carter signed the Alaska National Interest Lands Conservation Act into law. The landmark legislation instantly protected over 80 million acres and doubled the amount of land under control of the national parks. Ten new national parks and monuments were created in the process. Although controversial in Alaska, the move has been widely heralded as one of the greatest conservation measures in US history.

The Parks Today

Since Yellowstone was created in 1872, the National Park System has grown to encompass over 400 sites and more than 84 million acres. The parks today protect many of the continent's most sensitive ecosystems, some of the world's most remarkable landscapes, and America's most important historical and cultural landmarks. According to the National

2011
A proposed ban on the sale of plastic bottles in the Grand Canyon is blocked after Coca-Cola, an NPS donor, expresses displeasure.

2013
Congressional gridlock shuts down the federal government; all national parks are forced to close for a 16-day period.

2016
The National Park System celebrates the 100th anniversary of its founding.

Park Service, the total number of visitors to US national parks from 1904 to 2021 was 15,391,325,968. They are the country's greatest treasure.

Despite a steady increase in visitation, however, the parks still face a variety of threats and obstacles, including loss of biodiversity, declining air and water quality, climate disruption and insufficient funding. In 2011, the NPS released a Call to Action: an initiative to help the service prepare for its second century, with aims such as reducing greenhouse gas emissions by 20%, increasing community involvement and continuing to raise awareness of the parks among all Americans.

Hot Topics

While conservationists, policy makers and the NPS debate how to best protect the parks, nearly everyone agrees the parks need money – except, it seems, for Congress. With budget cuts and obstructionist gridlock becoming increasingly the norm in Washington, the NPS has begun to turn to private donors and corporate sponsorships in order to make up for the federal shortfall.

System-wide challenges are not the only matter garnering national attention. Congestion, crowds and cars remain a constant source of concern, and more and more parks are introducing free shuttles to combat traffic and reduce air pollution. And from the ongoing debate about snowmobiles in Yellowstone to the concern about melting glaciers in Glacier National Park, there are plenty of other park-specific issues fueling debate.

The Antiquities Act, National Monuments & Other NPS Sites

In 1906 Congress passed the Antiquities Act, which gives the president the authority to protect public land by designating it a National Monument. The Act was originally designed to protect Native American archaeological sites out West, but Theodore Roosevelt quickly realized that he could use it to protect any tract of land for any reason – and without opposition from lobbyists or political opponents in Congress. The Grand Canyon was the most famous example of Roosevelt's decisive stroke.

In 2015 there were 117 national monuments. More are designated every year, while others change status. Most are administered by the NPS. Other sites that come under NPS jurisdiction include National Historic Sites and Parks (eg Independence Hall), National Memorials (eg Lincoln Memorial), National Parkways, National Seashores, National Recreation Areas and National Preserves, which are like parks, except that fossil fuel extraction and sport hunting are permitted (many Alaskan parks hold a dual park–preserve status). In total the NPS currently administers over 423 natural and historic sites, including 63 national parks.

2019
White Sands National Park in New Mexico becomes the 62nd US national park.

2020
At the height of the coronavirus pandemic, park visitor numbers fall to 237 million, the lowest since 1980.

2021
Park visitor numbers rebound to 297.1 million.

DADE72/SHUTTERSTOCK ©

John Muir Trail

Outdoor Activities

We've yet to meet someone visiting a national park so they can hang around indoors. The outdoors is what the parks are all about, and getting out usually means getting active. With environments ranging from the peaks of Yosemite to the otherworldly deserts of Utah, the possibilities are endless.

Hiking

Nothing encapsulates the spirit of the national parks like hiking. Thousands of miles of trails crisscross the parks, offering access to their most scenic mountain passes, highest waterfalls, deepest canyons and quietest corners. Trails run the gamut of accessibility, from the flat, paved paths of Yosemite's **Loop Trails** to the 2,663-mile **Pacific Crest Trail**, which extends from Canada to Mexico, passing through seven national parks along the way.

Regardless of the style of the trail, you'll find that exploring on foot generally offers the best park experience. The relatively slow pace of walking brings you into closer contact with the wildlife, and allows you to appreciate the way different perspectives and the day's shifting light can alter the scenery. The satisfaction gained from completing a hike is also a worthy reward; it's one thing to look over the rim of the Grand Canyon; it's another to work up a sweat hiking back up from the canyon floor.

Each park chapter in this guide has its own Hiking or Activities section with descriptions of the parks' top hikes. We've done our best to cover a variety of trails, not just our favorites. Our goal with descriptions is less about navigation than it is about helping you choose which hikes to squeeze into your trip. Detailed trail descriptions and maps are readily available at visitor centers in every park, and they will complement this guide well. Know your limitations, know the route you plan to take, and pace yourself.

Backpacking

There are hundreds of amazing day hikes to choose from in the park system, but if you want the full experience, head out into the wilderness on an overnight trip. The claim that 99% of park visitors never make it into the backcountry may not be true everywhere, but you will unquestionably see far fewer people and witness exponentially more magic the farther from a road you go. Backcountry campsites are also much more likely to have openings than park lodges and car campsites (which fill up months in advance), making accommodations less of a headache.

Even if you have no backpacking experience, don't consider it out of reach. Most national parks have at least a few backcountry campsites within a couple of hours' walk of a trailhead, making them excellent options for first-time backpackers. You will need gear, however: an appropriate backpack, tent, sleeping bag and pad, stove, headlamp and food are all essential.

Familiarize yourself with the park rules and backcountry ethics before heading out. You will need a permit; if you have your heart set on a famous excursion, apply well in advance online. Most park visitor centers have a backcountry desk, where you can apply for walk-in permits, get trail information, learn about wildlife (bear canisters are generally required in bear country) and check conditions. Before hitting the trail, learn about low-impact camping principles at Leave No Trace (www.lnt.org).

Preparation & Safety

Walks can be as short or long as you like, but remember this when planning: be prepared. The wilderness may be unlike anything you have ever experienced, and designating certain parcels as 'national parks' has not tamed it.

The weather can be extraordinary in its unpredictability and sheer force. The summer sun is blazing hot, sudden thunderstorms can drop enough water in 10 minutes to create deadly flash floods, snow can fall at any time of year above the tree line, while ferocious wind storms can rip or blow away your poorly staked tent.

No matter where you are, water should be the number one item on your packing checklist – always carry more than you think you'll need. If you're doing any backpacking, make sure you have a way to purify water, and check with rangers ahead of time about the availability of water along the trail.

If your trip involves any elevation change, take the time to acclimatize before tackling a long hike, to avoid altitude sickness. Sunblock, a hat, ibuprofen and warm wind- and waterproof layers are all non-negotiable at high altitudes. Snow cover can last

Climbing Dawn Wall

In January 2015, climbers Tommy Caldwell and Kevin Jorgeson became the first to free-climb El Capitan's 3000ft Dawn Wall in Yosemite, a feat long thought impossible. The pair spent 19 days on the cliff face, sleeping on portaledges and documenting their progress with their phones.

Vernal Falls, Yosemite National Park

★ **Classic Day Hikes**

Vernal & Nevada Falls or Cathedral Lakes (Yosemite)

Wildrose Peak (Death Valley)

Angels Landing (Zion)

Fairyland Loop Trail (Bryce Canyon)

Widforss Trail (Grand Canyon)

KODIE GERRITSEN/SHUTTERSTOCK ©

through the end of June above 11,000ft; check with rangers to see if you'll need gaiters and snowshoes.

After the elements, getting lost is the next major concern. Most day hikes are well signed and visitors are numerous, but you should always take some sort of map. If you plan on going into the backcountry, definitely take a topographic (topo) map and a compass. You can pick up detailed maps in most visitor centers; National Geographic's *Trails Illustrated* series is generally excellent.

At lower elevations and in desert parks, always inquire about ticks, poison oak, poison ivy and rattlesnakes before heading out. Most day hikes are on well-maintained trails, but it's good to know what's out there.

And all hikers, solo or not, should always remember the golden rule: let someone know where you are going and how long you plan to be gone.

Rafting, Kayaking & Canoeing

Rafts, kayaks, canoes and larger boats are a wonderful way to get to parts of the parks that landlubbers can't reach. River-running opportunities abound in the parks, but none stand out quite like the **Colorado River**. The most famous trip along the Colorado is a three-week odyssey through the **Grand Canyon** – arguably the best possible way to visit – though you can also take a heart-thumping multiday excursion further upstream through the desert wilds of the **Canyonlands**.

For sea-kayaking, it's hard to beat **Channel Islands National Park**, especially around **Anacapa Island** and **Santa Cruz**. Combine it with a little birdwatching, and watch for whales, sea lions and even elephant seals. In the northern stretches of **Redwood**, the **Smith River** runs through pristine country with waters ideally suited to beginner kayakers or canoers.

For rafting, easily one of the best destinations in the US is the **Rio Grande**, in **Big Bend National Park**. Here the possibilities start from leisurely two-hour trips to multiday expeditions, but you'll generally need at least intermediate-level experience. **Boquillas Canyon** is the longest but easiest stretch of water, but **Colorado Canyon**, **Mariscal Canyon** and **Santa Elena Canyon** all have plenty of rapids; the latter features the famous IV Rock Slide rapid.

Rock Climbing & Mountaineering

There's no sport quite like rock climbing. From a distance it appears to be a feat of sheer strength, but balance, creativity, technical know-how and a Zen-like sangfroid are all parts of the game. Clinging by your fingertips 2000ft up on one of Yosemite's renowned big walls? Not the place to lose your cool. Thankfully, there are plenty of options for climbers

Colorado River, Canyonlands National Park

of all ages and levels that don't require the mind control of a Jedi. Sign up for a day of guided climbing – the **Yosemite Mountaineering School** (☏209-372-8344; www.travelyosemite. com; Half Dome Village; ◷8:30am-5pm Apr-Oct) is a great place to start.

Yosemite may get all the media, but experienced and beginner climbers alike know Joshua Tree as the most diverse climbing terrain in the US: there are more than 8000 established routes, from boulders to cliffs. Hidden Valley in particular is fertile climbing territory. Joshua Tree Rock Climbing School (p59) and Vertical Adventures (p59) both offer lessons and tours.

Other world-renowned destinations include **Zion**, **Capitol Reef**, and **Arches**.

Cycling & Mountain Biking

As a general rule, expect more options for two-wheeled fun just outside park boundaries. Many parks have bicycle rental shops close to the main entrance. On the down side, cycling within national parks can sometimes be challenging due to heavy traffic and steep grades. Anyone who's been grazed by an RV mirror can attest to that.

There are, however, some exceptions. As for most things, in California, **Yosemite** is your best bet: the 12 miles of paved pathways along the **Loop Trails** make for incredibly scenic and leisurely pedaling.

In Utah, you won't have to stray very far for some of the best mountain biking in the world. Mountain biking on trails is largely prohibited in the national parks, but some parks have dirt roads that substitute. **Canyonlands National Park** is particularly full of them. Forged by prospectors back in the 1950s, 70-mile **White Rim Road** is one of the best backcountry mountain-biking trails in the US; you'll need to be entirely self-sufficient. Other

Yosemite National Park

★ **Classic Backcountry Trips**

Nankoweap Trail (Grand Canyon)

High Sierra Camps Loop (Yosemite)

Redwood Creek Trail (Redwood)

Rae Lakes Loop (Kings Canyon)

Monarch Lakes (Sequoia)

fine Canyonlands mountain-biking adventures with some experience include **Salt Creek Canyon Trail** and **Elephant Hill**. There are lots of top, challenging trails on the desert slickrock outside **Arches** and **Zion**. In **Capitol Reef**, **Cathedral Valley Loop** is first-rate.

Over in Arizona, **Saguaro** has some decent options including the **Cactus Forest Loop Drive** and **Cactus Forest Trail**.

Winter Sports

Cross-Country Skiing & Snowshoeing

Come winter, trails and roads in many parks get blanketed with snow and the crowds disappear. It's a magical time to visit, and those willing to step into skis or snowshoes and brave the elements will be rewarded. Most of the best parks for both activities lie beyond the scope of this guide, taking you into the Rockies or Alaska. But in this, as in so many things, **Yosemite** is an exception and has some fine trails. Surprisingly, there's even cross-country skiing at the **Grand Canyon**.

In some parks, rangers lead snowshoe hikes, which can be an excellent entry to the sport and a great way to learn about the winter environment. Visitor centers are the best place to check for information.

Downhill Skiing & Snowboarding

Most of the best downhill skiing takes place outside the parks. One park, however, does have downhill ski resorts: **Badger Pass** in **Yosemite National Park** is an affordable, family-friendly resort.

Powell Geographic Expedition

John Wesley Powell led the first recorded descent of the Colorado River in 1869 – with only one arm. The 10-man survey team took four 21ft boats from Wyoming to Nevada in three months, passing through the Grand Canyon. One boat, lots of supplies and three men were lost along the way.

Swimming

With the exception of the higher-elevation parks, summer means heat, and heat means swimming. Alpine lakes make for wonderful but often frigid swimming (**Lake Tenaya** in **Yosemite** is a particularly cold example), and many of the larger lakes have beaches and designated swimming areas.

As river rats the world over will attest, nothing beats dipping into a swimming hole and drip-drying on a rock in the sun. But be careful – every year, swimmers drown in national park rivers. Always check with visitor centers about trouble spots and the safest places to swim. Unless you're certain about the currents, swim only where others are swimming.

Top places to get wet are **Zion's Virgin River**, the **Merced River** in **Yosemite Valley**, **Santa Cruz** in **Channel Islands**, and **Muir Rock** in **Kings Canyon**.

Fishing

For many, the idea of heading to the national parks without a fishing rod is ludicrous. Waters in **Yosemite's** high country, particularly the **Tuolumne River**, can be great for small, feisty trout.

Wherever you fish, read up on local regulations. Fishing permits are always required, and those caught fishing without one will be fined. (Children under 15 are generally not required to have a license.) Some waters, including many streams and rivers, are catch-and-release only, and sometimes bait-fishing is prohibited. Certain native fish, such as bull trout, kokanee salmon and wild steelhead, are often protected, and anglers in possession of these can be heavily fined. The best place to check regulations is online. For details, check the park's NPS website (www.nps.gov) and refer to the respective state's department of fish and game website. Find the latter by searching for the state plus 'fish and game.'

So Much to Do...

For those that want to try it all, here's some more fodder for fun:

- **Stargazing** Thanks to clear desert skies, stargazing is outstanding in Capitol Reef, Bryce, Great Basin, Carlsbad Caverns, and Big Bend. Also check park newspapers for nightly astronomy walks.

- **Canyoneering** Rope up and descend into Utah's mesmerizing slot canyons; with a guide, no experience is necessary.

- **Tide pooling** The Channel Islands are tide-pool heaven.

- **Caving** Join a subterranean tour at Carlsbad Caverns, Great Basin Pinnacles, and Sequoia.

Horseback & Mule Riding

Our most time-tested form of transport still makes for a wonderful way to experience the great outdoors. Horseback riding is possible in many of the parks, and outfitters within or immediately outside the parks offer everything from two-hour rides to full- and multiday pack trips. Rides run around $40 per hour or $80 per half-day.

Popular horseback excursions such as the descent into the **Grand Canyon** or the **High Sierra Camps** in **Yosemite** require reservations far in advance.

Black bear, Yosemite National Park

BJORN BAKSTAD/GETTY IMAGES ©

Wildlife

It's no coincidence that the establishment of many of the earliest national parks coincided with the first wave of near mass extinctions in the US: by the 1890s the passenger pigeon, bison, eastern elk, wolf, mountain lion and grizzly bear were all on the verge of disappearing forever. Today, some of these animals have made a comeback, thanks in large part to the protection afforded by the national parks.

Bears

If you see a bear on your trip to a national park in California and the Southwest, odds are it will be a black bear. These mostly vegetarian foragers are much more common than their larger, more elusive cousins, grizzly bears.

Black bears, which are sometimes brown or cinnamon-colored, roam montane and subalpine forests throughout the country and are surprisingly common. The Rockies and the Sierras have the highest populations, but black bears also roam the Southwest and California.

Black bears feed on berries, nuts, roots, grasses, insects, eggs, small mammals and fish, but can become a nuisance around campgrounds and mountain cabins where food is not stored properly. Black bears are usually not aggressive unless there are cubs nearby, but they will go after food or food odors.

Black bears are very adaptable and in some places, such as Yosemite, have become so accustomed to humans that they regularly roam campsites and break into cars at night for food. Make sure to store your food and trash properly, and use a bear canister if you plan on backpacking. Even though they're rarely dangerous, they can be intimidating: adult males weigh from 275lb to 450lb; females weigh about 175lb to 250lb. They measure 3ft high on all fours and can be taller than 5ft when standing on their hind legs.

The grizzly bear once ranged across the western US, but today its population in the lower 48 is estimated to be around 1500 to 1800. In the continental US, grizzlies are only found in the mountainous regions of Montana, Idaho, Wyoming and Washington.

The National Park Service (www.nps.gov) has excellent information on bears and how to handle encounters.

Bison, Elk & Bighorn Sheep

The continent's largest land mammal is the American bison (or buffalo). Some 60 million bison once roamed North America, but Euro-American settlers, in one of the saddest chapters of American history, reduced their numbers to about 300. Beginning in the 1860s, the US government and army encouraged their slaughter in order to deprive the Plains Indians of their primary means of survival. For many Americans traveling West, killing bison was also done for sport – as evidenced by the 'hunting by rail' trips organized by railroads, which left untold thousands of rotting buffalo corpses in their wake. By the 1890s, Yellowstone's bison herd was the only one remaining in the country, with poachers successfully reducing its numbers one by one.

What could have been a disaster instead became a turning point. Thanks to the determined intervention of George Bird Grinnell, editor of *Forest & Stream* and founder of the Audubon Society, and a young politician by the name of Theodore Roosevelt, Congress passed a law in 1894 granting national parks the power to protect all wildlife within their boundaries. Previous to this, poachers were simply expelled from park lands; now they could be arrested. Yellowstone's bison were gradually bred back from the brink of extinction, and today up to 5500 roam the park.

The only area of California and the Southwest that still has a wild bison population is in northern California. None of the national parks covered in this guide have bison populations, although you can see America's most iconic mammal at Black Butte Bison Ranch, in Tehama County, near Corning.

The Roosevelt elk, which is the largest surviving subspecies of elk, grows antlers up to 5ft long and weigh up to 700lb. These majestic herbivores graze along forest edges from northern California all the way to Alaska. They are commonly sighted in the prairie grasslands of Redwood National Park.

Bighorn sheep are synonymous with the Rocky Mountains, and have made a slow but steady comeback after nearing extinction in the 1800s. Today they are sighted throughout the Rockies, and in Joshua Tree, Zion and Bryce Canyon. During late-fall and early-winter breeding seasons, males charge each other at 20mph and clash their horns so powerfully that the sound can be heard for miles.

Wolves & Coyotes

The gray wolf was once the Rocky Mountains' main predator, but relentless persecution reduced its territory to a narrow belt stretching from Canada to the Northern Rockies. The wolf disappeared in California in the 1920s and the last wolf pack in Yellowstone was

Elk, Redwood National Park

MARTINA BIRNBAUM/SHUTTERSTOCK ©

★ Best Wildlife Sightings

Black bears Yosemite or Sequoia

Bighorn sheep Bryce Canyon

Roosevelt elk Redwood

Gray and humpback whales Channel Islands

Brazilian free-tailed bats Carlsbad Caverns

killed in 1924, but wolves were successfully reintroduced to the park beginning in 1995. The last official count in 2013 showed 95 wolves, though there are an estimated 500-plus in the Greater Yellowstone ecosystem. As of late 2021, the population had spread, with an estimated 20 wolves (across two wolf packs) thought to be living in California.

Altogether there are now more than 6000 wolves in the continental US (including close to 200 in the Southwest) and over 8000 in Alaska.

Coyotes and foxes are common in many of the parks. When it comes to coyotes, you're far more likely to hear them than see them. Listening to them howl at night as you doze off to sleep is an eerie yet wonderful experience.

Cats

North America's largest cat is the mountain lion (also known as a puma or cougar), an elusive and powerful predator. Highly adaptable, mountain lions are present in many parks, including Yosemite, Joshua Tree and Grand Canyon. According to state government estimates, California has the second-highest mountain lion population in the US (after Oregon) with between 4000 and 6000 cats. Other regional states with big populations include New Mexico (3500 to 4300), Arizona (2000 to 2700) and Nevada (2000). In a reminder of how adaptable mountain lions can be, *National Geographic* photographer Steve Winter took a famous photo of a mountain lion alongside the Hollywood sign above Los Angeles.

It's highly unlikely you'll spot a mountain lion, as they avoid human contact. If you're camping, however, you may hear one scream – it's an utterly terrifying sound in the darkness and a virtual guarantee that you won't fall back asleep until dawn. These powerful cats are about 150lb to 220lb of pure muscle, with short, tawny fur and long tails. In the Western US, the mountain lion hunts elk and even wild horses, as well as smaller mammals. One of the most adaptable of all wild-cat species, the mountain lion is found everywhere from tropical forests to rocky deserts, even up to an altitude of 13,100ft. The greatest threats to mountain lions are hunting and road accidents.

Bobcats are also present in most of these parks and are equally hard to spot.

Small Mammals

Small mammals often get short shrift on people's watch lists, but animals like beavers, pikas, marmots and river otters are a delight to see. Marmots, despite being little more than glorified ground squirrels, are enjoyable to watch hopping around on rocks in the high country. They are found in the subalpine regions of both the Rockies and the Sierras; one good place to look for them is the Monarch Lakes Hike in Sequoia National Park.

If bats are your thing, New Mexico's Carlsbad Caverns National Park has one of the more arresting nightly spectacles, when Brazilian free-tailed bats take to the skies on sunset from May to October.

Other critters you might come across include squirrels, voles, mice, chipmunks, raccoons, badgers, skunks, shrews and martens.

Birds

Many national parks are know for their bird-watching possibilities, but few can match Big Bend National Park in Texas, with more than 450 recorded species.

Birds of prey – including eagles, falcons, hawks, owls and harriers – are common in the parks, especially the western ones. Osprey, which nest and hunt around rivers and lakes, are a commonly spotted raptor. Keep your eyes peeled for bald eagles. In California, bald eagles have regained a foothold on the Channel Islands, and they sometimes spend the winter at Big Bear Lake near LA.

Most of the NPS park websites (www. nps.gov) have complete bird lists – bring binoculars for the best experience.

California Condors

With a 9ft wingspan, the California condor looks more like a prehistoric pterodactyl than any bird you've ever seen. In 1987, the condor became extinct in the wild when scientists took the drastic step of capturing all remaining wild condors in order to pursue a captive breeding program.

Return of the Wolf

The wolf is a potent symbol of America's wilderness. This smart, social predator is the largest species of canine – averaging more than 100lb and reaching nearly 3ft at the shoulder. An estimated 400,000 once roamed the continent from coast to coast, from Alaska to Mexico.

Wolves were not regarded warmly by European settlers. And as 19th-century Americans moved west, they replaced the native herds of bison, elk, deer and moose with domestic cattle and sheep, which wolves found equally tasty.

To stop wolves from devouring the livestock, extermination soon became official government policy. Eventually, only a few hundred gray wolves remained in the lower 48 states, in northern Minnesota and Michigan.

In 1944 naturalist Aldo Leopold called for the return of the wolf. His argument was ecology, not nostalgia. His studies showed that wild ecosystems need their top predators to maintain healthy biodiversity.

Protected and encouraged, wolf populations made a remarkable recovery. However, heavy pressure from ranchers has resulted in gray wolves losing their protected status in almost all states over the past few years. According to the Wolf Conservation Center, some 1700 wolves have since been killed.

Reintroductions into the Californian wild began a year later, followed by southern Utah and northern Arizona. Now considered a remarkable success story, the wild condor passed an important milestone in 2015 when more condors were born in the wild than had died, and the 2016 population reached 276, with a further 170 in captivity. By 2021, the estimated wild population had reached an encouraging 334, spread across California, Utah and Arizona.

These unusual birds – which fed on the carcasses of mastodons and saber-toothed cats in prehistoric days – are staging a minor comeback at the Grand Canyon. After several decades in which no condors lived in the wild there, a few pairs are now nesting on the canyon rim. Otherwise, the best bet for spotting them is Arizona's Vermilion Cliffs. In California, look skyward as you drive along the Big Sur coast or at Pinnacles National Park. Zion and Big Bend national parks in Utah are also possibilities.

In the Realm of Giants

Yosemite, Sequoia and Kings Canyon are home to the world's largest living things: giant sequoias. Although they aren't the tallest trees, nor the thickest, they are the biggest in terms of sheer mass. Living up to 3000 years, giant sequoias are also among the oldest living organisms. The General Sherman tree, in Sequoia, stands 275ft tall and measures 100ft around, making it the largest living single-specimen organism on earth. Think of it this way: according to the National Park Service, its trunk alone is equivalent to 15 blue whales or 25 military battle tanks. Now that's a big tree.

Trees & Plants

If you were to travel to every national park in this guide, you'd experience a vast array of plant life, from the bizarre Joshua trees of the Mojave Desert and saguaro cacti in Arizona, to the giant sequoias of California.

Saguaros

Perhaps the most famous cactus species of them all, the saguaro is a tree-like cactus native to Arizona's Sonoran Desert, the Whipple Mountains and Imperial County in California, and parts of Mexico. Arguably the best place to see them is Saguaro National Park, north of Tucson, AZ.

Saguaros can live for more than 150 years. They grow slowly, taking 50 years to reach 7ft, and do not start to grow their first side 'arm' until between 75 and 100 years of age. Saguaros have evolved to store large quantities of rainwater – they can draw down the water for hydration as needed, which enables them to survive in one of Western USA's most hostile environments. A fully hydrated giant saguaro can store more than a ton of water.

Not only is it illegal to shoot them in Arizona, it is also dangerous. In 1982 a vandal shot the arm off a 27ft-tall saguaro. The arm fell on the shooter and crushed him to death. The tragicomic tale was immortalized in the song 'Saguaro' by Texan band Austin Lounge Lizards.

Trees

The national parks protect some of the greatest forests in the world. Redwood has the planet's tallest trees, Yosemite's Mariposa Grove of giant sequoias is home to some of the planet's largest trees, while the park's high country holds subalpine forests that are nothing short of high-altitude fairylands.

In the drier, hotter climates of Zion, Bryce Canyon and Grand Canyon, trees are fewer, but still common. Many Zion visitors are surprised to find a lush riparian zone along the Virgin River that supports beautiful stands of cottonwoods and gorgeous bigtoothed maples. In the Mojave Desert is the strange Joshua tree, actually a giant yucca.

Smaller Plants

When it comes to the smaller plants of the national parks, none seem to make an impression like wildflowers do. If you're traveling in spring or summer, it's always worth doing a little research on your park of choice to find out what's blooming when. For example, wildflowers put on a spectacular show in Death Valley every spring, usually in late February and March. In the Sierras, wildflowers bloom in spring at lower elevations, in early summer up around Tuolumne Meadows, and as late as mid-July at the highest elevations.

On the Colorado Plateau (Zion, Bryce and Grand Canyon) wildflowers, such as desert marigolds and slickrock paintbrush, bloom for a short period in early spring. The plateau's most interesting plants are arguably the cacti and desert succulents that make this mostly desert region so unique. Although many plants are specific to the plateau, others are drawn from adjacent biological zones such as the Great Basin, Mojave Desert and Rocky Mountains.

Hetch Hetchy Reservoir, Yosemite National Park

NICHOLAY STANEV/SHUTTERSTOCK ©

Conservation

Protecting the national parks has been a challenge since the day Yellowstone was created in 1872. Thanks to the efforts of passionate individuals, the parks now safeguard some of the greatest natural treasures on the planet. But they face new, often concurrent, threats. Climate change, invasive species, overuse and irresponsible land use on park peripheries all jeopardize the national parks today.

Conserving California

In California, rapid development and unchecked growth have often come at great environmental cost. Starting in 1849, gold-rush miners hacked and blasted through the countryside in search of a lucky strike. More than 1.5 billion tons of debris and uncalculated amounts of poisonous mercury were carried downstream into the Central Valley, where rivers and streams became clogged and polluted. When you see forests in high Sierra gold country and salmon runs in the Sacramento Delta, you are admiring the resilience of nature and the work of many determined conservationists.

Water, or the lack thereof, has led to epic environmental struggles and catastrophes in California. Despite campaigning by John Muir, California's greatest environmental champion, the Tuolumne River was dammed at Hetch Hetchy in Yosemite National Park to supply

★ **Did you know?**

Over 200 national parks and monuments contain at least one endangered species.

Mountain yellow-legged frog

MICHELE D'AMICO SUPERSKY77/GETTY IMAGES ©

Bay Area drinking water. Pipelines diverting water supplies for arid Los Angeles have contributed to the destruction of Owens Lake and its fertile wetlands, and the degradation of Mono Lake in the Eastern Sierra.

Altered and compromised habitats make easy targets for invasive species, including highly aggressive species that upset California's precariously balanced ecosystems. In Sequoia and Kings Canyon National Parks, non-native trout have practically wiped out the mountain yellow-legged frog population, landing the frog on the candidate list for endangered species.

Although air quality in California has improved markedly in past decades, it's still among the worst in the country. In fact, Sequoia, Kings Canyon and Yosemite national parks have some of the dirtiest air of any of the country's parks.

The Southwest

Sustained droughts in the Southwest are contributing to forest fires of unprecedented size and widespread land degradation. Researchers warn that the long-term outlook of a prolonged megadrought remains a serious concern.

The construction of dams and human-made water features throughout the Southwest has radically altered the delicate balance of water that sustained life for millennia. In place of rich annual floods, dams now release cold waters in steady flows that favor the introduced fish and weedy plants that have overtaken the West's rivers.

In other areas, the steady draining of aquifers to provide drinking water for cows and sprawling cities is shrinking the water table and drying up unique desert springs and wetlands that countless animals once depended on during the dry season. Cows further destroy the fragile desert crust with their heavy hooves, and also graze on native grasses and herbs that are soon replaced by introduced weeds.

Development projects also put immense pressure on many locations by operating high-impact businesses just outside park boundaries. Conservationists battled for more than two decades to prevent Kaiser Ventures from creating the nation's largest landfill on the edge of Joshua Tree National Park. Grand Canyon is still affected by emissions from coal-fired power plants, which drift over the parks and contaminate the air. Sensitive riparian areas along the Grand Canyon's Colorado River have long been impacted by upriver damming and water holding.

Rising temperatures due to climate change have further effects. Scientists worry, for example, that due to rising temperatures in the Mojave Desert, Joshua trees may disappear almost entirely from Joshua Tree National Park within the next 60 to 90 years. And in Sequoia and Kings Canyon national parks, there is concern that changing temperatures and rainfall patterns may threaten the park's giant sequoias.

4x.QUAK/GETTY IMAGES ©

Shuttle bus, Zion National Park

FREE SHUTTLE

Visiting National Parks Sustainably

Park visitors can make a positive impact by traveling sustainably and getting involved with park associations. Whenever you can, ride park shuttles instead of driving your car. Skip high-impact park activities such as flight-seeing trips over the Grand Canyon. Conserve water in the desert parks and prevent erosion by always staying on trails. If you're backpacking, use biodegradable soaps (or skip them altogether) and follow the principles of Leave No Trace (www.lnt.org).

Nearly every national park has an associated foundation or other nonprofit supporting it. These organizations, which include the Yosemite Conservancy (www.yosemite.org), conduct everything from trail maintenance to habitat restoration. Members can volunteer or donate to programs that are critical to the parks' well-being.

The National Parks Conservation Association (www.npca.org) covers all of the parks. Since 1919, this nonprofit organization has been protecting and preserving America's national parks through research, advocacy and education.

Zabriskie Point, Death Valley National Park

Landscapes & Geology

Tectonic collisions, glaciation, volcanic eruptions, erosion – the forces of nature and time have worked wonders on the US, and nowhere is that geological history more beautifully evident than in the national parks of California and the Southwest.

California

South of Zion, the Colorado Plateau meets the Mojave Desert, which is home to the hottest, driest places in North America. Here you'll find Death Valley, which protects over 5000 sq miles of what is no less than a crazy quilted geological playground. Encompassing far more than Death Valley itself, the park contains giant sand dunes, marbled canyons, extinct volcanic craters and palm-shaded oases.

At the southernmost edge of the Mojave lies Joshua Tree, which straddles both the Mojave and the Sonoran deserts. The Mojave section of the park is home to a particularly striking member of the yucca family, the namesake Joshua tree.

Northwest of the California deserts, the Sierra Nevada is a 400-mile-long mountain range with tremendous biological and geological diversity. The Sierras are an uplifted,

Subterranean World

The national parks' caves are often overlooked by road-tripping families on summer vacations. After all, is walking around in a chilly, pitch-black tunnel really as appealing as hugging giant trees in Sequoia? Maybe not on the surface, but the thrill of exploring the underworld's bizarre formations should not be overlooked. Carlsbad Caverns in New Mexico is one of three enormous cave systems in the US; the others are Wind Cave (South Dakota) and Mammoth Cave (Kentucky). Rangers lead tours, plus you can hike down into Carlsbad's Big Room on your own. Other parks with smaller caves to explore include Pinnacles, Kings Canyon and Sequoia in California.

westward-tilting slab of granite that broke off from the Earth's crust and thrust upward roughly 10 million years ago.

Between two million and 10,000 years ago, glaciers 'flowed' from high-elevation ice fields, scouring out canyons and valleys and sculpting the range into a granite masterpiece. In Yosemite, evidence of glaciation is everywhere and is what makes the park so spectacular.

The Sierras' highest peaks stand within the areas protected by Yosemite, Sequoia and Kings Canyon, with Mt Whitney (14,505ft; in Sequoia) standing taller than any other peak in the lower 48.

Although located in northern California, the coastal Redwoods and Lassen Volcanic national parks are more closely related to the temperate rainforests and fiery peaks of the Pacific Northwest.

Geology & Earthquakes

California is a complex geologic landscape formed from fragments of rock and earth crust squeezed together as the North American continent drifted westward over hundreds of millions of years. Crumpled coastal ranges, fault lines rippling through the Central Valley and the jagged, still-rising Sierra Nevada mountains all reveal gigantic forces at work, as the continental and ocean plates crush together.

Everything changed about 25 million years ago, when the ocean plates stopped colliding and instead started sliding against each other, creating the massive San Andreas Fault. This contact zone catches and slips, rattling California with an ongoing succession of tremors and earthquakes.

In 1906 the state's most famous earthquake measured 7.8 on the Richter scale and demolished San Francisco, leaving more than 3000 people dead. The Bay Area was again badly shaken in 1989, when the Loma Prieta earthquake (6.9) caused a section of the Bay Bridge to collapse. In Los Angeles the last 'big one' was in 1994, when the Northridge quake (6.7) caused parts of the Santa Monica Fwy to fall down, resulting in damage that made it the most costly quake in US history. Shifting fault lines far from the large urban areas periodically register high on the Richter scale, like the 2019 Ridgecrest quake, which at 6.4, along with over 100,000 aftershocks, was the strongest in southern California in more than 20 years.

Southwest

At the southwest end of the Rockies, the mountains descend to the Colorado Plateau, a 130,000-sq-mile region centered on the arid Four Corners area of the United States. Home to Grand Canyon, Zion and Bryce Canyon – among numerous other parks – the Colorado Plateau is one of the world's densest concentrations of exposed rock. Arizona's Petrified Forest is a trove of Late Triassic–era fossils, which date back 225 million years.

★ **Rockstar Vistas**

Olmsted Point Yosemite

The Narrows Zion

Bryce Canyon Amphitheater Bryce Canyon

Bright Angel Point Grand Canyon

Hidden Valley Joshua Tree

View from Olmsted Point

JIM HAMMER/SHUTTERSTOCK ©

Unlike the Rocky Mountains to the east and the Sierras to the west, the plateau has remained stable for millions of years, during which water and wind slowly eroded the landscape, forming the spectacular canyons, arches, hoodoos and other rock formations you see today. From an aerial perspective, the plateaus and cliffs form a remarkable staircase that steps downward from the pink cliffs of Bryce Canyon, to the white and red cliffs of Zion, and finally to the chocolate cliffs abutting the Grand Canyon – each color represents a different geological era. This so-called Grand Staircase exposes the hundreds of millions of years of layered rock that make the region so visually awesome.

The Geological Backstory

The Colorado Plateau is an impressive and nearly impenetrable 150,000-sq-mile tableland lurking in the corner where Colorado, Utah, Arizona and New Mexico join. Formed in an ancient basin as a remarkably coherent body of neatly layered sedimentary rocks, the plateau has remained relatively unchanged even as the lands around it were compressed, stretched and deformed by powerful forces.

The most powerful indicators of the plateau's long-term stability are the distinct and unique layers of sedimentary rock stacked on top of each other, with the oldest dating back two billion years. In fact, the science of stratigraphy – the reading of Earth's history through its rock layers – stemmed from work at the Grand Canyon, where an astonishing set of layers has been laid bare by the Colorado River cutting across them. Throughout the Southwest, and on the Colorado Plateau in particular, layers of sedimentary rock detail a rich history of ancient oceans, coastal mudflats and arid dunes.

All other geographic features of the Southwest seem to radiate out from the plateau. To the east, running in a north–south line from Canada to Mexico, are the Rocky Mountains, the source of the mighty Colorado River, which gathers on the mountains' high slopes and cascades across the Southwest to its mouth in the Gulf of California. East of the Rocky Mountains, the eastern third of New Mexico grades into the Llano Estacado – a local version of the vast grasslands of the Great Plains.

In Utah, a line of mountains known collectively as the Wasatch Line bisects the state nearly in half, with the eastern half on the Colorado Plateau, and the western half in the Basin and Range Province. Northern Arizona is highlighted by a spectacular set of cliffs called the Mogollon Rim that runs several hundred miles to form a boundary between the Colorado Plateau to the north and the highland region of central Arizona. The mountains of central Arizona decrease in elevation as you travel into the deserts of southern Arizona.

Four deserts – the Sonoran, Mojave, Chihuahuan and Great Basin – stretch across the Southwest. Each is home to an array of well-adapted reptiles, mammals and plants. The Southwest's four distinct desert zones are superimposed on an astonishing complex of hidden canyons and towering mountains.

★ **Did you know?**

The Colorado Plateau is one of the world's densest concentrations of exposed rock.

Top: Park Avenue Trail, Arches National Park; Bottom left: View from Olmsted Point, Yosemite National Park; Bottom right: Bryce Canyon

Geology of the Grand Canyon

The Grand Canyon records two billion years of geologic history – a huge amount of time considering the earth is only about 4.5 billion years old. Extremely ancient rocks (among the oldest on the planet) exposed in the deep heart of the Grand Canyon show that the region was under water two billion years ago, and younger layers of rocks in southern Utah reveal that this region was continuously or periodically under water until about 60 million years ago.

The canyon itself, however, is young – a mere five to six million years old. Carved out by the powerful Colorado River as the land bulged upward, the 277-mile-long canyon reflects the differing hardness of the 10-plus layers of rocks in its walls. Shales crumble easily and form slopes, while resistant limestones and sandstones form distinctive cliffs.

Unique Landscape Features in the Southwest

Badlands Crumbling, mineral-filled soft rock; found in the Painted Desert at Petrified Forest National Park and Capitol Reef National Park.

Hoodoos Sculptured spires of rock weathered into towering pillars; showcased at Bryce Canyon National Park and Arches National Park.

Natural Bridges Formed when streams cut through sandstone layers; three bridges can be seen at Bryce Canyon National Park, Natural Bridges National Monument and Rainbow Bridge National Monument.

Goosenecks Early-stage natural bridges formed when a stream U-turns across a landscape; visible from Goosenecks Overlook at Capitol Reef National Park.

Mesas Hulking formations of layered sandstone where the surrounding landscape has been stripped away; classic examples can be found at Canyonlands National Park and on the Arizona–Utah border.

Behind the Scenes

Acknowledgements

Climate map data adapted from Peel MC, Finlayson BL & McMahon TA (2007) 'Updated World Map of the Köppen-Geiger Climate Classification', *Hydrology and Earth System Sciences*, 11, pp1633–44.

Cover photograph: Devil's Kitchen, Lassen National Park, California, SMcGuire45/Getty Images ©

This Book

This 1st edition of Lonely Planet's *California and Southwest USA's National Parks* was researched and written by Brett Atkinson, Amy Balfour, Loren Bell, Greg Benchwick, Celeste Brash, Jade Bremner, Gregor Clark, Jennifer Rasin Denniston, Michael Grosberg, Anthony Ham, Ashley Harrell, Anita Isalska, Mark Johanson, Bradley Mayhew, Carolyn McCarthy, Christopher Pitts, Brendan Sainsbury, Andrea Schulte-Peevers, Regis St Louis, Greg Ward and Karla Zimmerman.

This guidebook was produced by the following:

Commissioning Editor Angela Tinson

Production Editors Margaret Milton, Ronan Abayawickrema

Cartographer Alison Lyall

Book Designers Hannah Blackie, Clara Monitto

Assisting Editor Monique Choy

Cover Researcher Gwen Cotter

Thanks to Imogen Bannister, Liz Heynes, Sonia Kapoor, Katherine Marsh, Wayne Murphy, Dianne Schallmeiner, John Taufa, Juan Winata

Send Us Your Feedback

We love to hear from travellers – your comments keep us on our toes and help make our books better. Our well-travelled team reads every word on what you loved or loathed about this book. Although we cannot reply individually to your submissions, we always guarantee that your feedback goes straight to the appropriate authors, in time for the next edition. Each person who sends us information is thanked in the next edition.

Visit lonelyplanet.com/contact to submit your updates and suggestions or to ask for help. Our award-winning website also features inspirational travel stories and news.

Note: We may edit, reproduce and incorporate your comments in Lonely Planet products such as guidebooks, websites and digital products, so let us know if you are happy to have your name acknowledged. For a copy of our privacy policy visit lonelyplanet.com/legal.

Index

A

accessible travel 158
accommodations 17
activities 18-20, 36-7, 38-9, 234-9, see also individual activities
acute mountain sickness 23
Alpine 148-50
Angels Landing Trail 212
animals, 240-3, see also individual animals
Antiquities Act 233
Arches National Park 15, 26-7, 134-9, **135**
ATMs 16
Audubon Society 20
avalanches 23

B

backpacking 235
Balanced Rock Trail 136
bats 179, 242
bears 25, 240-1, 242
bicycle travel, see cycling
Big Bend National Park 26-7, 39, 140-5, 150, **141**
Big Morongo Canyon Preserve 63
bighorn sheep 241, 242
birds 243
birdwatching 20, 63, 142
bison 241
books 21
Bryce Amphitheater 8
Bryce Canyon 156-7, **157**
Bryce Canyon National Park 8, 26-7, 152-61, **153**
Bryce Point 152
Burning Man 20

C

cactuses 209

California 41-129, **43**
  climate 42
  highlights 42
  travel seasons 42
camping 17
canoeing 142, 236
canyoneering 39, 212, 239
Canyonlands National Park 15, 26-7, 39, 164-9, **164**
Capitol Reef National Park 26-7, 170-7, **171**
car travel 17, see also driving tours
Carlsbad Caverns 37
Carlsbad Caverns National Park 15, 26-7, 178-9, **179**
Cathedral Lakes 120-1, **120**
caves 37, 88, 104-5, 128, 178-9, 190, 249
cell phones 16
Channel Islands 87
Channel Islands National Park 14, 26-7, 44-9, **45**
Chapin Mesa 200
children, travel with 36-7
Chiricahua National Monument 207
Civilian Conservation Corps (CCC) 230, 231
Cliff Palace 10, 37, 198
climate 16, 18-20
climate change 227
climbing, see rock climbing
clothing 24-5
Coachella Valley 64, 66
Coachella Valley Music & Arts Festival 18
Colorado Plateau 250-1
Colorado River 39
compasses 25
conservation 245-7
costs 16, 17
Cottonwood Spring 66
COVID-19 2
coyotes 241-2

credit cards 16
cycling 17, 56-9, 209, 237-8

D

Dante's View 11
Dawn Wall 235
Death Valley National Park 11, 26-7, 50-5, **51**
Del Norte Coast Redwoods State Park 100
Delicate Arch 134-6
Desert Hot Springs 62-3
Devils Garden Trail 136
drinking water 23
driving tours
  Big Bend National Park 140-2
  Big Bend Scenic Loop 28-9, 146-51, **147**
  Capitol Reef National Park 170-3, 174-5, **175**
  Great Basin National Park 191
  Highway 24 174-5, **175**
  Newton B Drury Scenic Parkway 91
  Northern Redwood Coast 30-1, 96-101, **97**
  Palm Springs & Joshua Tree Oases 30-1, 62-7, **63**
  Yosemite, Sequoia & Kings Canyon 30-1, 124-9, **125**

E

earthquakes 249
economy 227
El Capitan 114
El Paso 146
elk 241, 242
Emerald Pools 212
environmental issues 225, 227, 233, 245, 246
equipment 24-5
events 18-20

F

Fairyland Loop Trail 154

family travel 36-7
festivals 18-20
films 21
fishing 239
Fruita 171-2
Fort Davis 146

G

General Grant Grove 68-70
General Sherman Tree 102
geography 166, 248-52
geology 170, 184, 193, 206-7, 225, 248-52
Glacier Point 117, 126
Glen Canyon National Recreation Area 206
Grand Canyon 6, 39
Grand Canyon National Park 26-7, 180-9, **181**
Grant, Ulysses S 228, 230
Great Basin National Park 26-7, 190-1, **191**
Guadalupe Mountains National Park 26-7, 192-7, **193**

H

Half Dome 112-14
health 22-3
Hermit Trail 39, 187, **187**
Hidden Valley 63-4
Highway 24 174-5, **175**
hiking 22-5, 32-3, 234-6
  Arches National Park 14-6
  Big Bend National Park 142
  Bryce Canyon National Park 152-4
  Canyonlands National Park 164-6
  Capitol Reef National Park 171
  Cathedral Lakes 120-1, **121**
  Death Valley National Park 52
  equipment 24-5
  Grand Canyon National Park 180, 186, 187, **186, 187**
  Hermit Trail 39, 187, **187**

Joshua Tree National Park 56
Kings Canyon National Park 74-5, **75**
Lassen Volcanic National Park 82-5
Monarch Lakes 106-7, **107**
Narrows, the 220-1, **221**
Pinnacles National Park 88
Rae Lake Loop 78-81, **79**
Redwood National Park 90-1
safety 22-3, 200, 235-6
Saguaro National Park 208-9
Sequoia National Park 106-7, 108-9, **107, 109**
Under the Rim Trail 162-3, **163**
Widforss Trail 186, **186**
Yosemite National Park 118-19, 120-1, **118, 120**
Zion National Park 210-12
history 47, 182, 195, 225, 228-33
Hoodoos 207
horseback riding 71, 239
Humboldt Lagoons State Park 98

I

internet 16-17
Island in the Sky 164

J

Jedediah Smith Redwoods State Park 100-1
Joshua Tree Music Festival 19
Joshua Tree National Park 7, 28-9, 56-61, **57**
Joshua trees 59

K

kayaking 236
  Big Bend National Park 142
  Channel Islands 47
  Redwood National Park 92
Kayenta Trails 212
Keys View 64
Kings Canyon National Park 28-9, 68-77, **69**

L

Lassen Peak 84
Lassen Volcanic National Park 13, 28-9, 82-5, **83**
Lava Beds National Monument 86
Lehman Cave 37, 190
Lincoln, Abraham 228, 229

M

maps 25
Marathon 150
Marfa 148
Marfa Lights 150
Mather, Stephen 229, 231
Maze, the 39, 165
McKittrick Canyon Trail 192-3
Mesa Arch 165
Mesa Verde National Park 10, 28-9, 198-203, **199**
meteor showers 20
Mineral King Valley 128
Mission 66 232
mobile phones 16
Monarch Lakes 106, **107**
money 16, 17
mountain biking 166, 237-8
mountain lion 242
mountaineering 236-7, *see also rock climbing*
Muir, John 230
Muir Woods National Monument 87
museums & galleries
  Ballroom Marfa 148
  Chinati Foundation 148
  El Paso Holocaust Museum 146
  El Paso Museum of Art 146
  Museum of the Big Bend 148-50
  Painted Desert Inn 205
  Palm Springs Art Museum 62
  White Sands Missile Test Center Museum 223

museums & galleries *continued*
    Yavapai Point & Geology
        Museum 184
music 21

N

Narrows, the 8, 210, 220-1, **221**
National Park Service 16, 231, 232
National Park Week 19
Natural Bridge 152
Natural Bridges National Monu-
    ment 207
Navajo Nation Fair 20
Needles, the 164-5

O

Oasis of Mara 64-6

P

Painted Desert 204-5
Palm Springs 62-7
park passes 16
Patrick's Point State Park 96
Petrified Forest National Park
    28-9, 37, 204-5, **205**
petroglyphs 173
Pioneer Days 20
Pinnacles National Park 28-9,
    88-9, **89**
planning 16-17, 18-20, 36-7, 22-3,
    235-6
Point Reyes National Seashore 87
politics 226, 227
Prada Marfa 151
Prairie Creek Redwoods State
    Park 100
Puebloan people 182, 200

R

rafting 39, 236
    Big Bend National Park 142
    Grand Canyon National Park
        180-2
Rainbow Bridge National
    Monument 206

Redwood Canyon 70
Redwood National Park 28,
    90-5, **91**
redwoods 12, 91
road trips, *see driving tours*
rock climbing 37, 236-7
    Capitol Reef National Park 173
    Joshua Tree National Park
        7, 59
    Pinnacles National Park 89
    Yosemite National Park 37
Roosevelt, Franklin Delano 231
Roosevelt, Theodore 230, 231

S

safe travel 22-3
    bears 25
    hiking 22-3, 200, 235-6
Saguaro National Park 28-9,
    208-9, 222-3, **209**
saguaros 209
Salton Sea 66
Samoa Peninsula 96
Santa Monica Mountains
    National Recreation Area 86
Scott, Walter E 52
Sequoia National Park 28-9,
    102-11, **103**
shuttle services 17
skiing & snowshoeing 238
    Mesa Verde 200
    Sierra Nevada 126
Southwest USA 132-223, **133**
    climate 132
    highlights 132
    travel seasons 132
stargazing 37, 142, 146, 179,
    191, 239
Sundance Film Festival 18
sustainability 245, 247
swimming 238-9

T

telephone services 16
Tenaya Lake 114

Terlingua 150-1
tipping 16
tortoises 215
travel within national parks 17
trees 104, 204, 244
Trees of Mystery 100
Trinidad 96
Tuolumne Meadows 115, 124

U

Utah Shakespeare Festival 20

V

visitor centers 17

W

water, drinking 23
waterfalls 19, 70, 75, 114-15
Wawona 126
weather 16, 18-20
Wetherill Mesa 200
whales 47, 92
White Sands National Park
    222-3, **223**
Widforss Trail 186, **186**
wi-fi 16
Wild Horse Sanctuary 85
wildflowers 18, 20, 244
wildlife 47, 91-2, 240-3
Wilson, Woodrow 231
Windows Trail 136

Y

Yosemite National Park 28-9, 37,
    112-23, **113**
Yosemite Valley 4, 112, 124-5
Yosemite Waterfalls 19, 114-15

Z

Zion Canyon 212, 216-17, **216**
Zion National Park 8, 28-9,
    210-19, **211**

DOUGLAS KLUG/GETTY IMAGES ©

Watching Wildlife, Channel Islands

Tossed like lost pearls off the coast, the Channel Islands have a history of habitation stretching back thousands of years. Marine life thrives on these islands, from coral reefs to giant elephant seals. Enjoy fantastic sea kayaking in Channel Islands National Park, or plan a posh getaway at the harborfront hotels of Catalina Island.

YAYA ERNST/SHUTTERSTOCK ©

STASS GRICKO/500PX/
GETTY IMAGES ©

9

Lassen Volcanic National Park

Anchoring the Cascades' chain of volcanoes to the south, this alien landscape bubbles over with roiling mud pots, noxious sulfur vents and steamy fumaroles. But Lassen also delights the senses with colorful cinder cones and azure crater lakes. Ditch the crowds and head to this off-the-beaten-path destination to discover fresh peaks to be conquered, pristine waters for dipping, forested campgrounds for comfort and boardwalks through Bumpass Hell that will leave you awestruck.